THE LEGACY OF SOCRATES

THE LEGACY
OF SOCRATES

Essays in Moral Philosophy

JAMES RACHELS

Edited by Stuart Rachels

Columbia University Press   New York

Columbia University Press
Publishers Since 1893
New York   Chichester, West Sussex
Copyright © 2007 Columbia University Press

Library of Congress Cataloging-in-Publication Data

Rachels, James, 1941–2003.
The legacy of Socrates : essays in moral philosophy / James Rachels ; edited by Stuart Rachels.
p.   cm.
Includes bibliographical references and index.
ISBN 0–231–13844–X (cloth : alk. paper)
1. Ethics. I. Rachels, Stuart, 1969– II. Title.
BJ21.R28 2006
170—dc22
2006019769

Columbia University Press books are printed on permanent and durable acid-free paper.
Printed in the United States of America
c 10 9 8 7 6 5 4 3 2 1

The world is getting better,
but slowly.

—*James Rachels, in conversation with Doug Lackey,*
as recalled by Lackey thirty-five years later

CONTENTS

BIOETHICS

ART

PREFACE

The essays in this book span thirty years and cover all the main themes of James Rachels' work: the importance of reason in moral decision making, the duty to relieve both human and animal suffering, the relevance of evolution to ethics, and a modest view about the value of human life. This book complements Jim's first collection of essays, *Can Ethics Provide Answers?* It also complements his other books, with two exceptions: the essay "Darwin, Species, and Morality" overlaps with *Created from Animals,* and most of the material in "Killing and Starving to Death" appears in *The End of Life.* All of the essays are written with a decent humanity that James Rachels' readers will recognize.

I am reprinting these essays exactly as Jim wrote them. Twice I have restored his work to its rightful form. "The Value of Human Life" was originally published without notes and with defective formatting. And when "Political Assassination" was published, it was changed without Jim's permission; I have changed it back. I did omit the last section of "Movies," about the movie literature, because it now seems dated. That essay, by the way, is my favorite of the bunch. Jim loved all kinds of movies, and those who knew him will hear his voice clearly in that piece.

In "Political Assassination," Jim asks at one point whether it would be wrong to kill a healthy person in order to save five people who need organ transplants. Jim thought up this now-famous example in the 1960s, but I have never seen it attributed to him. It goes mostly unattributed, though I have seen it credited to Judith Jarvis Thomson. When I asked my father if this bothered him, he said it didn't, but I hope philosophers will start attributing the example accurately.

In "Two Arguments Against Ethical Egoism," Jim tries to refute ethical egoism by pointing out its abhorrent implications. Sometime in the 1990s, he told me he had lost confidence in this argument. In particular, he said he'd changed his mind about the role that intuitions play in assessing moral theories. I wonder if the younger philosopher might have been right. At any rate, I include the essay with the caveat that it doesn't match Jim's later view.

Shortly before James Rachels died on September 5, 2003, I told him that I would edit a second volume of his essays. This book fulfills that promise. In compiling this collection, I have hoped that these essays will continue to influence philosophers while inspiring ordinary people to lead better lives.

Stuart Rachels
Birmingham, Alabama
January 2006

Acknowledgments

Many of these essays no longer existed on disk, so they had to be retyped from their original sources. I warmly thank Karissa Rinas for doing most of this typing and for doing it so well. Once we had all the essays on disk, my mother, Carol, read the published versions aloud to me while I proofread the computer copies. My debt to her is the greatest. Finally, I thank my cousin Joel Withrow, who cheerfully read half an essay to me while others were at a party upstairs wondering where he was.

The essays in this collection originally appeared in various books or journals. It is a pleasure to thank those who allowed us to reprint them.

1. "The Basic Argument for Vegetarianism" originally appeared in *Food for Thought: The Debate over Eating Meat,* edited by Steve F. Sapontzis, 70–80 (Amherst, N.Y.: Prometheus Books, 2004). © Steve F. Sapontzis. Reprinted by permission.

2. "Darwin, Species, and Morality" originally appeared in *The Monist* 70, no. 1 (January 1987): 98–113. © *The Monist: An International Quarterly Journal of General Philosophical Inquiry,* Peru, Illinois, 61354. Reprinted by permission.

3. "Drawing Lines" originally appeared in *Animal Rights: Current Debates and New Directions,* edited by Cass R. Sunstein and Martha C.

Nussbaum, 162–74 (New York: Oxford University Press, 2004). Reprinted by permission of Oxford University Press.

4. "The Value of Human Life" originally appeared in *Philosophical Inquiry* 24 (2002): 3–16. Reprinted by permission.

5. "Killing and Starving to Death" originally appeared in *Philosophy* 54 (1979): 159–71. Reprinted by permission of Cambridge University Press.

6. "Lives and Liberty" (coauthored with William Ruddick) originally appeared in *The Inner Citadel,* edited by John Christman, 221–33 (New York: Oxford University Press, 1989). Reprinted by permission of Oxford University Press.

7. "Political Assassination" originally appeared in *Assassination,* edited by Harold Zellner, 9–21 (Cambridge, Mass.: Schenkman, 1974). Reprinted by permission.

8. "The Legacy of Socrates," the 1992 Ireland Lecture at the University of Alabama at Birmingham, was originally published by the University of Alabama Press (Tuscaloosa, 1993). Reprinted by permission of the University of Alabama at Birmingham.

9. "Nietzsche and the Objectivity of Morals" originally appeared in *Philosophy Then and Now,* edited by N. Scott Arnold, Theodore M. Benditt, and George Graham, 385–412 (Oxford: Blackwell, 1998). Reprinted by permission of Blackwell Publishers.

10. "Two Arguments Against Ethical Egoism" originally appeared in *Philosophia* 4 (1974): 297–314. Reprinted by permission.

11. "The Principle of Agency" originally appeared in *Bioethics* 12 (1998): 150–61. Reprinted by permission of Blackwell Publishers.

12. "Baby M" originally appeared in *Bioethics* 1 (1987): 357–65. Reprinted by permission of Blackwell Publishers.

13. "Ethical Theory and Bioethics" originally appeared in *A Companion to Bioethics,* edited by Peter Singer and Helga Kuhse, 15–23 (Oxford: Blackwell, 1998). Reprinted by permission of Blackwell Publishers.

14. "Movies" originally appeared in *Stepping Out,* edited by Ada Long and Robert Yowell, 63–77 (Dubuque, Iowa: Kendall-Hunt, 1985). Reprinted by permission.

ANIMALS

ONE

THE BASIC ARGUMENT FOR VEGETARIANISM

I

In 1973, Peter Singer, who was then a young, little-known philosopher from Australia, published an article called "Animal Liberation" in the *New York Review of Books*.[1] The title suggested that there was a parallel between our treatment of animals and the unjust treatment of blacks and women. At first, it was hard to take the comparison seriously. Many proponents of "black liberation" and "women's liberation," as those movements were then known, found the comparison insulting, and most philosophers thought the topic was hardly worth discussing. But Singer kept at it, writing more articles and a now-famous book. It is now commonly said that the modern animal-rights movement grew out of those works. Thanks to Singer, many people, including me, became convinced that a fundamental change in our attitude toward animals was necessary. The indispensable first step was becoming a vegetarian.

The argument that persuaded me to become a vegetarian was so simple that it needs only a little elaboration. It begins with the principle that it is wrong to cause pain unless there is a good enough reason. The qualification is important because causing pain is not always wrong. My dentist causes me pain, but there's a good reason for it, and, besides, I consent. My children's doctor caused them pain when he gave them their shots, and they did not consent, but that was all right, too. However, as the principle says, causing pain is acceptable only when there is a good enough reason for it. Justification is required.

The second step in the argument is to notice that in the modern meat-production business, animals are made to suffer terribly. There is a reason for this suffering, too. We eat the meat, and it helps to nourish us. But there is a catch: we could just as easily nourish ourselves in other ways. Vegetarian meals are also good. Nonetheless, most people prefer a diet that includes meat because they like the way it tastes. The question, then, is whether our enjoyment of the way meat tastes is a good enough reason to justify the amount of suffering that the animals are made to endure. It seems obvious that it is not. Therefore, we should stop eating the products of this business. We should be vegetarians instead.

I will call this the Basic Argument. It has a limited application. It says nothing about animals raised on old-fashioned family farms or animals killed in hunter-gatherer societies. It addresses only the situation of people like us, in modern industrial countries. But it does point out, in a simple and compelling way, why those of us in the industrial countries should not support the meat-production business as it now exists.

When I emphasize the argument's simplicity, I mean that it does not depend on any controversial claims about health or on any religiously tinged notions of the value of life. Nor does it invoke any disputable ideas about "rights." Further claims of these kinds might strengthen the case for vegetarianism, but the Basic Argument does not depend on them. Nor does it rest on any contentious philosophical theory about the nature of morality. Philosophers sometimes misunderstand this when they think it is a merely utilitarian argument and that it can be refuted by refuting utilitarianism. But the Basic Argument is not tied to any particular theory about the nature of ethics. Instead, it appeals to a simple principle that every decent person already accepts, regardless of his or her stand on other issues. The most striking thing about the argument is that it derives such a remarkable conclusion from such a sober, conservative starting point.

The Basic Argument, then, is common ground for people of various moral and political persuasions. Matthew Scully is in most respects the antithesis of Peter Singer. Scully, a former speechwriter for various Republicans, including President George W. Bush, recently surprised his conservative friends by writing a book, *Dominion: The Power of Man, the Suffering of Animals, and the Call to Mercy*,[2] in which he details the cruelties of the mod-

ern factory farm—cruelties that are, in his words, "hard to contemplate."³
Scully reports:

> Four companies now produce 81 per cent of cows brought to market, 73 per cent
> of sheep, half our chickens, and some 60 per cent of hogs. From these latter,
> the 355,000 pigs slaughtered every day in America, even the smallest of mercies
> have been withdrawn. In 1967 there were more than a million hog farms in the
> country; today there are about 114,000, all of them producing more, more, more
> to meet market demand. About 80 million of the 95 million hogs slaughtered
> each year in America, according to the National Pork Producers Council, are
> intensively reared in mass-confinement farms, never once in their time on earth
> feeling soil or sunshine. Genetically engineered by machines, inseminated by
> machines, monitored, herded, electrocuted, stabbed, cleaned, cut, and packaged
> by machines—themselves treated as machines "from birth to bacon"—these
> creatures, when eaten, have hardly ever been touched by human hands.⁴

Scully visited some of these automated pig farms in North Carolina, and
his report is chilling. Sows have been engineered to weigh five hundred
pounds each. Pigs are crowded twenty each in pens only seven and one-
half feet square. The close confinement creates problems in managing the
animals. Pigs are intelligent and social animals who normally build nests
and keep them clean. They will not urinate or defecate in their nests, as
they must do in the pens. They form bonds with other animals. They want
to suck and chew, but in the pens, being deprived of a normal environment
in which they can do these things, they begin to chew on the tails of the
animals in front of them. In such close quarters, the victims cannot escape.
The chewing causes infection, and sick pigs are no good. The solution is
"tail docking," a procedure recommended by the U.S. Food and Drug Ad-
ministration, in which the pigs' tails are snipped (without anesthetic) by pli-
ers. The point is to make the tails more sensitive to pain, so that the animals
will make a greater effort to avoid their neighbors' attacks. Surveying the
whole setup, the operator of one such "farm" observes: "It's science driven.
We're not raising pets."⁵

When critics of the meat-production industry report such facts, their accounts are often dismissed as "emotional appeals." But that is a mistake.
It may be true that such descriptions engage our emotions. However, emo-
tionalism is not the point. The point is to fill in the details of the Basic Argument. The Basic Argument says that causing pain is not justified unless

there is a sufficiently good reason for it. In order to apply this principle to the case of factory farming, we need to know how much pain is involved. If only a little pain were being caused, a fairly insubstantial reason (such as our gustatory pleasure) might be sufficient. But if there is extensive suffering, that reason is not enough. Thus, these facts are a vital part of the argument, and it is necessary to keep them in mind when considering whether the argument is sound. For those of us who have no firsthand knowledge of the subject, reports by such relatively impartial observers as Matthew Scully are indispensable.

Another report recently appeared in the *New York Times Magazine*.[6] The author, Michael Pollan, went to a great deal of trouble to find out what happens to cattle who are raised and slaughtered for beef. "Forgetting, or willed ignorance, is the preferred strategy of many beef-eaters,"[7] he says, but Pollan wanted to see for himself the conditions in which the animals live and die. So he bought a steer—"No. 534"—at the Blair Brothers Ranch in South Dakota and followed its progress to the slaughterhouse. No. 534 spent the first six months of his life in pastures alongside his mother. Then, having been weaned and castrated, he was shipped to Poky Feeders, a feedlot operation in Garden City, Kansas.

"A cattle feedlot," says Pollan, "is a kind of city, populated by as many as 100,000 animals. It is very much a premodern city, however—crowded, filthy and stinking, with open sewers, unpaved roads and choking air."[8] Fecal dust floats in the air, causing irritation to the eyes and lungs. Searching for No. 534, Pollan found his animal standing in a "deep pile of manure."[9] Dried manure caked on the animals is a problem later, in the slaughterhouse, where steps must be taken to ensure that the meat does not become contaminated. In the feedlot itself, disease would kill the animals were it not for massive doses of antibiotics.

At the Blair Brothers Ranch, No. 534 ate grass and was given corn and alfalfa hay to fatten him up. In his last six weeks at the ranch, he put on 148 pounds. After being shipped to Poky Feeders, he would never eat grass again. His diet would be mostly corn and protein supplement, "a sticky brown goop consisting of molasses and urea."[10] Corn is cheap, and it produces "marbled" beef, although it is not what the animals naturally desire. In a grisly sort of forced cannibalism, the animals are also fed rendered cow parts. The animals could not live on this diet for long—it would "blow out their livers," said one of the feedlot operators. But they are slaughtered before this can happen. The diet is effective, however: the animals weigh more than 1,200 pounds when taken to the slaughterhouse.

No. 534 was slaughtered at the National Beef Plant in Liberal, Kansas, one hundred miles down the road from Poky Feeders. This is where Pollan's personal observations come to a stop. He was not allowed to watch the stunning, bleeding, and evisceration process; nor was he permitted to take pictures or talk to the employees.

Opposing cruelty should not be seen as a specifically liberal or conservative cause. Scully, the conservative Republican, emphasizes that one should oppose it "even if one does not accept [the animal-rights advocates'] whole vision of the world." He makes a point of distancing himself from Peter Singer, who champions various left-wing causes. Singer is wrong about the other issues, says Scully, but he is right about the animals.[11]

II

The Basic Argument seems to me obviously correct. But its very obviousness suggests a problem: If it is so simple and obvious, why doesn't everyone accept it? Why doesn't everyone who has this argument explained to them become a vegetarian? Of course, many people do, but most do not. Part of the explanation may be that it is natural for people to resist arguments that require them to do things they don't want to do. If you want to go on eating meat, you may pay no attention to arguments that say otherwise. Moreover, people generally do not respond to ethical appeals unless they see others around them also responding. If all your friends are eating meat, you are unlikely to be moved by a mere argument. It is like an appeal for money to provide vaccinations for third-world children. The argument that the vaccinations are more important than your going to a movie may be irrefutable, considered just as an argument. But when no one around you is contributing, and all your friends are going to the movie, you are likely to ignore the charitable appeal and spend the money on popcorn instead. It is easy to put the children out of mind.

All this may be true. But there is a more pressing problem about the Basic Argument—at least, a more pressing problem for me, as a philosopher. Many of my professional colleagues are unmoved by this argument, and I am not sure why. Those who study ethics, especially from a nonreligious point of view, often find the argument compelling. But others do not. This is puzzling because professional philosophers—those who teach in colleges and universities—study arguments dispassionately, and while they often disagree, they disagree about arguments only when the issues are tricky or obscure. But there is nothing tricky or obscure about the Basic Argument. Thus, I would expect that, on so simple a matter, there would be widespread agreement. Instead, many philosophers shrug the argument off.

The same is true of other academics who study cognitive science, psychology, and biology. They are at least as smart as I am, if not smarter, and they are morally decent people. Yet, while I think the Basic Argument is compelling, many of them do not. It is not that they think the argument makes a good point, even though they are unwilling to act on it. Rather, they find the argument itself unconvincing. How can this be?

Sometimes philosophers explain that the argument is unconvincing because it contains a logical gap. We are all opposed to cruelty, they say, but it does not follow that we must become vegetarians. It only follows that we should favor less-cruel methods of meat production. This objection is so feeble that it is hard to believe it explains resistance to the Basic Argument. It is true enough that if you are opposed to cruelty, you should prefer that the meat-production business be made less brutal. But it is also true that if you are opposed to cruelty, you have reason not to participate in social practices that are brutal as they stand. As it stands, meat producers and consumers cooperate to maintain the unnecessary system of pig farms, feedlots, and slaughterhouses. Anyone who finds this system objectionable has reason not to help keep it going. The point would be quickly conceded if the victims were people. If a product—curtains, let's say—were being produced by a process that involved torturing humans, no one would dream of saying: "Of course I oppose using those methods, but that's no reason not to buy the product. After all, the curtains are very nice."

Many in the animal-rights movement believe that scientists are blinded by the need to justify their own practices. The scientists are personally committed to animal experimentation. Their careers, or the careers of their colleagues, are based on it, and they would have to stop this research if they conceded that animals have moral claims on us. Naturally they do not want to do this. Thus, they are so biased in favor of current practices that they cannot see the evil in them. This explains why they cannot see the truth even in something so simple as the Basic Argument.

Perhaps there is something to this, but I do not want to pursue it. On the whole it is a condescending explanation that insults the scientists, cuts off communication with them, and prevents us from learning what they have to teach us. It should be noted, however, that the Basic Argument about vegetarianism is independent of any arguments about animal experimentation. Indeed, the case against meat eating is much stronger than the case against the use of animals in research. The researchers can at least point out that, in many instances, their work has a serious purpose that can benefit humankind. Nothing comparable can be said in defense of meat eating. Thus, even if some research using animals was justified, meat eating would still be wrong.

I believe a better explanation is in terms of the overall difference between how scientists and animal-rights advocates think about the nature of non-humans. Defenders of animal rights tend to see the differences between humans and nonhumans as slight. They frequently emphasize how much the animals are like us in order to argue that our ethical responsibilities to the animals are similar to our responsibilities to one another. Animals are pictured as intelligent and sociable creatures who love their children, who experience fear and delight, who sulk, play, mourn their dead, and much more. So how can it be denied that they have rights, just as we do? I have argued in this way myself, more than once.

Many scientists, however, see this as naive. They believe the differences between humans and other animals are vast—so vast, in fact, that putting humans in a separate moral category is entirely justified. Moreover, they feel they have some authority on this score. After all, the scientific study of animals is their professional concern. In light of this, how should we expect them to react when they are confronted by belligerent amateurs who insist they know better? It is only natural that the scientists should disregard the amateurs' arguments.

A case in point is the anthropologist Jonathan Marks, who teaches at the University of North Carolina at Charlotte. In 1993, Peter Singer and Paola Cavalieri, an Italian writer on animal issues, initiated a campaign known as the Great Ape Project, an effort to secure basic rights for our closest relatives, the chimpanzees, gorillas, and orangutans.[12] The rights being demanded were life, liberty, and freedom from torture. Marks was invited to participate in a debate about these demands, and he recorded his thoughts in an engaging book, *What It Means to Be 98% Chimpanzee*.[13] "Since their brains are closely related to our brains," Marks says, "it should come as no surprise that the apes can approach humans in their cognitive functions."[14] Despite this, "Apes are often objectified by callous and cynical entrepreneurs, who neither regard them nor treat them as the sentient, emotionally complex creatures they are."[15] Marks does not think this is acceptable. "Apes deserve protection," he says, "even rights."[16]

Reading these words, one would expect Marks to be an ally of Singer and Cavalieri. But he is not. The Great Ape Project, he thinks, is completely wrongheaded. Why? Marks' attempt at philosophical argument is unimpressive—he says the critical issues are that chimps, gorillas, and orangutans aren't human and that in any case we are politically powerless to guarantee such rights even for humans. Of course, these arguments get us nowhere. Everyone knows the animals aren't human; the point is that they are sufficiently like humans to deserve the same basic protections. And the fact that we cannot ensure rights for humans does not mean that we should stop thinking humans ought to have them.

The underlying reason for Marks' scorn of the animal-rights ideology becomes clear when he turns to the scientific study of animal behavior. The similarities between humans and other great apes, he intimates, is only superficial: "Where clever, controlled experimentation has been possible, it has tended strongly to show that in specific ways, ape minds work quite differently from human minds."[17] For support, he cites the work of the psychologist Daniel J. Povinelli, who argues that chimpanzees' conceptions of physical interactions (as, for example, when a hook is used to manipulate an object) are very different from humans' understanding.[18] Marks does not say how this fits with his earlier assertion that "[a]pes deserve protection, even rights," but clearly, in his view, the latter thought trumps the former.

We find this pattern repeated again and again: the scientists concede that the animal advocates have a bit of a point, but then the scientists want to talk about the facts. They think we do not know nearly enough about the details of how animal minds work to justify any firm moral conclusions. Moreover, such knowledge as we do have suggests caution: the animals are more different from us than it seems. The advocates of animal rights, on the other hand, think the facts are well enough established that we can proceed without further ado to the ethical conclusions. Anyone who suggests otherwise is viewed as dragging their feet, perhaps to avoid the unpleasant truth about the injustice of our behavior toward the animals.

What are we to make of all this? One obvious idea is that we should take seriously what the scientists tell us about what animals are like and adjust our moral conceptions accordingly. This would be an ongoing project. It would take volumes even to begin by considering what is currently known. But those volumes would be out of date by the time they were completed because new discoveries are being made all the time.

However, where the Basic Argument is concerned, the only relevant part of this project would be what science can tell us about the capacity of animals to experience pain. Jeremy Bentham famously said, "The question is not, Can they *reason?* nor Can they *talk?* but Can they *suffer?*"19 To this we might add that, contrary to Jonathan Marks, it is irrelevant whether chimps have a different understanding of physical interactions. It is irrelevant, that is, if we are considering whether it is acceptable to treat them in ways that cause them pain.

This point is easily misunderstood, so it is worth elaborating just a bit. Of course, the facts about an individual are important in determining how that individual should be treated. (This is true of humans as well as non-humans.) How an animal should be treated depends on what the animal is like—its nature, its abilities, and its needs. Different creatures have different characteristics, and these must be taken into account when we frame our ethical conceptions. The scientific study of animals gives us the factual information we need. But not every fact about an individual is relevant to every form of treatment. *What facts are relevant* depends on *what sorts of treatment* we are considering. To take a simple example, whether an animal can read is relevant if we are considering whether to admit him to university classes. But the ability to read is irrelevant in deciding whether it is wrong to operate on the animal without anesthesia. Thus, if we are considering whether it is wrong to treat pigs and cattle in the ways we have described, the critical issue is not whether their minds work in various sophisticated ways. The critical issue is, as Bentham said, whether they can suffer.

What does science tell us about this? The mechanisms that enable us to feel pain are not fully understood, but we do know a good bit about them. In humans, nociceptors—neurons specialized for sensing noxious stimuli—are connected to a central nervous system, and the resulting signals are processed in the brain. Until recently it was believed that the brain's work was divided into two distinct parts: a sensory system operating in the somatosensory cortex, resulting in our conscious experiences of pain, and an affective-motivational system associated with the frontal lobes, responsible for our behavioral reactions. Now, however, this picture has been called into question, and it may be that the best we can say is that the brain's system for processing the information from the nociceptors seems to be spread over multiple regions. At any rate, the human nociceptive system also includes endogenous opioids, or endorphins, which provide the brain with its natural pain-killing ability.

The question of which other animals feel pain is a real and important issue, not to be settled by appeals to common sense. Only a complete scientific understanding of pain, which we do not yet have, could tell us all that we need to know. In the meantime, however, we do have a rough idea of what to look for. If we want to know whether it is reasonable to believe that a particular kind of animal is capable of feeling pain, we may ask: Are there nociceptors present? Are they connected to a central nervous system? What happens in that nervous system to the signals from the nociceptors? And are there endogenous opiods? In our present state of understanding, this sort of information, together with the obvious behavioral signs of distress, is the best evidence we can have that an animal is capable of feeling pain.

Relying on such evidence, some writers, such as Gary Varner, have tentatively suggested that the line between animals that feel pain and those that do not is (approximately) the line between vertebrates and invertebrates.[20] However, research constantly moves forward, and the tendency of research is to extend the number of animals that might be able to suffer, not decrease it. Nociception appears to be one of the most primitive animal systems. Nociceptors have now been identified in a remarkable number of species, including leeches and snails.

The presence of a perceptual system does not, however, settle the question of whether the organism has conscious experiences connected with its operation. We know, for example, that humans have perceptual systems that do not involve conscious experience. Recent research has shown that the human vomeronasal system, which works through receptors in the nose, responds to pheromones and affects behavior even though the person is unaware of it. (It was long believed that this system was vestigial in humans, but it turns out that it is still working.) The receptors for "vomerolfaction" are in the nostrils, alongside the receptors for the sense of smell; yet the operation of one is accompanied by conscious experience, while the operation of the other is not.[21] We do not know why this is so. But this suggests at least the possibility that in some species there may be nociceptive systems that do not involve conscious experiences. In that case, those animals might not actually feel pain, even though various indications are present. Is this true of leeches and snails? Of snakes? Of hummingbirds? We may have strong hunches, but we don't really know.

Clearly, then, we still have a great deal to learn about the phenomenon of pain in the animal world, and the scientists who work in this area are right to caution us against quick and easy opinions. The ongoing study of animal pain is a fascinating subject in itself, and it has enormous importance for ethics. But should this make us less confident of the Basic Argument? If the issue was our treatment of snails and leeches, perhaps it should. But pigs and cattle are another matter. There is every reason to believe they feel pain—the facts about their nervous systems, their brains, their behavior, and their evolutionary kinship to human beings all point to the same conclusion as common sense: our treatment of them on factory farms and in the slaughterhouses is one of the world's great causes of misery. If further investigation were to prove otherwise, it would be one of the most astonishing discoveries in the history of science.

Strict vegetarians may want more than the Basic Argument can provide because the Basic Argument does not support sweeping prohibitions. If opposition to cruelty is our motive, we will have to consider the things we eat one at a time. Of course we should not eat beef and pork produced in the ways I have described, and we ought also to avoid factory-farm poultry, eggs, and milk. But free-range eggs and humanely produced milk are all right. Eating shrimp may also turn out to be acceptable. Moreover, from this point of view, not all vegetarian issues are equally pressing: eating fish may be questionable, but it is not nearly as bad as eating beef. This means that becoming a vegetarian need not be regarded as an all-or-nothing proposition. From a practical standpoint, it makes sense to focus first on the things that cause the most misery. As Matthew Scully says, whatever one's "whole vision of the world" may be, the pig farms, feedlots, and slaughterhouses are unacceptable.[22]

Notes

1. Peter Singer, "Animal Liberation," *New York Review of Books*, April 5, 1973, 17–21.

2. Matthew Scully, *Dominion: The Power of Man, the Suffering of Animals, and the Call to Mercy* (New York: St. Martin's Press, 2002).

3. Ibid., x.

4. Ibid., 29.

5. Ibid., 279.

6. Michael Pollan, "This Steer's Life," *New York Times Magazine*, March 31, 2002, 44–51, 68, 71–72, 76–77.

7. Ibid., 48.

8. Ibid., 50.

9. Ibid., 68.

10. Ibid., 50.

11. Scully, *Dominion*, 326–38.

12. Peter Singer and Paola Cavalieri, *The Great Ape Project: Equality and Beyond* (London: Fourth Estate, 1993).

13. Jonathan Marks, *What It Means to Be 98% Chimpanzee: Apes, People, and Their Genes* (Berkeley: University of California Press, 2002).

14. Ibid., 189.

15. Ibid., 185.

16. Ibid., 188.

17. Ibid., 195.

18. Daniel J. Povinelli, *Folk Physics for Apes: The Chimpanzee's Theory of How the World Works* (Oxford: Oxford University Press, 2000).

19. Jeremy Bentham, *The Principles of Morals and Legislation* (New York: Hafner, 1948; originally published in 1789), 311.

20. Gary Varner, *In Nature's Interests? Interests, Animals Rights, and Environmental Ethics* (New York: Oxford University Press, 1998).

21. L. Monti-Bloch, C. Jennings-White, and D. L. Berliner, "The Human Vomeronasal Organ: A Review," *Annals of the New York Academy of Sciences* 855 (1998): 373–89.

22. I have learned a great deal from Colin Allen's essay "Animal Pain," as yet unpublished. It is the best discussion of the question of animal pain known to me. [*Editor's note:* This paper was published in *Nous* 38, no. 4 (December 2004): 617–43.]

TWO

DARWIN, SPECIES, AND MORALITY

I

"Man in his arrogance thinks himself a great work worthy the interposition of a deity. More humble and I think truer to consider him created from animals."[1] Thus wrote Darwin in his notebooks for 1838, twenty-one years before he was to publish *The Origin of Species*. He would go on, of course, to support this idea with overwhelming evidence, and it is commonly said that, in doing so, he brought about a profound change in our conception of ourselves. After Darwin, we can no longer think of ourselves as occupying a special place in creation—instead, we must realize that we are products of the same evolutionary forces that shaped the rest of the animal kingdom. We are not a great work. We were created from animals. And this, it is said, has deep philosophical significance.

Curiously, though, it is not *philosophers* who say such things. Anthropologists, journalists, and poets might believe that there is a big philosophical lesson to be learned from Darwin, but by and large the philosophers themselves have not agreed. If we examine the most influential works of philosophy written in the twentieth century, we find little discussion of Darwin or his theory. When the subject is broached, it is usually to explain that Darwinism does *not* have some philosophical implication it is popularly thought to have. The philosophers seem to agree with Wittgenstein's assessment: "The Darwinian theory," he said, "has no more to do with philosophy than any other hypothesis of natural science."[2]

Why are philosophers so indifferent to Darwin? Among moral philosophers, it may be in part a reaction to the exaggerated character of claims that once were made. When Karl Marx first read *The Origin*, he declared that "Darwin's book is very important and serves me as a basis in natural selection for the class struggle in history."[3] Later socialists made similar judgments, often claiming to find in Darwinism the "scientific basis" of their political views. Meanwhile, capitalists were also claiming Darwin: the idea of "the survival of the fittest" was invoked time and again to justify competitive economic systems.[4] Exasperation with such nonsense might very well provoke a reaction like Wittgenstein's.

There is another, more general reason for skepticism about drawing philosophical conclusions from Darwinism. That is the old problem of the relation of fact and value, of "is" and "ought." Darwin's theory, if it is correct, tells us what *is* the case with respect to the evolution of species; and so, strictly speaking, no conclusion follows from it regarding any matter of value. It does not follow, merely because we are descended from apes, that we ought to think less of ourselves, that our lives are less important, or that human beings are "merely" one kind of animal among others. Nor does it follow that the main tenets of religion are false. As has often been observed, natural selection could be the means chosen by God for the purpose of making man. If so, man could still be regarded as the divinely blessed crown of creation.

Nevertheless, the nagging thought remains that Darwinism does have unsettling consequences. The feeling that Darwin's discovery undermines traditional religion, and some parts of traditional morality, will not go away, despite the nice logical points about what follows from what. I believe this feeling is justified. There is a connection between Darwin's theory and these larger matters, but the connection is more subtle than a straightforward logical implication. Darwin himself had a good sense of this. In 1880, two years before he died, he wrote—wisely, in my opinion—"Though I am a strong advocate for free thought on all subjects, yet it appears to me (whether rightly or wrongly) that direct arguments against Christianity and Theism produce hardly any effect on the public; and freedom of thought is best promoted by the gradual illumination of men's minds, which follows from the advancement of science. It has, therefore, been always my object to avoid writing on religion, and I have confined myself to science."[5] Thus, even if Darwin's theory is not a "direct argument" against Christianity and theism, he saw it as having a clear long-range influence on such beliefs.

The idea that Darwinism undermines religion is, of course, familiar, even though it is by no means obvious how it does so. I will not discuss the relation between Darwinism and religion. Instead, I will focus on the other, less well-explored idea: that Darwinism also undermines some aspects of traditional morality. Traditional morality depends, at crucial points, on the assumption that there is something morally special about being human— the fact that a being is human, rather than, say, canine or bovine, makes a big difference, according to traditional morality, in how it may be treated. My thesis is that "the gradual illumination of men's minds," of the sort provided by Darwin's theory, must lead inevitably to the conclusion that this assumption is false.

II

When Darwin wrote *The Origin of Species,* he studiously avoided the question of whether human beings have evolved. There was resistance enough to the idea that *any* species might be transformed into another, and he did not want to complicate matters needlessly by considering the emotionally charged question of human origins. He did, however, issue a warning. At the very end of the book, after having discussed dozens of other species for more than 450 pages, Darwin predicted that, as a result of his investigations, "Much light will be thrown on the origin of man and his history."[6]

That light was to come in two later works, *The Descent of Man* (1871) and *The Expression of the Emotions in Man and Animals* (1872), in which Darwin considered the specific question of human origins. He was convinced, of course, that man is subject to the same laws that govern the rest of nature, and that we, like the other animals, are descended from more primitive forms. But the most impressive evidence of this—the fossil remains of early hominids—had not yet been discovered. Therefore, Darwin had to argue for this conclusion indirectly, by stressing the similarities between humans and the other animals. We are so much like them, he said, that if *they* have evolved, then it is only reasonable to think that *we* have evolved also.

What were those similarities? First, like the other animals, man is subject to slight variations from individual to individual (no two people are exactly alike), and these variations are heritable. Man also reproduces in greater numbers than can survive. These facts alone would be enough to clinch the case, in Darwin's view, for these are just the facts that enable natural selection to operate. But there is more. Any species with an extended range will tend to diversify; individualized, geographically separated varieties will appear. This happens with man: Africans, Eskimos, and Japanese are, to the biologist's trained eye, distinct varietal forms. Moreover, as biologists had always known, it is easy to fit man into the great classificatory scheme: he is a primate, a mammal, and so on. Once these classifications are seen as related to lines of evolutionary descent, it is clear that man also belongs to a particular line of descent.

Darwin was aware, however, that this sort of evidence would not be enough to convince the skeptics. From ancient times, man has thought himself special because of his higher intellectual capacities. Man is the rational animal. How could *that* be explained on evolutionary grounds? Even some evolutionists, such as Alfred Russel Wallace, thought this was impossible. Wallace, who had independently formulated the theory of natural selection, held that the theory did not apply to humans. Darwin disagreed and sought to explain even man's proudest characteristics as the products of natural selection. Once again, he tried to make this plausible by emphasizing the similarities between human and nonhuman animals.

What makes man rational? One popular answer is that it is his linguistic ability. Because we are masters of a complex language, we can formulate thoughts, draw inferences, and in general understand ourselves and what is going on around us in a sophisticated way. Darwin argues, however, that our use of language differs in degree, not in kind, from the systems of signals used by other animals. Our language, he thought, is probably just the natural extension of some such primitive system:

> I cannot doubt that language owes its origin to the imitation and modification of various natural sounds, the voices of other animals, and man's own instinctive cries, aided by signs and gestures.... We may conclude from a widely-spread analogy, that this power would have been especially exerted during the courtship of the sexes—would have expressed various emotions, such as love, jealousy, triumph—and would have served as a challenge to rivals. It is, therefore, probable that the imitation of musical cries by articulate sounds may have given rise to words expressive of various complex emotions.... May not some unusually wise ape-like animal have imitated the growl of a beast of prey, and thus told his

fellow-monkeys the nature of the expected danger? This would have been a first step in the formation of a language.[7]

Although Darwin thought language could be explained in this way, he was skeptical about its importance. Even if other animals do *not* have a language as impressive as man's, this does not prevent them from being rational. In his early notebooks, Darwin makes a note to himself: "Forget the use of language and judge only by what you see."[8] When we look at the *behavior* of nonhuman animals, it seems to show reason, regardless of whether the use of language is involved: "The orang in the Eastern islands, and the chimpanzee in Africa, build platforms on which they sleep; and as both species follow the same habit, it might be argued that this was due to instinct, but we cannot feel sure that it is not the result of both animals having similar wants and possessing similar powers of reasoning."[9] Today we might make the same point in somewhat different terms: our best theory of animal behavior involves attributing to them desires and beliefs. Desires and beliefs, taken together, form reasons for action. Thus, when we explain the animal's behavior like this (the animal wants certain benefits and realizes that by building a platform it can obtain those benefits, etc.), we are seeing its conduct as rational.

Now I do not wish to defend or even to discuss in any detail Darwin's specific ideas about language or rationality. But I do want to call attention to the moral implications of his way of thinking. Darwin's strategy of argument brings him into direct conflict with traditional morality, which holds that humans and nonhumans are in separate moral categories. The traditional moral view is expressed by another nineteenth-century thinker, the Jesuit Joseph Rickaby, when he writes that we have no duties to mere animals because they are not the kind of beings toward whom we *could* have duties: "Brute beasts...are of the order of *things*.... We have then no duties of charity, nor duties of any kind, to the lower animals, as neither to sticks nor stones."[10] Darwin, however, could never regard nonhuman animals as mere things. His strategy leads him at every point to stress their similarities to human beings. He even goes so far as to assert: "There is no fundamental difference between man and the higher mammals in their mental faculties."[11] (He did admit that there are differences of degree, but stressed that these were *only* matters of degree.) But if man and animal are so much alike, how can it be right to treat them so differently? How can it be right to place them in different moral categories? Why shouldn't the same moral rules that determine how *we* should be treated also determine how *they* should be treated?

Darwin himself may have been aware of this implication. His personal feelings about the mistreatment of animals were unusually strong and matched in some ways his feelings about the mistreatment of humans. Reflecting on his father's character, one of Darwin's sons wrote: "The two subjects which moved my father perhaps more strongly than any others were cruelty to animals and slavery. His detestation of both was intense, and his indignation was overpowering in case of any levity or want of feeling on these matters."[12] It is surprising that a man of science—especially a naturalist who had killed countless animals for specimens—should have such feelings about cruelty to animals. What of the uses of animals for research? Darwin wrote in a letter, "You ask my opinion on vivisection. I quite agree that it is justifiable for real investigations on physiology; but not for mere damnable and detestable curiosity. It is a subject which makes me sick with horror, so I will not say another word about it, else I shall not sleep tonight."[13] It would be wrong to count Darwin as an advocate of "animal rights"; his feelings were far too ambiguous for that. He was sickened by vivisection—and at times visitors to the Darwin home were forbidden to bring up the subject—but he also thought it justifiable "for real investigations." Once he supported an effort to secure legislative controls on the use of animals in research, but later he refused to support another such effort.[14] Regardless of such wavering, however, it seems clear that he was troubled by prevailing attitudes toward animals.

Darwin *seems* to have connected his feelings about animals with his more general biological view about the kinship of species (although I do not wish to make too strong a claim about this). There are hints of a connection in passages such as this one from an early notebook: "If we choose to let conjecture run wild then animals our fellow brethren in pain, disease, death, suffering and famine, our slaves in the most laborious works, our companions in our amusements, they may partake from our origin in one common ancestor, we may be all netted together."[15]

However, if Darwin was ambiguous, others close to him were not. Asa Gray, the Harvard professor of botany who was Darwin's friend and defender in America, made the connection between biology and ethics explicit. In a lecture at the Yale Theological School, delivered less than a decade after publication of *The Descent of Man*, he said: "We are sharers not only of animal but of vegetable life, sharers with the higher brute animals in common instincts and feelings and affections. It seems to me that there is a sort of meanness in the wish to ignore the tie. I fancy that human beings may be more humane when they realize that, as their dependent associates live a life in which man has a share, so they have rights which man is bound to respect."[16]

III

Asa Gray's address raised the fundamental moral issue: Is the fact that a being is a member of a certain species in and of itself a morally good reason for treating it in a certain way? Is the fact that a being is *human* a reason for treating it with greater consideration than is given members of other species? There are (at least) three possible answers.

1. *Unqualified Speciesism.* First, it might be held that mere species alone is morally important. On this view, the bare fact that an individual is a member of a certain species, unsupplemented by any other consideration, is enough to make a difference in how that individual should be treated.

This is not a very plausible way of understanding the relation between species and morality, and generally it is not accepted even by those who are sympathetic to what I am calling "traditional morality." Consider, for example, the old science-fiction story "The Teacher from Mars" by Eando Binder.[17] The main character is a Martian who has come to earth to teach in a school for boys. Because he is "different"—seven feet tall, thin, with tentacles and leathery skin—he is taunted and abused by the students until he is almost driven out. Then, however, an act of heroism makes the boys realize they have been wrong, and the story ends happily with the ringleader of the bullies vowing to mend his ways.

Written in 1941, the story is a not so thinly disguised morality tale about racism. But the explicit point concerns species, not race.[18] The teacher from Mars is portrayed as being, psychologically, exactly like a human: he is equally as intelligent and equally as sensitive, with just the same cares and interests as anyone else. The only difference is that he has a different kind of body. And surely *that* does not justify treating him with less respect. Having appreciated this point, the reader is then expected to draw the obvious conclusion: the fact that there are physical differences between whites and blacks—skin color, for example—should make no moral difference either.

However, it has been suggested by some philosophers that species alone *can* make a difference in our moral duties toward a being. In his review of Tom Regan's *The Case for Animal Rights*,[19] Robert Nozick speculates that in a satisfactory moral scheme, "perhaps it will turn out that the bare species characteristic of simply being human...will command special respect only from other humans—this is an instance of the general principle that the members of any species may legitimately give their fellows more weight than they give members of other species (or at least more weight than a neutral view would grant them). Lions, too, if they were moral agents, could not then be criticized for putting other lions first."[20] Nozick illustrates the point with his own science-fiction example: "denizens of Alpha Centauri" would be justified in giving greater weight to the interests of other such Alpha Centaurians than they give to our interests, he says, even if we were like them in all other relevant respects. But this isn't at all obvious—in fact, it seems wrong on its face. If we substitute an Alpha Centaurian for a Martian in Binder's story, it makes no difference. Treating him less well because he is "different" (in this case, a member of a different species) still seems like unjustified discrimination.

What of the "general principle" Nozick suggests? It seems to be an expanded version of something that most people find plausible—namely, that one is justified in giving special weight to the interests of one's family or neighbors. If it is permissible to have special regard for family or neighbors, why not one's fellow species members? The problem with this way of thinking is that there are lots of groups to which one naturally belongs, and these group memberships are not always (if they are ever) morally significant. The progression from family to neighbor to species passes through other boundaries on the way—through the boundary of race, for example. Suppose it were suggested that we are justified in giving the interests of our own race greater weight than the interests of other races? ("Blacks, too," it might be said, "could not then be criticized for putting other blacks first.") This would rightly be resisted, but the case for distinguishing by species alone is little better. As Binder's story suggests, Unqualified Speciesism and racism are twin doctrines.

2. *Qualified Speciesism.* But there is a more sophisticated view of the relation between morality and species, and it is this view that defenders of traditional morality most often adopt. On this view, species alone is not regarded as morally significant. However, species membership is correlated with *other* differences that *are* significant. Humans, it might be said, are

in a special moral category because they are rational, autonomous agents. (Other special human qualities are sometimes mentioned, but, at least since Kant, this one has been most popular.) It is this fact, rather than the "mere" fact that they are human, that qualifies them for special consideration. This is why their interests are more important, morally speaking, than the interests of other species, although, presumably, if the members of any other species were rational, autonomous agents, they would also go into the special moral category and would qualify for the favored treatment. However, defenders of traditional morality insist that, as a matter of fact, no other species has this characteristic. So humans alone are entitled to full moral consideration.

Darwin, as we have seen, resisted the idea that humans have characteristics that are not shared by other animals. Instead, he emphasized the continuities between species: if man is more rational than the apes, it is only a matter of degree, not of kind. But let us set this point aside and grant for the purpose of argument that humans are the only fully rational, autonomous agents. What would follow from this assumption? I want to make two comments.

(a) The first comment has to do with the logical structure of Qualified Speciesism. It is important to see *exactly* what function the reference to man's rationality is supposed to serve. The reference to rationality comes at a certain point in the discussion of morality and species, and has a certain purpose. Let us see what that purpose is.

The discussion begins with the observation that we use nonhuman animals in a variety of ways: to name a few, we raise and eat them as food; we use them in laboratories, not only for medical and psychological experiments, but to test products such as soap and cosmetics; we dissect them in classrooms for educational purposes; we use their skins as clothing, rugs, and wall decorations; we make them objects of our amusement in zoos, circuses, and rodeos; we use them as work animals on farms; we keep them as pets; and we have a popular sport that consists of tracking them down and killing them for the pleasure of it.

Next, it is noted that we would think it deeply immoral if *humans* were used in any of these ways. But this leads to a problem. Ever since Aristotle, it has been recognized as a fundamental rule of moral reasoning that

> When individuals are treated differently, we need to be able to point to a difference between them that justifies the difference in treatment.

Thus, we have to face this question: What is the difference between humans and nonhumans that justifies us in treating nonhumans so differently?

This is where the reference to rationality comes in. Qualified Speciesism attempts to answer this question by pointing to the fact that humans are rational autonomous agents, while the other animals are not—*that* is what is supposed to justify treating nonhuman animals differently.

But now notice this crucial point: we treat nonhumans in a *variety* of ways in which we think it would be wrong to treat humans. In the attempt to justify this, Qualified Speciesism mentions *one* difference between humans and nonhumans. Will this work? Is the fact that humans are rational, while other animals are not, relevant to *all* the differences in treatment?

As a general rule, relevant differences vary with the different kinds of treatment. A difference between individuals that justifies *one* sort of difference in treatment might be completely irrelevant to justifying *another* difference in treatment. Suppose, for example, the admissions committee of a law school accepts one applicant but rejects another. Asked to justify this, they might explain that the first applicant had excellent college grades and test scores, while the second applicant had a miserable record. Or, to take a different sort of example, suppose a doctor treats two patients differently: he gives one a shot of penicillin and puts the other's arm in a plaster cast. Again, this can be justified by pointing to a relevant difference between them: the first patient had an infection, while the second had a broken arm.

Now, suppose we switch things around. Suppose the law school admissions committee is asked to justify admitting A while rejecting B and replies that A had an infection, but B had a broken arm. Or suppose the doctor is asked to justify giving a shot of penicillin to A, but putting B's arm in a cast, and replies that A had better college grades and test scores. Both replies are, of course, silly, for it is clear that what is relevant in the one context is irrelevant in the other.

We might express this point in a general principle:

> *Whether a difference between individuals justifies a difference in treatment depends on the kind of treatment that is in question. A difference that justifies one kind of difference in treatment need not justify another.*

Once this principle is made explicit, it seems obvious and indisputable. But once it is accepted, Qualified Speciesism is seen to be untenable.

Does the fact that someone is a rational, autonomous agent make a difference in how he should be treated? Certainly it may. For such a being, the self-direction of his own life is a great good, valued not only for its instrumental worth, but for its own sake. Thus, paternalistic interference may be seen as an evil. To take a simple example: a woman might have a certain conception of how she wants to live her life. This conception might involve taking risks that we think are foolish. We might therefore try to change her mind; we might call attention to the risks and argue that they are not worth it. But suppose she does not accept our arguments: Are we then justified in forcibly preventing her from living her life as she chooses? It may be argued that we are not justified, for she is, after all, a rational, autonomous agent. But suppose we contrast this case with how we may treat someone who is *not* a fully rational being—a small child, for example. Then we feel perfectly justified in interfering with his conduct to prevent him from taking foolish risks. The fact that the child is not (yet, anyway) a fully rational agent justifies us in treating him differently than we would treat someone who is a fully rational agent.

The same would be true if the comparison were between a (normal adult) human being and a nonhuman animal. If we forcibly intervened to protect the animal from danger, but did not do so for the human, we might justify this by pointing to the fact that the human is a rational autonomous being who knew what she was doing and who had the right to make her own choice, while this was not true of the animal. But this difference is not relevant to justifying just *any* kind of difference in treatment. Suppose what is in question is not paternalistic interference, but putting chemicals in rabbits' eyes to test the "safety" of a new shampoo. Why, it might be asked, is it all right to treat rabbits in this way, when we would not treat humans similarly? To reply that humans are rational agents while rabbits are not is comparable to noting that the rejected law school applicant had a broken arm rather than an infection.

Therefore, the observation that humans are rational agents cannot justify the whole range of differences between our treatment of humans and our treatment of nonhumans. It can (at best) justify *some* differences in treatment, but not others. So, as a justification of our general practice of treating nonhumans "differently," Qualified Speciesism fails.

It might be thought that Qualified Speciesism could be saved by mentioning a bigger set of differences between humans and nonhumans. Rickaby, for example, points out that "Man alone speaks, man alone worships, man alone hopes to contemplate for ever," and so on.[21] Couldn't a *combination* of such unique characteristics justify placing man in a special moral category? The logical problem, however, would remain: we would have to ask, for each kind of treatment, whether man's ability to speak, to worship, or to hope for eternal contemplation is really relevant. What do these things have to do with putting chemicals in a rabbit's eyes? Just as there is no one difference between the species that can justify all the differences in treatment, there is no reason to think that a list of such differences could do the job, either.

(b) A different sort of problem is raised by humans who lack the characteristics that supposedly place man in a privileged moral position. Qualified Speciesism says that the interests of humans count for more because they are rational agents. But some humans, perhaps because they have suffered brain damage, are not rational agents. Granting this, the natural conclusion would be that their status is the status of mere animals, and that they may be used as nonhuman animals are used (perhaps as laboratory subjects or as food?).

Of course, traditional moralists do not accept any such conclusion. The interests of humans are regarded as important no matter what their "handicaps" might be. The traditional view is, apparently, that moral status is determined by what is normal for the species. Therefore, because rationality is the norm, even nonrational humans are to be treated with the respect due to the members of a rational species.

This idea—that how individuals should be treated is determined by what is normal for their species—has a certain appeal because it does seem to express our moral intuition about defective humans. "We should not treat a person worse merely because he has been so unfortunate," we might say about someone who has suffered brain damage. But the idea will not bear close inspection. Suppose (what is probably impossible) that a chimpanzee learned to read and speak English. And suppose he eventually was able to converse about science, literature, and morals. Finally he wants to attend university classes. Now there might be various arguments about whether to permit this, but suppose someone argued as follows: "Only humans should be allowed to attend these classes. Humans can read, talk, and understand science. Chimps cannot." But this chimp *can* do those things. "Yes, but *normal* chimps cannot, and that is what matters." Is this a good argument? Regardless of what other arguments might be persuasive, *this* one is weak. It assumes that we should determine how an individual is to be treated not on the basis of *its* qualities, but on the basis of *other* individuals' qualities. This chimp is not permitted to do something that requires reading, despite the fact that he can read, because other chimps cannot. That seems not only unfair, but irrational.

3. *Moral Individualism.* All this argues for a quite different approach, one that abandons the whole project of trying to justify a "separate moral category" for humans. On this approach, how an individual may be treated is determined not by considering his group memberships, but by considering his own particular characteristics. If A is to be treated differently than B, the justification must be in terms of A's individual characteristics and B's individual characteristics. Treating them differently cannot be justified by pointing out that one or the other is a member of some preferred group.

Where does this leave the relation between species and morality? What of the important differences between humans and other animals? Are they now to be considered irrelevant? The picture that emerges is more complex, but also more true to the facts, than traditional morality. The fact is that human beings are not simply "different" from other animals. In reality, there is a complex pattern of similarities and differences. The matching moral idea is that insofar as a human and a member of another species are similar, they should be treated similarly, while to the extent that they are different, they should be treated differently. This will allow the human to assert a right to better treatment whenever there is some difference between him and other animals (or other humans!) that justifies treating him better. But it will *not* permit him to claim greater rights simply because he is human or because humans in general have some quality that he lacks or because he has some characteristic that is irrelevant to the particular type of treatment in question.

There is a striking parallel between this Moral Individualism and Darwin's view about the nature of species. Before Darwin, when species were thought to be immutable, naturalists believed that membership in a species was determined by whether the organism possessed the qualities that defined the *essence* of the species. This essence was something real and determinate, fixed by nature itself, and the systems of classification devised by biologists were viewed as accurate or inaccurate depending on how well they corresponded to this fixed order of nature. Evolutionary biology implies a very different view. Darwin argued that there are no fixed essences; there is only a multitude of organisms that resemble one another in some ways, but differ in others. The only reality is the individual.[22] How those individuals are grouped—into species, varieties, and so on—is more or less arbitrary. In *The Origin of Species,* he wrote: "I look at the term species, as one arbitrarily given for the sake of convenience to a set of individuals closely resembling each other, and that it does not essentially differ from the term variety, which is given to less distinct and more fluctuating forms. The term variety, again, in comparison with mere individual differences, is also applied arbitrarily, and for mere convenience sake."[23] Thus, Darwinian biology substitutes individual organisms, with their profusion of similarities and differences, for the old idea of determinate species; while Moral Individualism substitutes the view that our treatment of those organisms must be sensitive to those similarities and differences for the old view that what matters is the species to which the organism belongs.

IV

How does "the gradual illumination of men's minds," of the sort provided by Darwin's theory, lead to the rejection of speciesism? We might think of it as a historical process that has four stages.

In the first stage, traditional morality is comfortably accepted because it is supported by a worldview in which everyone (or, so nearly everyone as makes no difference) has confidence. The moral view is simple. Human beings, as Kant put it, have "an intrinsic worth, i.e., *dignity,*" which makes them valuable "above all price," while other animals "are there merely as means to an end. That end is man."[24] The worldview that supported this ethical doctrine had several familiar elements. The universe, with the earth at its center, was seen as created by God primarily to provide a home for humans, who were made in his image. The other animals were created by God for their use. Humans, therefore, are set apart from other animals and have a radically different *nature.* This justifies their special moral standing.

In the second stage, the worldview begins to break up. This had begun to happen, of course, long before Darwin—it was already known, for example, that the earth is not the center of the cosmos, and, indeed, that considered as a celestial body it seems to be nothing special. But Darwin completed the job by showing that humans, far from being set apart from the other animals, are part of the same natural order and, indeed, are actually kin to them. By the time Darwin was done, the old worldview was virtually demolished.

This did not mean, however, that the associated moral view would be immediately abandoned. Firmly established moral doctrines do not lose their grip overnight, sometimes not even overcentury. As Peter Singer observes, "If the foundations of an ideological position are knocked out from under it, new foundations will be found, or else the ideological position will just hang there, defying the logical equivalent of the law of gravity."[25]

We are now in the third stage, which comes when people realize that, having lost its foundations, the old moral view needs to be reexamined. In his review of Regan's book Nozick remarks that "Nothing much should be inferred from our not presently having a theory of the moral importance of species membership that no one has spent much time trying to formulate because the issue hasn't seemed pressing."[26] The issue hasn't seemed pressing because philosophers have not yet fully assimilated the implications of the collapse of the old worldview.

It still might turn out that traditional morality is defensible if new support can be found for it. Nozick and a host of others think this is likely. Philosophers such as Singer and Regan take a different view: "the gradual illumination of men's minds" must lead to a new ethic in which species membership is seen as relatively unimportant. For the reasons given above, I think that on this broad issue the revisionists are right. The most defensible view seems to be some form of Moral Individualism, according to which what matters is the individual characteristics of organisms and not the classes to which they are assigned. Whatever the outcome of the debate, the issue can no longer be avoided. What has made it "pressing" is not simply a faddish interest taken by some philosophers in animal welfare; rather, it is an issue pressed upon us by the disintegration of the pre-Darwinian way of understanding nature. The fourth and final stage of the historical process will be reached if and when a new equilibrium is found in which our morality can once again comfortably coexist with our understanding of the world and our place in it.

Notes

1. Quoted in Ronald W. Clark, *The Survival of Charles Darwin: A Biography of a Man and an Idea* (New York: Random House, 1984), 178, from Notebook "C" in the Darwin papers held at Cambridge University Library. Clark's biography is an excellent compendium of information about various matters relating to Darwin.

2. Ludwig Wittgenstein, *Tractatus Logico-Philosophicus*, translated by D. F. Pears and B. F. McGuiness (London: Routledge and Kegan Paul, 1961), 4.1122, 49.

3. Letter to Lassalle, January 16, 1861, quoted in Clark, *The Survival of Charles Darwin*, 212.

4. C. Antony Flew, *Evolutionary Ethics* (London: Macmillan, 1967), 5.

5. Quoted in Erhard Lucas, "Marx and Engels; Auseinandersetzung mit Darwin zur Differenz zwischen Marx und Engels," *International Review of Social History* 9 (1964): 433–69. The quotation is from a letter written by Darwin, supposedly to Marx. However, there is now some reason to believe the letter was actually written to Edward Aveling, Marx's son-in-law.

6. Charles Darwin, *On the Origin of Species by Means of Natural Selection, or The Preservation of Favoured Races in the Struggle for Life* (London: John Murray, 1859), 488.

7. Charles Darwin, *The Descent of Man and Selection in Relation to Sex* (New York: Random House Modern Library Edition, 1977), 463.

8. "Darwin's Early and Unpublished Notebooks," in Howard E. Gruber, *Darwin on Man: A Psychological Study of Scientific Creativity* (London: Wildwood House, 1974), 296.

9. *The Descent of Man*, 446.

10. Joseph Rickaby, S. J., *Moral Philosophy* (London, 1892), reprinted in Tom Regan and Peter Singer, eds., *Animal Rights and Human Obligations* (Englewood Cliffs, N.J.: Prentice-Hall, 1976), 179. According to such figures as Aquinas, Descartes, Kant, and Rickaby, the so-called interests of nonhumans count for *nothing*, morally speaking; if it is sometimes wrong to "mistreat" them, it is only because the interests of humans are somehow involved. There is another, less radical view, taken by most contemporary defenders of traditional morality: namely, that while the interests of nonhumans count for *something*, they count for much less than the interests of humans. In the present context, this difference is unimportant; the arguments given here apply equally to both.

11. *The Descent of Man*, 446.

12. Quoted in Clark, *The Survival of Charles Darwin*, 76. For more about Darwin's attitude toward animals, see pp. 76–77.

13. Letter to Ray Lankester, March 22, 1871, in Francis Darwin, ed., *The Life and Letters of Charles Darwin* (London: John Murray, 1887), 3:200.

14. See *The Collected Papers of Charles Darwin*, edited by Paul H. Barrett (Chicago: University of Chicago Press, 1977), 2:226.

15. Darwin's "B" Notebook, in the Darwin papers held at Cambridge University Library, p. 121. Quoted in Clark, *The Survival of Charles Darwin*, 76.

16. Asa Gray, *Natural Science and Religion: Two Lectures Delivered to the Theological School of Yale College* (New York: Charles Scribner's Sons, 1880), 54. Gray's view contrasts sharply with that of another of Darwin's champions, T. H. Huxley. In reply to the charge that Darwin was undermining human dignity, Huxley declared: "no-one is more strongly convinced than I am of the vastness of the gulf between civilized man and the brutes.... Our reverence for the nobility of manhood will not be lessened by the knowledge, that Man is, in substance and in structure, one with the brutes." T. H. Huxley, *Evidence as to Man's Place in Nature* (London: Williams and Norgate, 1863), chap. 2, 129–30, 132. Darwin, who was in close contact with both men, must have been aware of their different views of the moral implications of his theory. But we do not know what he himself made of this.

17. The story is included in *My Best Science Fiction Story*, edited by Leo Marguiles and Oscar J. Friend (New York: Pocket Books, 1954).

18. It's an interesting twist: today, writers such as Singer take it for granted that racism is wrong and argue by analogy that speciesism is wrong also, whereas in 1941 Binder took it as obvious that speciesism was wrong and expected his readers to get the point that racism was wrong. See Peter Singer, *Animal Liberation* (New York: New York Review of Books, 1975), chap. 1.

19. Tom Regan, *The Case for Animal Rights* (Berkeley: University of California Press, 1983).

20. Robert Nozick, "About Mammals and People," *New York Times Book Review*, November 27, 1983, 29. For a fuller discussion of Nozick's arguments, see my *End of Life: Euthanasia and Morality* (Oxford: Oxford University Press, 1986), chap. 4.

21. Rickaby, *Moral Philosophy*, 179.

22. For the pre-Darwinian naturalist, variations were of little interest, except as curiosities. It was, after all, the "standard" specimen that best represented the eternal essence of the species that the naturalist was trying to learn about. But for the evolutionary biologist, variation is the very stuff of nature—it is what makes natural selection possible.

23. *The Origin of Species*, 52. For a recent defense of the idea that there are several equally valid ways species might be identified, each serving a legitimate need of biologists, see Philip Kitcher, "Species," *Philosophy of Science* 51 (1984): 308–33.

24. Immanuel Kant, *Foundation of the Metaphysics of Morals*, translated by Lewis White Beck (Indianapolis, Ind.: Bobbs-Merrill, 1959), 47; and *Lectures on Ethics*, translated by Louis Infield (New York: Harper and Row, 1963), 239–40.

25. Singer, *Animal Liberation*, 231.

26. Nozick, "About Mammals and People," 29.

THREE

DRAWING LINES

When people are skeptical of the idea that we have moral responsibilities with respect to animals or that we should have laws protecting them, they will ask, "But where do we draw the line?" They may have two things in mind: (1) Where do we draw the line with respect to the *kinds of animals* to whom we have duties or on whom we should confer legal protection? Do we have duties to fish? Snails? Insects? Viruses? (2) Where do we draw the line with respect to the *kinds of duties* we should acknowledge? Do we have a duty not to harm them? To protect them from harm? To feed them? I will begin by discussing the first question. But as we shall see, the two are related. If we understand the right way to answer one, we will know how to answer the other.

Here is an example of line drawing in the law. The U.S. Animal Welfare Act, enacted in 1966 and amended several times since then, instructs the secretary of agriculture to take steps to protect animals used in various ways, including research. Originally, the act defined *animal* as follows:

> The term "animal" means any live or dead dog, cat, monkey (nonhuman primate mammal), guinea pig, hamster, rabbit, or such other warm-blooded animal, as the Secretary may determine is being used, or is intended for use, for research, testing, experimentation, or exhibition purposes or as a pet; but such term excludes horses not used for research purposes and other farm animals, such as, but not limited to livestock or poultry, used or intended for use as food or fiber,

or livestock or poultry used or intended for improving animal nutrition, breeding, management or production efficiency, or for improving the quality of food
or fiber. With respect to a dog the term means all dogs including those used for
hunting, security, or breeding purposes. (Animal Welfare Act as Amended [7
U.S.C. 2132(g)])

Of course, this is not intended as a proper definition of *animal,* but only a
specification of which animals are included within the scope of the act.

Mice, rats, and birds are not specifically mentioned, but they seem to be
included because they are "warm-blooded animals." However, soon after
the act was passed, the secretary of agriculture issued a regulation that excluded them from its scope. There the matter stood until the 1990s, when
the Humane Society of the United States and some other pro-animal groups
challenged the regulation in court, arguing that there is no legal basis for
exempting these species. The court agreed, and the Department of Agriculture began to draft new regulations that would have brought the mice,
rats, and birds back under the act's somewhat feeble protections. At this
point, Senator Jesse Helms of North Carolina stepped in and proposed an
amendment to the act that would make the new regulations unnecessary.
He proposed to change the definition of *animal* so that "birds, rats of the
genus *Rattus,* and mice of the genus *Mus*" would be specifically excluded.[1]
The Helms amendment was adopted without debate and was signed into
law by President George W. Bush in May 2002.

Why shouldn't mice, rats, and birds have the same status as guinea pigs,
hamsters, and rabbits? On what grounds could such distinctions be made?
For the American Association of Universities (AAU) and others who supported Senator Helms' proposal, the issue appears to have been entirely practical. More than 90 percent of laboratory animals are mice, rats, or birds, so if
they don't count, there will be enormously less paperwork needed to comply
with federal regulations.[2] On the Senate floor, Mr. Helms also mentioned the
"paperwork burden."[3] Of course, there is nothing wrong with modifying a
policy for the sake of efficiency, especially if the administrative burden would
be great and there is no important matter of principle involved.

The problem is that, for those on the other side, there are important matters of principle involved. The principles are ethical. Central among them is
the idea that the interests of animals are important for their own sakes and
that it is indecent of humans not to respect those interests. It is problematic
whether ethical principles should be enforced by law, especially when they

are not shared by everyone, and I will say nothing about that. But I will assume that at least part of the motivation behind the Animal Welfare Act is a concern for the animals' own interests. This is consistent with the language of the act, which lists as its first purpose "to insure that animals intended for use in research facilities or for exhibition purposes or for use as pets are provided humane care and treatment" (7 U.S.C. 2131[1]).

The fact that the Animal Welfare Act does not treat all animals as equals will not offend most people. Most people—and by this I mean people who are at least moderately thoughtful about such matters—think of some animals as more worthy of protection than others. They seem to think in terms of a hierarchy in which the animal's rank depends, more or less, on its perceived degree of similarity to humans. Thus, the mistreatment of primates is seen as a serious matter, and dogs and cats also rate high, but snakes and fish count for little. The act's original definition of *animal* reflects this view: "cold-blooded" animals were never included.

Theories of Moral Standing

Theories of moral standing try to answer the question, "To whom do we have direct duties?" A *direct* duty is a duty to an individual as contrasted with a duty that merely involves the individual. If I promise you that I will feed your cat while you are away, the duty created by the promise is not a duty to your cat, even though it involves the cat; it is a duty to you. No one doubts that there can be duties involving animals. The question is whether we have duties *to* them, and if so, why.

The concept of moral standing was introduced by philosophers in the 1970s to deal with a number of issues that had arisen, such as the treatment of animals, but also abortion, euthanasia, and the environment. Philosophers thought they could make progress in these areas by establishing the moral standing of animals, fetuses, comatose persons, trees, and so on. The notion of "standing" was, of course, borrowed from the law.[4] Just as legal standing means that you have the right to bring your claims before a court, moral standing means that, from a moral point of view, you have claims that must be heard—that your interests constitute morally good reasons why you may or may not be treated in this or that way. So a key question became: "What qualifies one for moral standing?" Here is a quick summary of four main kinds of theories that have been proposed:

1. The first thought that occurred to many philosophers was that simply being human confers moral standing. This had the advantage of being nondiscriminatory, at least as far as humans were concerned. It echoed the rhetoric of the civil rights movement, which proclaimed that people of all races have equal rights "simply in virtue of being human," with no other qualification necessary. But only a little reflection was needed to see that this statement can't be taken literally. Even if it were true that all and only humans have full moral standing, we should be able to say *what it is* about being human that gives us this special status. Simply being human cannot be what does the job.

2. A more substantial type of theory connects moral standing with such qualities as self-consciousness, autonomy, and rationality—humans, it was said, have full moral standing because they have such characteristics. These theories have a long history from Aristotle, who believed that human rationality gives us a supremely important place in the scheme of things, to Kant, who held that only self-conscious beings can be direct beneficiaries of obligations. Recently, Kantians such as Christine Korsgaard have argued that exercising one's capacity for rational choice necessarily involves acknowledging the special moral status of human beings.[5]

3. Still another idea is that *having moral standing* and *being a moral agent* go together—the same characteristics that make for one make for the other. Thus, you have moral standing if you have the capacity for moral judgment and action. This type of theory is especially attractive to contractarians, who see moral obligations as arising from agreements between people who are then expected to keep their bargains. John Rawls asks to whom the duties of justice are owed, and he replies: "The natural answer seems to be that it is precisely the moral persons who are entitled to equal justice.... They are capable of having (and are assumed to acquire) a sense of justice, a normally effective desire to apply and to act upon the principles of justice, at least to a certain minimum degree.... Those who can give justice are owed justice."[6]

However, there is a problem with theories that emphasize qualities like self-consciousness, autonomy, and moral agency: they set the bar too high. Although the proponents of these theories emphasize that moral standing is not limited by definition to normal adult humans—it is at least possible for some nonhuman animals (as well as hypothetical extraterrestrials) to be self-conscious, autonomous persons, or to be moral agents—it turns out that in fact only normal adult humans uncontroversially satisfy such demanding criteria. This means, for one thing, that these theories make unwelcome discriminations among human beings. They leave us with a problem about what to say about babies and mentally handicapped people, who may not be self-conscious, autonomous moral agents. Moreover, animals, as is frequently noted, can feel pain even if they do not possess the fancier qualities. So it seems wrong to torture them; and it seems wrong because of what is being done to them.

4. For this reason, many philosophers, especially utilitarians, were attracted to a more modest theory that says that to have moral standing, it is only necessary that one be able to feel pain. Thus, Mark Bernstein writes: "The realm of the morally considerable is constituted by those individuals with the capacity for modifiable, hedonic conscious experience. If we use 'phenomenology' or 'sentience' as abbreviations for this capacity, we can say that experientialism dictates that all and only those with moral standing are phenomenological or sentient individuals."[7]

Finally, we may note that in working their way toward a conception of moral standing, many writers take a detour through the concept of personhood. They take "What qualifies one for moral standing?" and "What is a person?" to be essentially the same question. I believe that Joseph Fletcher was the first to produce a list of "conditions for personhood" with an eye to addressing ethical issues,[8] but others soon followed. Mary Anne Warren's list of person-making qualities in her much-anthologized 1973 paper on abortion is perhaps the most famous.[9] Warren produced an account of what it means to be a person—where *person* is not just a biological category, but denotes individuals with the psychological and "personal" dimensions of human beings—in order to argue that because fetuses lack the characteristics of persons, they do not have the full moral rights of persons. This became a familiar strategy. In 1988, some of the literature that had been generated was gathered into an anthology called *What Is a Person?* and its editor wrote: "The problems of personhood...are central to issues in ethics ranging from the treatment or termination of infants with birth defects to the question whether there can be rational suicide. But before questions on such issues as the morality of abortion, genetic engineering, infanticide, and so on, can be settled, the problems of personhood must be clarified and analyzed.... What qualities/attributes must a being have to be considered a person? Why are those qualities, and not others, significant?"[10]

Connecting moral standing with personhood provides an intuitively plausible way of identifying the characteristics that are important for moral standing. We are confident that persons have moral standing, and so, if certain qualities are central to personhood, it is reasonable to conjecture that those qualities are also central to moral standing. If those qualities happen to be the grand, impressive features of human nature that have always led humans to regard themselves as special, so much the better. In this way, the appeal to such qualities as rationality, autonomy, self-consciousness, and moral agency were made to seem less arbitrary.

Characteristics and Types of Treatment

The theories I have mentioned will be familiar to anyone who is acquainted with the literature produced by moral philosophers since the 1970s. I have summarized these theories without going into any detail about them because I want to make a general point about their structure. Despite differences in detail, the theories have this in common: they all assume that the answer to the question of how an individual may be treated depends on whether the individual qualifies for a general sort of status, which in turn depends on whether the individual possesses a few general characteristics. But no answer of this form can be correct. In what follows, I will explain why this is so and why it is important.

Each of the theories offers an account of the relation between (1) how individuals may be treated and (2) facts about them—facts about their capacities, abilities, and other characteristics, such as whether they are rational, self-conscious, or sentient. But what, exactly, is the relation between the facts about an individual and how the individual may be treated? Let us consider how this works, first for normal adult humans, where our intuitions are firmest.

Facts about people often figure into the reasons why they may or may not be treated in this or that way. Adam may be ejected from the choir because he can't sing. Betty may be given Prozac because she is depressed. Charles may be congratulated because he has just gotten engaged. Doris may be promoted because she is a hard worker. Notice, however, that a fact that justifies one type of treatment may not justify a different type of treatment: Unless something unusual is going on, we cannot justify giving Betty Prozac on the grounds that she can't sing or throwing Adam out of the choir because he has become engaged.

The same is true of the more impressive characteristics that are mentioned in the theories of moral standing. Autonomy and self-consciousness are not ethical superqualities that entitle the bearer to every possible kind of favorable treatment. Like musical ability and betrothal, they are relevant to some types of treatment, but not to others.

Autonomy

Humans are rational, autonomous agents who can guide their own conduct according to their desires and their conceptions of how they ought to live. Does this fact make a difference in how they may be treated? Of course it does. Suppose someone wants to live her life in a way that involves risks we think are foolish. We may try to change her mind; we may point out the risks and argue that they are not worth it. But may we compel her to follow our advice? We may not, for she is, after all, a rational, autonomous agent.

It is different for someone who is not fully rational—a small child, for example. Then we may prevent her from harming herself. The fact that the child is not yet a fully rational agent justifies us in treating her differently than we would treat someone who is a fully rational agent.

Once we understand why autonomy makes a difference in how someone may be treated, it becomes clear in the cases in which it does make a difference that possession of this quality is not relevant in other sorts of cases. Suppose the treatment at issue is not paternalistic interference, but torture: Why would it be wrong to poke you with a stick? The answer is not that you are autonomous; the answer is that it would cause you pain.

Self-consciousness

To be self-conscious is to be able to make oneself the object of one's thoughts, to have beliefs about oneself, and to be able to reflect on one's own character and conduct. As the term is used by most philosophers, *self-consciousness* also includes the capacity for conceiving of oneself as extended through time—for understanding that one has a past and a future.

There are, therefore, a number of goods that self-consciousness makes possible: self-confidence, hope for the future, satisfaction with your life, the belief that you are someone of value, and the knowledge that you are loved and appreciated by other people. Without self-consciousness, there could be no sense of pride or self-worth. Considered in this light, it is no wonder that some philosophers have singled-out self-consciousness as a supremely important human quality.

At the same time, a person who has this capacity is thereby vulnerable to a special range of harms. Because you are capable of reflecting on your own conduct and your own place in the world, you may feel embarrassed, humiliated, guilty, and worthless. Because you can think about your own future, you may despair and lose hope. Your capacity for self-referential beliefs and attitudes makes it possible for you to feel that your life and activities have no meaning, and you can believe, rightly or wrongly, that other people have no regard for you.

This being so, there are ways of treating people that are objectionable on grounds that involve their capacity for self-consciousness. I should not do things that would embarrass or humiliate you. I should not unjustly curse you or hold you in contempt. I should not question or criticize you in ways that would cause you debilitating self-doubt or self-loathing. I should not belittle you in ways that would injure your self-respect. I should not treat you in such a way as to take away your hope for the future.

Moral Agency

Humans have the capacity for moral judgment and action, and this, it is often said, gives them an especially noble nature that sets them apart from other animals. But, self-congratulation aside, how is the possession of this capacity relevant to how an individual may be treated? Here are three ways of treating people that are appropriate if they are moral agents.

First, and most obviously, moral agents may merit praise or blame for what they do. Beings who lack a sense of right and wrong are not eligible for such responses.

Second, the fact that someone has moral capacities may be important when we need to influence his or her conduct. When we are dealing with moral agents, we can reason with them—we can influence their behavior by appealing to their sense of right. This may be better than bribes, threats, or other cajolery not only because it respects their autonomy, but because such influence might be more stable and longer-lasting. Demands for social justice, for example, are more effective in the long run if they address people's consciences than if they are merely exercises of power.

Third, moral agency includes the capacity for cooperating with others, and so moral agents are individuals with whom we can make agreements.

This is the critical capacity for rational-choice contractarians, who believe that moral obligations exist only as a result of such agreements. But general views aside, it is important in everyday life to discern whom one can trust and with whom one can profitably cooperate. So this is another respect in which someone's being a moral agent makes a difference in our dealings with him or her.

The Ability to Feel Pain

The ability to feel pain is perhaps the most obviously relevant characteristic anyone possesses. The fact that jabbing you with a stick would cause you pain is a complete and sufficient reason why I should not do it. This reason does not need to be supplemented or reinforced by considerations having to do with your dignity as a rational being, your autonomy, or anything like that. It is enough that being jabbed hurts.

Of course, your interests as an autonomous agent may be affected by debilitating pain. Chronic pain may prevent you from leading the kind of life you want to lead, and even a short experience of intense pain may have lasting psychological effects. But this only means that in the case of autonomous beings there is an additional reason why torture is wrong. The additional reason does not replace the original one, nor is one a mere shorthand for the other.

But regardless of how important the ability to feel pain may be, when other types of treatment are involved, it may be irrelevant: what entitles you to remain in the choir is not the same as what makes it objectionable to poke you with the stick.

We may draw the following conclusions from all this: there is no characteristic or reasonably small set of characteristics that sets some creatures apart from others as meriting respectful treatment. That is the wrong way to think about the relation between an individual's characteristics and how he or she may be treated. Instead, we have an array of characteristics and an array of treatments, with each characteristic relevant to justifying some types of treatment but not others. If an individual possesses a particular characteristic (such as the ability to feel pain), then we may have a duty to treat it in a certain way (not to torture it), even if that same individual does not possess other characteristics (such as autonomy) that would mandate other sorts of treatment (refraining from coercion).

We could spin these observations into a theory of moral standing that would compete with the other theories. Our theory would start like this: there is no such thing as moral standing *simpliciter.* Rather, moral standing is always moral standing with respect to some particular mode of treatment. A sentient being has moral standing with respect to not being tortured. A self-conscious being has moral standing with respect to not being humiliated. An autonomous being has moral standing with respect to not being coerced. And so on. If asked toward whom it is appropriate to direct fundamental moral consideration,[11] we could reply: it is appropriate to direct moral consideration toward any individual who has any of the indefinitely long list of characteristics that constitute morally good reasons why he or she should or should not be treated in any of the various ways in which individuals may be treated.

You may think this isn't a very appealing theory. It is tedious; it lacks the crispness of the other theories; it doesn't yield quick and easy answers to practical questions; and, worse, it isn't exciting. But it is the truth about moral standing. (I believe it was Bertrand Russell who once said it wasn't his fault if the truth wasn't exciting.)

It would do no harm, however, and it might be helpful for clarity's sake, to drop the notion of "standing" altogether and replace it with a simpler conception. We could just say that the fact that doing so-and-so would cause pain to someone (to any individual) is a reason not to do it. The fact that doing so-and-so would humiliate someone (any individual) is a reason not to do it. And so on. Sentience and self-consciousness fit into the picture like this: someone's sentience and someone's self-consciousness are facts about them that explain why they are susceptible to the evils of pain and humiliation.

We would then see our subject as part of the theory of reasons for action. We would distinguish three elements: what is done to the individual; the reason for doing it or not doing it, which connects the action to some benefit or harm to the individual; and the pertinent facts about the individual that help to explain why he or she is susceptible to that particular benefit or harm.

Action: Poking you with a sharp stick
Reason for not doing that: It would cause you pain.
Facts about you that explain why you are capable of feeling pain: You have
conscious experiences and a nervous system of a certain kind; you
are sentient.

Action: Telling your husband's friends that he is impotent
Reason for not doing that: It would humiliate him.

Facts about him that explain why he is capable of being humiliated: He has attitudes and beliefs about himself and about how others regard him; he is self-conscious.

So, part of our theory of reasons for action would go like this. We always have reason not to do harm. If treating an individual in a certain way harms him or her, that is a reason not to do it. The fact that he or she is autonomous or self-conscious or sentient simply helps to explain why he or she is susceptible to particular kinds of harms.

Kinds of Animals and the Animal Welfare Act

How will a morally decent human treat nonhuman animals? The answer will depend, in part, on what we think nonhumans are like, and most of us are willing to attribute a fairly broad range of morally important characteristics to them. Ever since Darwin taught us to see ourselves as kin to the other animals, we have increasingly come to think of them as like us in morally significant ways.[12] We believe that monkeys have cognitive and social abilities similar to our own, that all sorts of animals are self-conscious, and that dogs have qualities such as courage and loyalty. And even if the "lower animals" do not have these impressive qualities, we think it is undeniable that they can at least feel pain.

There are, of course, those who are skeptical about this consensus. Daniel Dennett chides animal-rights advocates for assuming too much and trusting their intuitions too easily. Even the consciousness of animals, he says, can be doubted:

> Cog, a delightfully humanoid robot being built at MIT, has eyes, hands, and arms that move the way yours do—swiftly, relaxedly, compliantly. Even those of us working on the project, knowing full well that we haven't even begun to program the high level processes that might arguably endow Cog with consciousness, get an almost overwhelming sense of being in the presence of another conscious observer when Cog's eyes still quite blindly and stupidly follow one's hand gestures. Once again, I plead for symmetry: when you acknowledge the power of such elegant, life-like motions to charm you into an illusion, note that it ought to be an open question, still, whether you are also being charmed by your beloved dog or cat, or the noble elephant. Feelings are too easy to provoke for them to count for much here.[13]

It is a stretch to doubt the consciousness of "your beloved dog or cat," and there is no evidence that would compel such a major change in how we think of those animals. Indeed, Dennett does not say there is any such evidence: he only pleads for us not to preclude the possibility. The plea for open-mindedness is hard to fault. Nonetheless, I believe the most reasonable approach, when formulating ethical and social policies, is to assume that the prevailing consensus is correct except where we have good evidence to the contrary.

43

On the fundamental question of whether animals can feel pain, scientific investigations tend to confirm the commonly held belief that most animals, especially the "higher" animals, do feel pain. The mechanisms that enable us to feel pain are not fully understood, but we do know a good bit about them. In humans, nociceptors—neurons specialized for sensing noxious stimuli—are connected to a central nervous system, and the resulting signals are processed in the brain. Until recently it was believed that the brain's work was divided into two distinct parts: a sensory system operating in the somatosensory cortex, resulting in our conscious experiences of pain, and an affective-motivational system associated with the frontal lobes, responsible for our behavioral reactions. Now, however, this picture has been called into question, and it may be that the best we can say is that the brain's system for processing the information from the nociceptors seems to be spread over multiple regions. At any rate, the human nociceptive system also includes endogenous opiods, or endorphins, which provide the brain with its natural "pain-killing" ability.

The question of which other animals feel pain is a real and important issue, not to be settled by appeal to "common sense," as Dennett insists. Only a complete scientific understanding of pain, which we do not yet have, could tell us all that we need to know. In the meantime, however, we do have a rough idea of what to look for. If we want to know whether it is reasonable to believe that a particular kind of animal is capable of feeling pain, we may ask: Are there nociceptors present? Are they connected to a central nervous system? What happens in that nervous system to the signals from the nociceptors? And are there endogenous opiods? In our present state of understanding, this sort of information, together with the obvious behavioral signs of distress, is the best evidence we can have that an animal is capable of feeling pain.[14]

It is harder to devise experimental tests for the presence of other, more sophisticated capacities. Yet there is some evidence even for such capacities as self-consciousness. One idea is to see whether animals can recognize themselves in mirrors (after it has been established that they know how mirrors work and can recognize other objects in mirrors). In 1970, the psychologist Gordon Gallup devised a clever experiment to test this. While chimpanzees were unconscious, he placed a red mark on one of their eyebrows and ears. Then, he showed each chimp a full-length mirror. The chimps would immediately rub the marked spots and examine their fingers. We are apt to agree with Gallup that this provides strong evidence that the chimps are self-aware. However, Gallup's experiment was subsequently tried on other species, with very different results. Surprisingly, gorillas and monkeys failed the test. But more recently, using a modified form of the Gallup test, Marc Hauser has shown that cotton-top tamarins do show mirror self-recognition.[15]

It is clear, then, that we should proceed cautiously. But bearing all this in mind, let us return to our question: "How will a morally decent human treat nonhuman animals?" No general answer is possible because animals are different from one another—a chimpanzee has little in common with a mockingbird. So how, for example, may a chimpanzee be treated? Once again, it depends on what sort of treatment we have in mind. There are lots of ways of treating chimps, just as there are lots of ways of treating people. This means that if we seriously want to know how chimps may be treated, we will have to consider a long list of treatments and relevant characteristics.

Is there anything about a chimp that makes it objectionable to poke it with a stick? Yes—the chimp can feel pain. Is there anything about a chimp that makes it objectionable to confine it to a barren cage? Yes—chimps are active, intelligent creatures that cannot thrive without a stimulating environment. Is there anything about a female chimp that makes it objectionable to separate her from her babies? Yes—chimpanzee mothers and babies are emotionally bonded in much the same way as are human mothers and babies.

Is there anything about chimps that makes it objectionable to exclude them from college classrooms? No—they lack the intellectual capacities necessary to participate in college classes. Is there anything about chimps that makes it objectionable to exclude them from the choir? No—they can't sing. Is there anything about a chimp that makes it impermissible to forcibly vaccinate it against a disease? No—the chimp lacks the cognitive capacities that would enable it to choose for itself in the relevant sense.

Obviously, we could continue in this way indefinitely. The point, though, is that there is no general answer to the question of how chimps may be treated. There are only the various ways of treating them and the various considerations that count for and against those treatments. Among other things, this means that the question "Where do we draw the line?" is misguided. As we noted at the outset, the question may be taken in two ways: (1) Where do we draw the line with respect to the kinds of animals to whom we have duties? and (2) Where do we draw the line with respect to which duties we have? But in neither instance is there one place to draw the line. There is only an indefinitely long series of lines: where causing pain is concerned, we draw the line between individuals who can feel pain and individuals who cannot; where separating mothers and babies is concerned, we draw the line between mothers who are bonded with their babies (and babies who need their mothers), and those who are not; and so on.

For purposes of public policy, however, we may need to draw rough lines, and we can do this by attending to the characteristics that are typical of the members of various species and the kinds of treatment that they are likely to receive in relevant contexts. For example, if the relevant context is laboratory research, in which the animals are liable to be separated from their own kind, kept for long periods in sterile cages, and caused a lot of pain, and we are seeking to ensure "humane care and treatment," then it is reasonable to draw the line between species whose members are social, are intelligent, and can feel pain, and species whose members lack those qualities.

The Animal Welfare Act's list of included and excluded species is a jerry-rigged affair that looks like the result of compromise and political bargaining. But in some respects it isn't bad. When the context is "research, testing, [and] experimentation," the secretary of agriculture is authorized to ensure "humane care and treatment" for "dog[s], cat[s], monkey[s] (nonhuman primate mammal[s]), guinea pig[s], hamster[s], rabbit[s], or such other warm-blooded animal[s]." The six kinds of animals mentioned by name appear to be no more than examples of the kinds intended; the language of the act includes all "warm-blooded animals" such as guinea pigs, hamsters, or rabbits. This category seems to capture the social, intelligent, and sensitive animals about whom we should be concerned when they are taken into the laboratory. At the same time, the act's protections do not extend to snakes, snails, or fish, where the presence of the relevant qualities seems less certain. And what of the Helms amendment? In this context, if a mouse or a rat isn't relevantly similar to a guinea pig or a hamster, what is? The Helms amendment is contrary not only to good sense, but to the intent of the original legislation. Its adoption was a lamentable step backward.

Notes

1. The amendment replaced the words "excludes horses not used for research purposes" with "excludes birds, rats of the genus *Rattus*, and mice of the genus *Mus* bred for use in research, horses not used for research purposes."

2. Letter from AAU president Nils Hasselmo to Senator Helms, February 21, 2002.

3. *Congressional Record*, February 12, 2002, S624.

4. I believe that Christopher Stone's book *Should Trees Have Standing?* (Los Altos, Calif.: William Kaufmann, 1972) prompted the borrowing.

5. Christine Korsgaard, *The Sources of Normativity* (Cambridge: Cambridge University Press, 1996).

6. John Rawls, *A Theory of Justice* (Cambridge, Mass.: Harvard University Press, 1971), 505, 510.

7. Mark Bernstein, *On Moral Considerability: An Essay on Who Morally Matters* (New York: Oxford University Press, 1998), 24.

8. Joseph Fletcher, "Indicators of Humanhood: A Tentative Profile of Man," *Hastings Center Report* 2 (November 1972): 1–4.

9. Mary Anne Warren, "On the Moral and Legal Status of Abortion," *The Monist* 57 (1973): 43–61. Warren's more recent views are presented in her book *Moral Status: Obligations to Persons and Other Living Things* (Oxford: Clarendon Press, 1997).

10. Michael F. Goodman, ed., *What Is a Person?* (Clifton, N.J.: Humana Press, 1988), vii.

11. See Arthur Kuflick, "Moral Standing," in *Routledge Encyclopedia of Philosophy* (London: Routledge, 1998), 6:550.

12. See James Rachels, *Created from Animals* (Oxford: Oxford University Press, 1990).

13. Daniel Dennett, *Brainchildren* (Cambridge, Mass.: Bradford Books, 1998), 340.

14. The best treatment of these issues of which I am aware is an (as yet) unpublished paper by Colin Allen, "Animal Pain," from which I have learned a great deal. [*Editor's note:* This paper was published in *Nous* 38, no. 4 (December 2004): 617–43.]

15. Marc Hauser, *Wild Minds: What Animals Really Think* (New York: Henry Holt, 2000), 100–109.

LIVES

FOUR

The Value of Human Life

Human life, said Kant, is valuable "above all price,"[1] and few would disagree, at least in the abstract. But in the context of particular ethical issues—suicide, abortion, capital punishment, euthanasia, the treatment of defective newborns—the meaning and application of this principle are uncertain. How should we think about the value of human life? Can we achieve a reasonable understanding of this principle that will give us some insight into its basis and allow us to judge, in various instances, what follows from it and how much weight it will bear?

The Simple View

We may begin with the most obvious sort of value that a life has—namely, the *Personal Value* that a life has for its subject. This is the value that my life has for me and your life has for you.

The idea that something has value "for you" is easily misunderstood. It can be taken in two ways. First, it may suggest that we are dealing only with personal opinions and tastes—something is good "for you" just in case you believe it is important or you care about it. (Others, of course, may not believe it is important and may not care about it, so it would not be good "for them.") Often, this notion is introduced to insinuate that, despite your fondness for something, it has no real value: "Yes, I suppose country music is good, for you." This interpretation of the relativizing clause comes most immediately to mind, and it is tempting to understand the Personal Value of human life in this way.

But there is a second interpretation. Consider the sense in which your eyes are important to you. It is not merely that you believe they are valuable, nor is it merely that you care about them. Your eyes are important to you in the sense that *you are the one who benefits from them* and *you are the one who would be harmed if anything happened to them*. In a perfectly plain sense, you—not me or your neighbor or your cousin Harry—are the one who stands to lose if your eyes are damaged. The loss would be real and not just a matter of opinion or taste. You really would be worse off without them.

Your life has value "for you" in this second sense. You would be harmed by its loss, just as you would be harmed by the loss of your eyesight or your hearing. The loss of your life, of course, is more comprehensive, inasmuch as your life includes virtually everything you hold dear—your enjoyments, activities, relationships, desires, aspirations, projects, achievements, and a great deal more. That is why your death would be, from your own point of view, not just unfortunate but catastrophic.

We can be a little more specific about what we value when we value our lives. There is a difference between being alive, in the merely biological sense, and having a life, in the sense of a biography that includes enjoyments, activities, and all the rest. This is worth noting because, while the practical issues of life and death often concern the preservation of mere biological life, it is biographical life that is important to us. The point may seem obvious, but if an argument is needed, one is not hard to find. Consider this thought-experiment. Suppose we are given a choice between *(a)* dying now and *(b)* lapsing into a dreamless coma from which we will never awaken and dying after ten years. Which would we choose? Most of us would prefer the first option, both because we would find the prospect of a vegetable existence undignified and because we would not want to put our loved ones through the pointless ordeal of caring for our unconscious bodies. But in an obvious sense the choice is indifferent: when we enter the coma, our biographical lives are over in the same way as if we had died. In the coma, of course, we would still be alive; and if being alive mattered, then we should prefer that option. The reason we do not is that being alive has no value for us if it does not enable us to have some sort of biographical life.

In addition to the Personal Value that a life has for its subject, there is also the *Social Value* that one's life has for others. People have friends and family to whom their lives are important. This is in part an instrumental value; other people may depend on them in various ways. But this value may be more than merely instrumental; their friends and family may love them and value them for their own sakes. The Social Value of most people's lives is limited, but some people's lives may have great Social Value because of what they contribute to society as a whole.

The idea that lives have Personal Value and Social Value is relatively uncontroversial. It is accepted by almost everyone. Now one possible view is that these two kinds of value are all that exist. The *Total Value* of a life, we might say, is just the sum of its Personal Value and its Social Value.[2] We may call this the Simple View.

If we take this view, there will be practical implications. Suppose, for example, the issue is whether we may transplant the organs of an anencephalic baby to other infants. This is obviously desirable in at least one respect: it could save the lives of the babies who need transplants. But many moralists argue that this would be impermissible because taking the organs would kill the anencephalic baby. As one commentator put it, "It's unethical to kill person A to save person B."[3] If we take the Simple View, however, we may not appeal to the value of the infant's life as an argument against the transplants. The anencephalic infant's life has no Personal Value because she can never have a life in the biographical sense—indeed, she can never even know she exists. And her brief existence would be Socially Valuable only if her organs were used to benefit the other babies. These considerations do not settle the issue, for there may be additional arguments to be considered. Nonetheless, if the Simple View is correct, then *insofar as the value of human life is concerned*, there is no objection to taking the organs.

The same goes for suicide. On August 19, 1935, the American writer Charlotte Perkins Gilman, who was dying of cancer, took her own life. She left this note:

Human life consists in mutual service. No grief, pain, misfortune or "broken heart" is excuse for cutting off one's life while any power of service remains. But when all usefulness is over, when one is assured of an unavoidable and imminent death, it is the simplest of human rights to choose a quick and easy death in place of a slow and horrible one.

Public opinion is changing on this subject. The time is approaching when we shall consider it abhorrent to our civilization to allow a human being to lie in prolonged agony which we should mercifully end in any other creature. Believing this choice to be of social service in promoting wiser views on this question, I have preferred chloroform to cancer.[4]

Gilman's reasoning appeals directly to the Simple View. Suicide was permissible, she said, because the life remaining to her was devoid of value to her or to anyone else. Once again, there may be other reasons against suicide, having nothing to do with the value of her life; but if the Simple View is correct, then the value of life would itself pose no objection to the chloroform.

Enriched Views

Many people believe there is more to the value of a human life than the Simple View allows. They believe that human life is sacred in some deep sense not captured by the Simple View. Thus, they would prefer an Enriched View, which says that human life has an *Additional Value,* beyond its Personal Value and its Social Value. We do not need, at this point, to specify what this Additional Value consists in. There may be different ideas about this, associated with different varieties of Enriched Views. At this point, we only need to note that an Enriched View would provide the resources to support different moral judgments than the ones supported by the Simple View.

When it is said, for example, that an anencephalic baby's life has no Personal Value and no Social Value apart from the use of its organs, many people doubt that this can be the whole story. The fact that a human life is destroyed, they think, must provide *some* objection to killing the infant, no matter how meager its life is. Therefore, the Simple View seems, to them, too anemic to account for life's value. An Enriched View would permit them to say that the baby's life still has some sort of value, even if it has no Personal Value or Social Value.

Hume and Kant famously disagreed about suicide, and one aspect of their disagreement was that Hume endorsed the Simple View, while Kant wanted an Enriched View. In his essay "Of Suicide" (1741), Hume asked why a man may not dispose of his own life: "Is it because human life is of so great importance that 'tis a presumption for human prudence to dispose of it? But the life of a man is of no greater importance to the universe than that of an oyster."[5] Thus, Hume argued, if a person's life is no longer of value to himself or to others, suicide is permissible.

Kant's view was more complex. In his most famous works, such as the Foundations of the Metaphysics of Morals (1785), Kant connected the prohibition of suicide to the idea that we could not consistently will that self-destruction (as a means to escape troubles) be universally practiced. He also argued that suicide is incompatible with treating persons as ends-in-themselves. These are difficult arguments that require some effort to understand, much less to evaluate. In his lectures to students, however, Kant relied on simpler considerations. "Sophistication," he explained, "even though well meant, is not a good thing. It is not good to defend either virtue or vice by splitting hairs." And in the case of suicide, he told them, the critical issue is that "humanity is worthy of esteem." We may kill animals to put them out of misery, but not humans, for "man is not a thing, not a beast. If he disposes over himself, he treats his value as that of a beast."[6]

And what, exactly, is "the value of a beast"? Kant's idea, if I may put it this way, is that the Simple View is good enough for animals, but not for people. For "beasts," the Total Value of their lives is nothing more than the value their lives have for them (if any) plus the value their lives have for us. So if the beasts' lives have become unbearable to them, and they are no longer useful to us, there is no objection to destroying them as a kindness. But human life is different. Even if its Personal Value and Social Value are gone, there remains something of worth that may not be destroyed. For this reason, Kant opposed suicide absolutely.

Value and Reasons

Despite its familiarity, the notion of a "value" is somewhat obscure. What sort of thing is a value? What does it mean to say that something "is valuable" or "has value"? At least in the present context, I will take this to be a shorthand way of saying something about reasons. Reasons are needed to support moral judgments; if it is said that we *ought* to do thus-and-so, we can ask why and expect an answer. Sometimes the answer will be that we should (or should not) do so-and-so because it would protect (or imperil) human life.

Thus, we may understand the thought that life "has value" like this: to say that human life has value is to say that *the fact that a human being would be killed* is a reason against doing certain kinds of things. Conversely, *the fact that someone's life would be protected or preserved* is a reason in favor of doing other kinds of things. Why may I not shoot my neighbor? Because it would kill him. Why should I give blood? Because it would save someone's life. To say that human life is valuable is just to say that such considerations are good reasons for and against various sorts of actions.

But we can go a step further and explain why these are good reasons. Someone would be killed—so what? We could say that killing a person is wrong because

(a) Her consciousness would be obliterated. She would experience no more enjoyments and engage in no more activities. Her personal relationships would be abruptly concluded. Her projects would be cancelled. Her desires would be forever unsatisfied; her hopes unfulfilled. Moreover,

(b) Her family and friends, and perhaps many others, would be worse off.

These, of course, are the considerations associated with Personal Value and Social Value. They explain why killing is wrong and why preserving life is good. Thus, to say that a human life has Personal Value or Social Value simply adds detail to our account of reasons—it explains why preserving life is important. The idea that there is a third kind of value is just the thought that there is something more to the explanation than (a) and (b), and, moreover, that this "something more" provides an extra reason for protecting life.

Is There Something More?

Is the Simple View sufficient, or do we need an Enriched View to account for the value of human life? Does human life have an Additional Value beyond its Personal Value and its Social Value?

Traditionally, the idea that human life has a special value was connected with religious ideas about the nature and origin of human beings. Human life is morally special because humans are made in the image of God and have a special place in God's affections and in God's plan. It is possible to support the idea of a third kind of value in this way. There would then be three kinds of reasons for thinking your life is important: reasons connected with your interests; reasons connected with other people's interests; and reasons connected with the fact that you are God's child.

This explains why religious ethics and secular ethics are often in conflict, especially when secular ethics relies on the Simple View. (And the Simple View sometimes seems to be the default position of secular ethics.) The reason they come into conflict is not that religious ethicists believe moral precepts are divine commands or anything like that, although of course they may. Rather, on almost any issue where human life is at stake, religious ethicists will think there are relevant considerations—a third reason for valuing human life—to which secular ethicists are blind.

But suppose we set aside religious conceptions and ask whether it is possible to provide a secular justification for saying that human life has an Additional Value. This is one of the most important unresolved issues in moral theory, and there are several ways in which it might be approached.

The Appeal to Fundamental Principles

One strategy is to assert that the value of human life is one's fundamental principle and as such it requires no further support. After all, if something is a fundamental principle, it cannot be justified by appeal to further principles because then it would not be fundamental—instead, the further principles would be fundamental. So, where fundamental principles are concerned, the demand for support is misguided. Asserting the principle is all one can do.

But it does not appear that the special value of human life is fundamental in this sense. One problem is that fundamental principles should be transparent. We should be able to see their point immediately, with no explanation required. The badness of pain is an example. We do not have to explain the undesirability of pain by reference to anything else; anyone who has experienced pain will understand that it is bad just because of what it is like. But the Additional Value of human life is not like that.

Moreover, it seems unreasonable to suppose that if human life has an extra value, then this value is unconnected with the facts about human beings. Humans are rational, autonomous, emotionally complex, social beings who occupy a particular place in the natural order. Surely, the extra value of human life, if it exists, must be explained by reference to what human beings are or what they add to the universe.

This problem can be posed in the abstract, but it also comes up in connection with such practical issues as animal rights. In the debate about animal rights, traditionalists insist that human life is more valuable than animal life, and the defenders of animal rights want to know why. What is it about humans that makes their lives more important than, say, the life of a chimpanzee? If the answer is "nothing," then the traditional ethic is arbitrary—it endorses treating humans differently even though there is nothing about them that justifies it. On the other hand, if a feature of human life is mentioned—if, for example, it is said that human life is more valuable because humans are rational beings—then we have appealed to a more fundamental principle, namely the principle that the lives of rational beings have value. We can then ask whether that principle is reasonable. We can ask why rationality is so important, and we can consider whether any beings other than humans are rational in the required sense. So we are not stuck with an undebatable "first principle." There is lots to discuss.

The Descriptivist Method in Ethical Theory

Many people believe that human life must have an Additional Value because they are convinced that certain ethical judgments are true, and those judgments cannot be true unless human life has the Additional Value. For example, to some people it seems obvious that the anencephalic infant's organs should not be taken. To them, taking the organs seems horrible, and the reason seems intimately connected with the fact that the infant is a precious little baby, a human being despite her awful disability. But we could not account for the horribleness if we did not assume that the baby's life has a value beyond its Personal and Social Value.

Much the same may be said of suicide. Charlotte Perkins Gilman was a wonderful human being, we might think. How could it be right for such a person to be destroyed? If we feel it was not right, and our reason has to do with the value of her life, we will need something more than the Simple View; and so the Additional Value may be posited.

This procedure may seem insufficiently critical; nonetheless, many philosophers have adopted it. They use a descriptivist method that consists, essentially, in positing whatever principles are needed to support either their own judgments or the prevailing moral consensus. First, they make observations about what is "obviously true" or what people commonly believe; then they consider what sorts of principles and values must be assumed in order for those beliefs to be true; and, finally, the resulting system of beliefs-plus-principles is displayed as the finished philosophical product. (A variation is for the writer to present made-up cases to evoke intuitive responses from the reader; and then the writer suggests principles to "account for" the presumed responses.) The procedure may be associated with an intuitionist ethical theory; or it may be justified by reference to "reflective equilibrium's" being the test of moral acceptability. Either way, this approach allows us to introduce whatever principles we need to support whatever judgments we care to make, and it creates the false impression that the judgments are "justified" because the cooked-up principles support them. The judgments require the principles, and the principles support the judgments. It's a very small circle.

The Appeal to an Aristotelian Worldview

We could justify thinking of human life as important "to the universe" if we adopted an Aristotelian view of what the universe is like. Aristotle conceived the world to be an orderly, rational system, with each thing having its own proper place and serving its own special purpose. The rain falls so that the plants can grow, the plants exist for the sake of the animals, and the animals exist for the sake of humans, whose well-being is the point of the whole arrangement. "[W]e must believe, first that plants exist for the sake of animals, second that all other animals exist for the sake of man, tame animals for the use he can make of them as well as for the food they provide; and as for wild animals, most though not all of these can be used for food or are useful in other ways; clothing and instruments can be made out of them. If then we are right in believing that nature makes nothing without some end in view, nothing to no purpose, it must be that nature has made all things specifically for the sake of man."[7]

For more than a thousand years, these thoughts formed part of the best available theory of what the world was like. They made it reasonable to believe that human life had a special cosmic importance.

It may seem pointless to bring this up today because the Aristotelian worldview is inconsistent with modern science, and so it is no longer an option for scientifically-minded people. Nevertheless, it is instructive to notice how well the idea that human life has an Additional Value fits the Aristotelian cosmology. The two go together so naturally that it is tempting to conclude that the idea of Additional Value is nothing but a vestige left over from the days when people thought of the world in Aristotelian terms.

The Appeal to Evolution

The worldview of modern science seems inhospitable to Additional Value. Still, there is at least one philosopher who has suggested otherwise. In *Life's Dominion*, Ronald Dworkin says that the doctrine of the sacredness of human life can be separated from its traditional theistic moorings and given a secular justification. Dworkin gives a surprising (and, some might think, a peculiar) account of how the secular justification might go. An atheist, he says, might appeal to evolution in the same way that theists appeal to God. Within the theistic framework, the sacredness of human life is seen as a product of its history: it is sacred because it comes from God. From a nontheistic standpoint, we may also view human life as sacred because of its history: it is sacred because it is the product of evolution. Thus, the workings of evolution may be regarded as having the same sort of ethical significance as the creative action of God.

According to Dworkin, this is exactly what thoughtful people believe. "The natural processes of evolution and development themselves have a normative significance for us," he says.[8] Some people think of evolution as creative by analogy with artistic creation, or they think of nature as acting for a purpose. Among other things, this explains why we care about the extinction of species. "We see the evolutionary process through which species were developed as contributing, in some way, to the shame of what we do when we cause their extinction now." Therefore, "We consider it a kind of cosmic shame when a species that nature has developed ceases, through human actions, to exist."[9]

But humans are not just one species among others—our species has greater intrinsic value. Why? "[W]e treat the preservation and prosperity of our own species as of capital importance," Dworkin says, "because we believe that we are the highest achievement of God's creation, if we are conventionally religious, or of evolution, if we are not."[10]

What are we to make of all this? First, we should note that it isn't clear to what extent Dworkin actually believes what he is saying. In *Life's Dominion*, his overall project is descriptive—he wants to demonstrate that there is no big gap between religious and secular ideas about the value of life by showing that even atheists believe that life is, in some sense, sacred. The thoughts about evolution are meant to explain how nonreligious people might also have a reverence for human life. When Dworkin has finished setting out these thoughts, he comments that "It is not my present purpose to recommend or defend any of these widespread convictions."[11] Nonetheless, he also emphasizes that "there is nothing irrational or disreputable"[12] about these beliefs.

Evolutionary biologists, however, might think that there is something irrational or disreputable about this use of their science. The idea that evolution has a "normative significance" was popular in the late nineteenth century, when scientists recognized the value of the evolutionary approach but were put off by the materialistic implications of Darwin's natural selection. Thus, they tried to identify other mechanisms that would explain evolutionary change as the result of a process that is purposive or creative. These efforts failed, and as the evolutionary synthesis of the twentieth century emerged, natural selection, with its mechanistic account of how change takes place, was its centerpiece.

Thus, while Dworkin may be right that many people believe humanity is "evolution's highest achievement," this belief has no basis in contemporary evolutionary science. Evolution operates by random variation and natural selection. It does not aim at any particular outcome, nor does it incorporate any principle of "progress" toward "higher levels" of development. There is no drive toward increased complexity, emergent consciousness, or anything like that. These are all misconceptions, and the idea that human beings are the "highest achievement of evolution" is the greatest misconception of all. In fact, if we insist on identifying evolutionary successes, the durable cockroach is a better candidate. As the nineteenth-century critics of Darwinism realized, the idea that humans are the products of natural selection does not provide a basis for affirming the special value of humanity. Instead, it provides grounds for doubting it.[13]

The Kantian Argument

Kant, as we have noted, held that human life is valuable "above all price," and he gave a long, complicated argument to prove it. Christine Korsgaard, one of the most prominent contemporary Kantians, has usefully summarized the argument. In *The Sources of Normativity*, she writes:

He started from the fact that when we make a choice we must regard its object as good.... He asked what it is that makes these objects good, and, rejecting one form of realism, he decided that the goodness was not in the objects themselves. Were it not for our desires and inclinations—and for the various physiological, psychological, and social conditions which gave rise to those desires and inclinations—we would not find their objects good. Kant saw that we take things to be important because they are important to us—and he concluded that we must therefore take ourselves to be important. In this way, the value of humanity itself is implicit in every human choice. If complete normative scepticism is to be avoided—if there is such a thing as a reason for action—then humanity, as the source of all reasons and values, must be valued for its own sake.[14]

Korsgaard, who endorses this line of thought, concludes that "You must value your own humanity if you are to value anything at all."[15] Or, more flatly: "It follows from this argument that human beings are valuable. Enlightenment morality is true."[16]

The argument seems to involve these steps:

1. As human beings, we must make choices, and we cannot make choices without taking at least some things to be valuable.
2. Objects are not valuable "in themselves"—if they are valuable at all, it must be because of their relation to our desires and inclinations.
3. Nothing can be valuable in virtue of its relation to our desires and inclinations unless *we* are valuable.
4. Therefore, we must take ourselves to be valuable.
5. Therefore, we are valuable.

But there is an obvious problem with this, as Korsgaard notes: "You might want to protest against that last step," she says. "How do we get from the fact that we find ourselves to be valuable to the conclusion that we are valuable?"[17]

How, indeed? It looks like an insuperable difficulty. The Kantian argument, if it is successful, shows only that we must believe ourselves to be valuable. But what shows that this belief is true? Korsgaard responds that we must remember the difference between first-person and third-person perspectives:

Value, like freedom, is only directly accessible from within the standpoint of reflective consciousness. And I am now talking about it externally, for I am describing the nature of the consciousness that gives rise to the perception of value. From this external, third-person perspective, all we can say is that when we are in the first-person perspective we find ourselves to be valuable, rather than simply that we are valuable. There is nothing surprising in this. Trying to actually see the value of humanity from the third-person perspective is like trying to see the colours someone sees by cracking open his skull. From outside, all we can say is why he sees them.[18]

Does this solve the problem? It depends on whether the internal/external distinction will do the job required of it. A first-person, "internal" perspective is, presumably, the way things look to whoever is actually solving a problem or making a choice. In order to capture the first-person perspective, we would have to re-create the experiences and thoughts of that person, experiencing and thinking them as though they were our own. The third-person perspective, on the other hand, provides a description, "from the outside," of what the person is experiencing and thinking. Thus, from the first-person perspective, one would say, simply, "Humanity is valuable," while from the third-person perspective one would say, "He finds humanity to be valuable."

This may be true, but how does it help? It may be useful to digress for a moment and consider a different sort of issue. Suppose the question is not whether human life is valuable, but whether there is a largest prime number. There is a way anyone could come to know with absolute certainty. He could work through Euclid's famous proof:

(Euclid's Proof) Take any finite list of prime numbers, and multiply them together. Then add one. Call the resulting number n. n is not evenly divisible by any of the numbers on the list because there will always be a remainder of one. Therefore, either n is itself a prime number, or it is divisible by some prime not on the list. Either way, there is at least one prime not on the list. Since this will be true no matter what list we begin with, it follows that there are an infinite number of primes.

From a first-person ("internal") point of view, this reasoning proves the point. When you grasp this reasoning, you know that there is no largest prime. But the reasoning contains no reference to you, your decisions, your thought processes, or anything of the kind. When you are going through the proof, you are not thinking about yourself. You are just thinking about

the numbers. From a third-person ("external") point of view, however, someone who was describing what you are doing would describe you and your
thought processes.

The same is true when practical issues are at stake. Should your dog be
given an anesthetic when the veterinarian performs surgery? The relevant
reasoning is obvious:

> (The Argument about the Anesthetic) The anesthetic would have no ill effects; it
> would just render the animal temporarily unconscious and insensitive to pain.
> On the other hand, if we perform the operation without first administering the
> anesthetic, the dog will be in agony. That would be terrible. Therefore, the anes-
> thetic should be administered.

Once again, from a first-person point of view, this reasoning proves the
point. When you grasp this reasoning, you know why the anesthetic must
be given. But the reasoning contains no reference to you, your decisions,
your thought processes, or anything of the sort. When you are thinking this
through, you are not thinking about yourself. You are just thinking about
the dog and the effects of the anesthetic. From a third-person point of view,
however, someone who was describing what you are doing would mention
you and your thought processes.

But now notice this: when someone comes to believe something as a
result of reasoning, and a third-person account explains "from the outside"
how that happened, the first-person reasoning will be embedded within
the third-person account. The third-person account of *how the student comes
to know that there is a largest prime number* will include a description of the
student's working through Euclid's proof; and a third-person account of
how you come to know that the anesthetic should be given will include a description of your thinking through the above argument. Thus, the embedded
first-person arguments are critical. Without them, we have only biography.
The third-person account without an embedded first-person argument may
provide information about how the subject forms his beliefs, but it will not
justify any conclusions about prime numbers or anesthetics.

It is fair enough to say that the Kantian argument explains practical reason
from a third-person, "outside" point of view. The critical question, however, is
what is the *first-person argument* that proves humanity is valuable? What is the
argument about humanity that is analogous to Euclid's Proof or the Argument
about the Anesthetic? The striking fact is that there is no such argument em-

bedded within the Kantian account. If we try to extract one, we get something like the following. (The third-person argument describes what happens when someone makes a choice, so the first-person reasoning must start from some choice. We need an example, so I will imagine that someone is making the choice about the anesthetics. But any example would do since we are told that "the value of humanity itself is implicit in *every* human choice.")

1. The anesthetic should be administered before the dog is operated on.
2. It would not be true that the anesthetic should be given were it not for human desires and inclinations.
3. If humanity weren't valuable, then human desires and inclinations would not suffice to make it true.
4. Therefore, humanity is valuable.

But this is not sound. The second premise is false because the explanation of why it would be terrible for the dog to be operated on without an anesthetic makes no reference at all to "human desires and inclinations." The explanation is given in the Argument about the Anesthetic, and that argument says nothing about us or our desires, just as the argument about prime numbers says nothing about us or our thought processes. It is tempting to reply that if we did not have certain desires and inclinations, we would not believe the anesthetic should be given—but that only throws us back into a third-person perspective.

It appears, then, that the Kantian analysis does not have a sound first-person argument embedded within it. And failing that, it provides no good argument for the value of humanity. It gives an (unlikely) account of why so many people have believed humanity is valuable, but that is all.

What Human Beings Add to the Universe

Finally, here is a line of thought, inspired by an argument of G. E. Moore's, that seems to provide the most promising defense of the third kind of value. Moore believed that beauty is good in itself, independent of any enjoyment it affords observers. To prove this, he once suggested a thought-experiment. Imagine, he said, two worlds, both without conscious beings, but one of them lovely and the other a slag heap. Isn't the former better? And wouldn't we have good reason to prefer that the first existed, even if no observer ever viewed it?

Let us imagine one world exceedingly beautiful. Imagine it as beautiful as you can; put into it whatever on this earth you most admire—mountains, rivers, the sea; trees, and sunsets, stars and moon. Imagine these all combined in the most exquisite proportions, so that no one thing jars against another, but each contributes to increase the beauty of the whole. And then imagine the ugliest world you can possibly conceive. Imagine it simply one heap of filth, containing everything that is most disgusting to us, for whatever reason, and the whole, as far as may be, without one redeeming feature.... Supposing them quite apart from any possible contemplation by human beings; still, is it irrational to hold that it is better that the beautiful world should exist, than the one which is ugly? Would it not be well, in any case, to do what we could to produce it rather than the other? Certainly I cannot help thinking that it would; and I hope that some may agree with me in this extreme instance.[19]

And what about the value of humanity? Taking our cue from Moore, we might imagine two worlds: our own world and a world just like ours but with no human beings in it. Which is better? In the world without humans, there could be natural beauty, but there would be

no love:
no moral striving;
no friendship;
no courage or generosity or loyalty;
no great literature or art;
no knowledge or understanding;
no appreciation of the vastness and beauty of nature;
no baseball; no movies; no rock and roll;
and the list could go on.

Moreover, the world with humans has an additional, more profound feature: it is aware of itself. Humanity is the bit of the universe that has become conscious and that can look around and register what it sees. Without human beings, the universe is insensate and mindless.[20]

Thus, the world without humans would be worse because it would be lacking these things. Hume was wrong when he said that "The life of a man has no greater importance to the universe than that of an oyster."[21] Without humanity, the universe would be impoverished and unaware of itself.

As I said, this may be the best we can do in providing substance and support for the "third kind of value." Nonetheless, there are two serious

64

problems with this line of thought. First, it may be true that without humans there would be no love, striving, generosity, and loyalty. But, equally, there would be no hatred, cruelty, greed, and betrayal. If the former make the world better, the latter make it worse; and to make our argument persuasive, we would need some reason to think the former are more numerous or more important. Second, the suspicion remains that these things are good because of the way that they enrich our lives—they are good because they are good for us, not because they somehow ennoble the universe.

Suppose, however, we set those worries aside, and we say that humanity does have an Additional Value and that it consists in the fact that human beings add these qualities to the universe. Where would that leave us with respect to an ethic of life and death?

Such an account would confer surprisingly little value on ordinary human lives. It could explain very nicely what would be wrong with wiping out the whole human race. Then, love, baseball, and all the other good things would be eliminated from the universe. But, from this point of view, while humanity in general might be important, individual human lives will not matter much. So long as there are a sufficient number of people to supply the universe with the good things, the addition or subtraction of individuals would be of little consequence. As for the examples we considered earlier, this view would provide no reason for keeping handicapped babies alive, for their existence adds nothing to the world in terms of art, knowledge, moral striving, and the rest; and it would provide no objection to suicide—or even murder, for that matter—if the individual to be killed would not be missed from the point of view of the universe's supply of the good things. This means that in making judgments about the value of people's lives, we would be left to make our calculations on the basis of their Personal and Social Value. In other words, for practical purposes, we would be left with the Simple View.

Is the Simple View Enough?

Many people believe that an ethic that recognizes only Personal and Social Value is impoverished because it lacks a sufficiently robust sense of the moral preciousness of human life. But the more modest ethic might actually be better than one that encourages an exaggerated sense of the cosmic importance of human beings. It might be superior in at least two ways.

First, the Simple View discourages speciesism. A pernicious consequence of the sanctity-of-human-life ethic has always been the downgrading and mistreatment of nonhuman animals. But if we were to give up the Aristotelian notion that we are somehow cosmically important (while they are not), we would be in a better position to appreciate that insofar as nonhumans have lives and interests similar to our own, they have a moral standing similar to our own. Our lives are important to us; their lives—at least, the lives of the intelligent, social animals—are similarly important to them. This does not mean, of course, that humans and nonhumans must always be treated in the same way, for there will often be differences between them that justify differences in treatment. It does not even mean that in a situation of forced choice, we would not be justified in preferring the life of a human over that of a nonhuman. But it does mean, as Peter Singer puts it, that the comparable interests of humans and nonhumans must be given comparable moral consideration.[22] The reason this point is so often resisted is that people are in the grip of the notion that humanity is somehow "special" in some occult or hard-to-define sense.

Second, an ethic focused on the Personal and Social Value of our lives would be concerned with what is good for us rather than with some abstract value that we are said to instantiate. The ethic that says we have an Additional Value initially seems very flattering—we may like the idea that we are really splendid in some grand cosmic way—but, paradoxically, it appeals to the great value of our lives to justify actions and policies that are not in our best interests. Suicide and euthanasia are conspicuous examples: someone dying horribly must linger on because his or her life is held to be so precious. If I were in that position, I would wish that my life were not thought to be so valuable. The Personal and Social Value of my life are important to me; but when my own interests are at stake, to say that my life has some grander sort of worth is an unwelcome compliment.

Notes

1. Immanuel Kant, *Foundations of the Metaphysics of Morals*, translated by Lewis White Beck (Indianapolis: Bobbs-Merrill, 1959; originally published in 1785), 53.

2. Some philosophers argue that it is wrong to speak of "adding" values. If they are right, then we should just say that Personal Value and Social Value are all that exist.

3. David Briggs, "Baby Theresa Case Raises Ethics Questions," *Champaign-Urbana News-Gazette*, March 31, 1992, A6.

4. Quoted in "Charlotte Gilman Dies to Avoid Pain," *New York Times*, August 20, 1935, 44.

5. David Hume, "Of Suicide," in *Essays Moral, Political, and Literary* (Oxford: Oxford University Press, 1963; originally published in 1741–42), 590.

6. All the quotations in this paragraph are from Immanuel Kant, *Lectures on Ethics*, translated by Louis Infield (New York: Harper and Row, 1963), 151–52.

7. Aristotle, *The Basic Works of Aristotle*, edited by Richard McKeon (New York: Random House, 1941), 40.

8. Ronald Dworkin, *Life's Dominion* (New York: Alfred A. Knopf, 1993), 78.

9. Ibid., 75.

10. Ibid., 82.

11. Ibid., 81.

12. Ibid., 80.

13. For more on this, see James Rachels, *Created from Animals* (Oxford: Oxford University Press, 1990).

14. Christine M. Korsgaard, *The Sources of Normativity* (Cambridge: Cambridge University Press, 1996), 122.

15. Ibid., 123.

16. Ibid.

17. Ibid., 124.

18. Ibid.

19. G. E. Moore, *Principia Ethica* (Cambridge: Cambridge University Press, 1903), 83–84.

20. I am leaving aside the important question of whether humans are the only beings in the universe with the ability to understand, love, be courageous, produce art, and so on. If other such beings exist, then this argument is unsound. Indeed, nonhuman animals on earth have some of the relevant capacities, although not enough of them to make humans superfluous.

21. Hume, "Of Suicide," 590.

22. See Peter Singer, *Unsanctifying Human Life* (Oxford: Blackwell, 2002), especially chap. 15.

FIVE

KILLING AND STARVING TO DEATH

Although we do not know exactly how many people die each year of malnu-trition or related health problems, the number is very high, in the millions.[1] By giving money to support famine relief efforts, each of us could save at least some of them. By not giving, we let them die.

Some philosophers have argued that letting people die is not as bad as killing them because in general our "positive duty" to give aid is weaker than our "negative duty" not to do harm.[2] I maintain the opposite: letting die is just as bad as killing.[3] At first, this may seem wildly implausible. When reminded that people are dying of starvation while we spend money on trivial things, we may feel a bit guilty, but certainly we do not feel like murderers. Philippa Foot writes: "Most of us allow people to die of starva-tion in India and Africa, and there is surely something wrong with us that we do; it would be nonsense, however, to pretend that it is only in law that we make a distinction between allowing people in the underdeveloped countries to die of starvation and sending them poisoned food. There is worked into our moral system a distinction between what we owe people in the form of aid and what we owe them in the way of non-interference."[4] No doubt this would be correct if it were intended only as a description of what most people believe. Whether this feature of "our moral system" is rationally defensible is, however, another matter. I shall argue that we are wrong to take comfort in the fact that we "only" let these people die because our duty not to let them die is equally as strong as our duty not to kill them, which, of course, is very strong indeed.

Obviously, this Equivalence Thesis is not morally neutral, as philosophical claims about ethics often are. It is a radical idea that, if true, would mean that some of our "intuitions" (our prereflective beliefs about what is right and wrong in particular cases) are mistaken and must be rejected. Neither is the view I oppose morally neutral. The idea that killing is worse than letting die is a relatively conservative thesis that would allow those same intuitions to be preserved. However, the Equivalence Thesis should not be dismissed merely because it does not conform to all our prereflective intuitions. Rather than being perceptions of the truth, our "intuitions" might sometimes signify nothing more than our prejudices or selfishness or cultural conditioning. Philosophers often admit that, in theory at least, some intuitions might be unreliable—but usually this possibility is not taken seriously, and conformity to prereflective intuition is used uncritically as a test of the acceptability of moral theory. In what follows, I shall argue that many of our intuitions concerning killing and letting die *are* mistaken and should not be trusted.

I

We think that killing is worse than letting die not because we overestimate how bad it is to kill, but because we underestimate how bad it is to let die. The following chain of reasoning is intended to show that letting people in foreign countries die of starvation is very much worse than we commonly assume.

Suppose there were a starving child in the room where you are now—hollow eyed, belly bloated, and so on—and you have a sandwich at your elbow that you don't need. Of course, you would be horrified; you would stop reading and give her the sandwich or, better, take her to a hospital. And you would not think this an act of supererogation: you would not expect any special praise for it, and you would expect criticism if you did not do it. Imagine what you would think of someone who simply ignored the child and continued reading, allowing her to die of starvation. Let us call the person who would do this "Jack Palance," after the very nice man who plays such vile characters in the movies. Jack Palance indifferently watches the starving child die; he cannot be bothered even to hand her the sandwich. There is ample reason for judging him very harshly, without putting too fine a point on it: he shows himself to be a moral monster.

When we allow people in faraway countries to die of starvation, we may think, as Mrs. Foot puts it, that "there is surely something wrong with us." But we most emphatically do not consider ourselves moral monsters. We think this, in spite of the striking similarity between Jack Palance's behavior and our own. He could easily save the child; he does not; and the child dies. We could easily save some of those starving people; we do not; and they die. If we are not monsters, there must be some important difference between him and us. But what is it?

One obvious difference between Jack Palance's position and ours is that the person he lets die is in the same room with him, while the people we let die are mostly far away. Yet the spatial location of the dying people hardly seems a relevant consideration.[5] It is absurd to suppose that being located at a certain map coordinate entitles one to treatment that one would not merit if situated at a different longitude or latitude. Of course, if a dying person's location meant that we *could not* help, that would excuse us. But, since there are efficient famine relief agencies willing to carry our aid to the faraway countries, this excuse is not available. It would be almost as easy for us to send these agencies the price of the sandwich as for Palance to hand the sandwich to the child.

The location of the starving people does make a difference, psychologically, in how we feel. If there were a starving child in the same room with us, we could not avoid realizing, in a vivid and disturbing way, how it is suffering and that it is about to die. Faced with this realization, our consciences probably would not allow us to ignore the child. But if the dying are far away, it is easy to think of them only abstractly or to put them out of our thoughts altogether. This might explain why our conduct would be different if we were in Jack Palance's position, even though, from a moral point of view, the location of the dying is not relevant.

There are other differences between Jack Palance and us that may seem important, having to do with the sheer numbers of people, both affluent and starving, that surround us. In our fictitious example, Jack Palance is one person confronted by the need of one other person. This makes his position relatively simple. In the real world, our position is more complicated, in two ways: first, in that there are millions of people who need feeding, and none of us has the resources to care for all of them; and second, in that for any starving person we *can* help, there are millions of other affluent people who can help as easily as we.

On the first point, not much needs to be said. We may feel, in a vague sort of way, that we are not monsters because no one of us could possibly save *all* the starving people—there are just too many of them, and none of us has the resources. This is fair enough, but all that follows is that, individually, none of us is responsible for saving everyone. We may still be responsible for saving someone or as many as we can. This is so obvious that it hardly bears mentioning; yet it is easy to lose sight of, and philosophers have actually lost sight of it. In his article "Saving Life and Taking Life," Richard Trammell says that one morally important difference between killing and letting die is "dischargeability."[6] By this he means that while each of us can discharge completely a duty not to kill anyone, no one among us can discharge completely a duty to save everyone who needs it. Again, fair enough; but all that follows is that since we are bound to save only those we can, the class of people we have an obligation to save is much smaller than the class of people we have an obligation not to kill. It does *not* follow that our duty with respect to those we can save is any less stringent. Suppose Jack Palance were to say: "I needn't give this starving child the sandwich because, after all, I can't save everyone in the world who needs it." If this excuse will not work for him, neither will it work for us with respect to the children we could save in India or Africa.

The second point about numbers was that for any starving person we can help, there are millions of other affluent people who can help as easily as we. Some are in an even better position to help since they are richer. But by and large these people are doing nothing. This also helps to explain why we do not feel especially guilty for letting people starve. How guilty we feel about something depends, to some extent, on how we compare with those around us. If we were surrounded by people who regularly sacrificed to feed the starving, and we did not, we would probably feel ashamed. But because our neighbors do not do any better than we, we are not ashamed.

But again, this does not imply that we should not feel more guilty or ashamed than we do. A psychological explanation of our feelings is not a moral justification of our conduct. Suppose Jack Palance were only one of twenty people who watched the child die. Would that decrease his guilt? Curiously, I think many people assume it would. Many people seem to feel that if twenty people do nothing to prevent a tragedy, each of them is only one-twentieth as guilty as he would have been if he had watched the trag-

71

edy alone. It is as though there is only a fixed amount of guilt, which divides. I suggest, rather, that guilt multiplies, so that each passive viewer is fully guilty if he could have prevented the tragedy but did not. Jack Palance watching the girl die alone would be a moral monster; but if he calls in a group of his friends to watch with him, he does not diminish his guilt by dividing it among them. Instead, they are all moral monsters. Once the point is made explicit, it seems obvious.

The fact that most other affluent people do nothing to relieve hunger may very well have implications for one's own obligations. But the implication may be that one's own obligations *increase* rather than decrease. Suppose Palance and a friend were faced with two starving children, so that if each did his "fair share," Palance would have to feed only one of them. But the friend will do nothing. Because he is well off, Palance could feed both of them. Should he not? What if he fed one and then watched the other die, announcing that he has done *his* duty and that the one who died was his friend's responsibility? This shows the fallacy of supposing that one's duty is only to do one's fair share, where this is determined by what would be sufficient *if* everyone else did likewise.

To summarize: Jack Palance, who refuses to hand a sandwich to a starving child, is a moral monster. But we feel intuitively that we are not so monstrous, even though we also let starving children die when we could feed them almost as easily. If this intuition is correct, there must be some important difference between him and us. But when we examine the most obvious differences between his conduct and ours—the location of the dying, the differences in numbers—we find no real basis for judging ourselves less harshly than we judge him. Perhaps there are some other grounds on which we might distinguish our moral position with respect to actual starving people from Jack Palance's position with respect to the child in my story. But I cannot think of what they might be. Therefore, I conclude that if he is a monster, then so are we—or at least, so are we after our rationalizations and thoughtlessness have been exposed.

This last qualification is important. We judge people, at least in part, according to whether they can be expected to realize how well or how badly they behave. We judge Palance harshly because the consequences of his indifference are so immediately apparent. By contrast, it requires an unusual effort for us to realize the consequences of our indifference. It is normal behavior for people in the affluent countries not to give to famine relief, or if they do give, to give very little. Decent people may go along with this normal behavior pattern unthinkingly, without realizing or without comprehending in a clear way just what this means for the starving. Thus, even though those decent people may act monstrously, we do not judge them monsters. There is a curious sense, then, in which moral reflection can transform decent people into indecent ones: for if a person thinks things through and realizes that he is, morally speaking, in Jack Palance's position, his continued indifference is more blameworthy than before.

The preceding is not intended to prove that letting people die of starvation is as bad as killing them. But it does provide strong evidence that letting die is much worse then we normally assume, and so that letting die is much *closer* to killing than we normally assume. These reflections also go some way toward showing just how fragile and unreliable our intuitions are in this area. They suggest that if we want to discover the truth, we are better off looking at arguments that do not rely on unexamined intuitions.

II

Before arguing that the Equivalence Thesis is true, let me explain more precisely what I mean by it. I take it to be a claim about what does or does not count as a morally good reason in support of a value judgment: the bare fact that one act is an act of killing while another act is an act of "merely" letting someone die is not a morally good reason in support of the judgment that the former is worse than the latter. Of course, there may be *other* differences between such acts that are morally significant. For example, the family of an irreversibly comatose hospital patient may want their loved one to be allowed to die, but not killed. Perhaps the reason for their preference is religious. So we have at least one reason to let the patient die rather than to kill him—the reason is that the family prefers it that way. This does not mean, however, that the distinction between killing and letting die is *itself* important. What is important is respecting the family's wishes. (It is often right to respect people's wishes even if we think those wishes are based on false beliefs.) In another sort of case, a patient with a painful terminal illness may want to be killed rather than allowed to die because a slow, lingering death would be agonizing. Here we have a reason to kill and not let die, but once again the reason is not that one course is intrinsically preferable to the other. The reason is, rather, that the latter course would lead to more suffering.

It should be clear, then, that I will *not* be arguing that every act of letting die is equally as bad as every act of killing. There are lots of reasons why a particular act of killing may be morally worse than a particular act of letting die, or vice versa. If a healthy person is murdered from a malicious motive, while a person in an irreversible coma is allowed to die upon a calm judgment that maintaining him alive is pointless, certainly this killing is very much worse than this letting die. Similarly, if an ill person who could be saved is maliciously allowed to die, while a terminal patient is killed, upon his request, as an act of kindness, we have good reason to judge the letting die worse than the killing. All I want to argue is that whatever reasons there may be for judging one act worse than another, the simple fact that one is killing whereas the other is only letting die is not among them.

The first stage of the argument is concerned with some formal relations between moral judgments and the reasons that support them. I take it to be a point of logic that moral judgments are true only if good reasons support them; for example, if there is no good reason why you ought to do some action, it cannot be true that you ought to do it. Moreover, when there is a choice to be made from among several possible actions, the preferable alternative is the one that is backed by the strongest reasons.

But when are the reasons for or against one act stronger than those for or against another act? A complete answer would have to include some normative theory explaining why some reasons are intrinsically weightier than others. Suppose you are in a situation in which you can save someone's life only by lying: the normative theory would explain why "Doing A would save someone's life" is a stronger reason in favor of doing A than "Doing B would be telling the truth" is in favor of doing B.

However, there are also some purely formal principles that operate here. The simplest and least controversial such principle is this:

(i) If there are the *same* reasons for or against A as for or against B, then the reasons in favor of A are neither stronger nor weaker than the reasons in favor of B; and so A and B are morally equivalent—neither is preferable to the other.

Now, suppose we ask why killing is morally objectionable. When someone is killed, there may of course be harmful effects for people other than the victim himself. Those who loved him may grieve, and those who were depending on him in one way or another may be caused hardship because he, being dead, will be unable to perform as expected. However, we cannot explain the wrongness of killing purely or even mainly in terms of the bad effects for the survivors. The primary reason why killing is wrong is that something very bad is done to the victim himself: he ends up dead; he no longer has a good—his life—which he possessed before. But notice that exactly the same can be said about letting someone die. The primary reason why it is morally objectionable to let someone die, when we could save him, is that he ends up dead; he no longer has a good—his life—which he possessed before. Secondary reasons again have to do with harmful effects on those who survive. Thus, the explanation of why killing is bad mentions features of killing that are also features of letting die, and vice versa. Since there are no comparably general reasons in favor of either, this suggests that

> (ii) There are the same reasons for and against letting die as for and against killing.

And if this is true, we get the conclusion:

> (iii) Therefore, killing and letting die are morally equivalent—neither is preferable to the other.

The central idea of this argument is that there is no morally relevant difference between killing and letting die—that is, no difference that may be cited to show that one is worse than the other. The argument therefore contains a premise—(ii)—that is supported only inductively. The fact that the explanation of why killing is wrong applies equally well to letting die, and vice versa, provides strong evidence that the inductive generalization is true. Nevertheless, no matter how carefully we analyze the matter, it will always be possible that there is some subtle, morally relevant difference between the two that we have overlooked. In fact, philosophers who believe that killing is worse than letting die have sometimes tried to identify such differences. I believe that these attempts have failed; here are three examples.

I. The first is one that I have already mentioned. Trammell urges that there is an important difference in the "dischargeability" of duties not to kill and not to let die. We can completely discharge a duty not to kill anyone, but we cannot completely discharge a duty to save everyone who needs aid. This is obviously correct, but it does not show that the Equivalence Thesis is false, for two reasons. In the first place, the difference in dischargeability shows only that the class of people we have a duty to save is smaller than the class of people we have a duty not to kill. It does not show that our duty with respect to those we *can* save is any less stringent. In the second place, if we *cannot* save someone and that person dies, then we do not let him die. It is not right to say that I let Joseph Stalin die, for example, since there is no way I could have saved him. So if I cannot save everyone, then neither can I let everyone die.

2. It has also been urged that in killing someone, we are *doing* something—namely, killing him—whereas in letting someone die we are not doing anything. In letting people die of starvation, for example, we only *fail* to do certain things, such as sending food. The difference is between action and inaction, and somehow this is supposed to make a moral difference.[7]

There are also two difficulties with this suggestion. First, it is misleading to say, without further ado, that in letting someone die we do nothing, for there is one very important thing that we do: we let someone die. "Letting someone die" is different, in some ways, from other sorts of actions, mainly in that it is an action we perform *by way of* not performing other actions. We may let someone die by way of not feeding him, just as we may insult someone by way of not shaking his hand. (If it is said, "I didn't do anything; I simply refrained from taking his hand when he offered it," it may be replied, "You did do one thing—you insulted him.") The distinction between action and inaction is relative to a specification of *what* actions are or are not done. In insulting someone, we may *not* smile, speak, shake hands, and so on—but we *do* insult or snub the person. And in letting someone die, the following may be among the things that are not done: we do not feed the person, we do not give medication, and so on. But the following is among the things that are done: we let him die.

Second, even if letting die were only a case of inaction, why should any moral conclusion follow from *that* fact? It may seem that a significant conclusion follows if we assume that we are not responsible for inactions. However, there is no general correlation between the action-inaction distinction and any sort of moral assessment. We ought to do some things, and we ought not do others, and we can certainly be morally blameworthy for not doing things as well as for doing them—Jack Palance was blameworthy for not feeding the child. (In many circumstances, we are even legally liable for not doing things: tax fraud may involve only "inaction"—failing to report certain things to the Internal Revenue Service—but what of it?) Moreover, failing to act can be subject to all the other kinds of moral assessment. Not doing something may, depending on the circumstances, be right, wrong, obligatory, wise, foolish, compassionate, sadistic, and so on. Since there is no general correlation between the action-inaction distinction and *any* of these matters, it is hard to see how anything could be made out of this distinction in the present context.

3. My final example is from Trammell again. He argues that "optionality" is a morally relevant difference between killing and letting die. The point here is that if we fail to save someone, we leave open the option for someone else to save him, whereas if we kill, the victim is dead and that is that. This point, I think, has little significance. For one thing, while "optionality" may mark a difference between killing and *failing to save,* it does not mark a comparable difference between killing and *letting die.* If X fails to save Y, it does not follow that Y dies; someone else may come along and save him. But if X lets Y die, it does follow that Y dies; Y is dead, and that is that.[8] When Palance watches the child die, he does not merely fail to save the child; he lets her die. And when we fail to send food to the starving, and they die, we let them die—we do not merely fail to save them.

The importance of "optionality" in any particular case depends on the actual chances of someone else's saving the person we do not save. Perhaps it is not so bad not to save someone if we know that someone else *will* save him. (Although even here, we do not behave as we ought, for we ought not simply to leave what needs doing to others.) And perhaps it even gets us off the hook a little if there is the *strong chance* that someone else will step in. But in the case of the world's starving people, we know very well that no person or group of persons is going to come along tomorrow and save all of them. We know that there are at least some people who will *not* be saved if we do not save them. So, as an excuse for not giving aid to the starving, the "optionality" argument is clearly in bad faith. To say of those people after they are dead that someone else *might* have saved them, in the very weak sense in which that will be true, does not excuse us at all. The others who might have saved them but did not are as guilty as we; however, that does not diminish our guilt: as I have already remarked, guilt in these cases multiplies, not divides.

I need now to say a few more things about the counterintuitive nature of the Equivalence Thesis.

The fact that this view has radical implications for conduct has been cited as a reason for rejecting it. Trammell complains that "Denial of the distinction between negative and positive duties leads straight to an ethic so strenuous that it might give pause even to a philosophical John the Baptist."9 Suppose John is about to buy a phonograph record, purely for his enjoyment, when he is reminded that with this five dollars a starving person could be fed. On the view I am defending, he ought to give the money to feed the hungry person. This may not seem exceptional until we notice that the reasoning is reiterable. Having given the first five dollars, John is not free to use another five to buy the record. For the poor are always with him: there is always *another* starving person to be fed and then another and then another. "The problem," Trammell says, "is that, even though fulfillment of one particular act of aid involves only minimal effort, it sets a precedent for millions of such efforts."10 So we reach the bizarre conclusion that it is almost always immoral to buy phonograph records! And the same goes for fancy clothes, cars, toys, and so on.

This sort of reductio argument is of course familiar in philosophy. Such arguments may be divided into three categories. The strongest sort shows that a theory entails a contradiction, and since contradictions cannot be tolerated, the theory must be modified or rejected. Such arguments, when valid, are of course devastating. Second, an argument may show that a theory has a consequence that, while not inconsistent, is nevertheless demonstrably false—that is, an independent proof can be given that the offensive consequence is unacceptable. Arguments of this second type, while not quite so impressive as the first, can still be irresistible. The third type of reductio is markedly weaker than the others. Here, it is merely urged that some consequence of a theory is counterintuitive. The supposedly embarrassing consequence is perfectly consistent, and there is no proof that it is false; the complaint is only that it goes against our unreflective, pretheoretical beliefs. Now sometimes even this weak sort of argument can be effective, especially when we have not much confidence in the theory or when our confidence in the pretheoretical belief is unaffected by the reasoning that supports the theory. However, it may happen that *the same reasoning that leads one to accept a theory also persuades one that the pretheoretical beliefs were wrong.* (If this did not happen, philosophy would always be in the service of what we already think; it could never challenge and change our beliefs and would be, in an important sense, useless.) The present case, it seems to me, is an instance of this type. The same reasoning that leads to the view that we are as wicked as Jack Palance and that killing is no worse than letting die also persuades (me, at least) that the prereflective belief in the rightness of our affluent lifestyle is mistaken.[11]

So I want to say about all this what H. P. Grice once said at a conference when someone objected that his theory of meaning had an unacceptable implication. Referring to the supposedly embarrassing consequence, Grice said, "See here, that's not an *objection* to my theory—*that's* my theory!"[12] Grice not only accepted the implication, he claimed it as an integral part of what he wanted to say. Similarly, the realization that we are morally wrong to spend money on inessentials when that money could go to feed the starving is an integral part of the view I am defending. It is not an embarrassing consequence of the view; it is (part of) the view itself.

There is another way in which the counterintuitive nature of the Equivalence Thesis may be brought out. It follows from that thesis that if the *only* difference between a pair of acts is that one is killing, while the other is letting die, those actions are equally good or bad—neither is preferable to the other. Defenders of the distinction between positive and negative duties have pointed out that in such cases our intuitions often tell us just the opposite: killing seems obviously worse. Here is an example produced by Daniel Dinello:

Jones and Smith are in a hospital. Jones cannot live longer than two hours unless he gets a heart transplant. Smith, who has had one kidney removed, is dying of an infection in the other kidney. If he does not get a kidney transplant, he will die in about four hours. When Jones dies, his one good kidney can be transplanted to Smith, or Smith could be killed and his heart transplanted to Jones.... It seems clear that it would, in fact, be wrong to kill Smith and save Jones, rather than letting Jones die and saving Smith.[13]

And another from Trammell:

If someone threatened to steal $1000 from a person if he did not take a gun and shoot a stranger between the eyes, it would be very wrong for him to kill the stranger to save his $1000. But if someone asked from that person $1000 to save a stranger, it would seem that his obligation to grant this request would not be as great as his obligation to refuse the first demand—even if he has good reason for believing that without his $1000 the stranger would certainly die.... In this particular example, it seems plausible to say that a person has a greater obligation to refrain from killing someone, even though the effort required of him ($1000) and his motivation toward the stranger be assumed identical in both cases.[14]

The conclusion we are invited to draw from these examples is that, contrary to what I have been arguing, the bare difference between killing and letting die *must be* morally significant.

Now Dinello's example is badly flawed since the choice before the doctor is not a choice between killing and letting die at all. If the doctor kills Smith in order to transplant his heart to Jones, he will have killed Smith. But if he waits until Jones dies and then transfers the kidney to Smith, he will *not* have "let Jones die." The reason is connected with the fact that not every case of not saving someone is a case of letting him die. (Joseph Stalin died, and I did not save him, but I did not let Stalin die.) Dinello himself points out that in order for it to be true that X lets Y die, X must be "in a position" to save Y, but not do so.[15] (I was never in a position to save Stalin.) Now the doctor is in a position to save Jones only if there is a heart available for transplantation. But no such heart is available—Smith's heart, for example, is not available since Smith is still using it. Therefore, since the doctor is not in a position to save Jones, he does not let Jones die.[16]

Trammell's example is not quite so easy to dismiss. Initially, I share the intuition that it would be worse to kill someone to prevent one thousand dollars from being stolen than to refuse to pay one thousand dollars to save someone. Yet on reflection I have not much confidence in this feeling. What is at stake in the situation described is the person's thousand dollars and the stranger's life. But we end up with the *same* combination of lives and money, no matter which option the person chooses: if he shoots the stranger, the stranger dies, and he keeps his thousand dollars; and if he refuses to pay to save the stranger, the stranger dies, and he keeps his thousand dollars. It makes no difference either to the person's interests or to the stranger's interests which option is chosen. Why, then, do we have the curious intuition that there is a big difference here?

I conceded at the outset that most of us believe that in letting people die we are not behaving as badly as if we were to kill them. I think I have given good reasons for concluding that this belief is false. Yet giving reasons is often not enough, even in philosophy. For if an intuition is strong enough, we may continue to rely on it and assume that *something* is wrong with the arguments opposing it, even though we are not sure exactly what is wrong. It is a familiar remark: "X is more certain than any argument that might be given against it." So in addition to the arguments, we need some account of why people have the allegedly mistaken intuition and why it is so persistent. Why do people believe so firmly that killing is so much worse than letting die, both in fictitious cases such as Trammell's and in the famine-relief cases in the real world? In some ways, the explanation of this is best left to the psychologists; the distinctly philosophical job is accomplished when the intuition is shown to be false. However, I shall hazard a hypothesis since it shows how our intuitions can be explained without assuming that they are perceptions of the truth.

Human beings are to some degree altruistic, but they are also to a great degree selfish, and their attitudes on matters of conduct are largely determined by what is in their own interests and what is in the interests of the few other people they especially care about. In terms of both the costs and the benefits, it is to their own advantage for people in the affluent countries to regard killing as worse than letting die. First, the *costs* of never killing anyone are not great: we can live very well without ever killing. But the cost of not allowing people to die when we could save them would be very great. For any one of us to take seriously a duty to save the starving would require that we give up our affluent lifestyles; money could no longer be spent on luxuries while others starve. On the other side, we have much more to *gain* from a strict prohibition on killing than from a like prohibition on letting die. Since we are not in danger of starving, we will not suffer if people do not regard feeding the hungry as so important; but we would be threatened if people did not regard killing as very, very bad. So both the costs and the benefits encourage us, selfishly, to view killing as worse than letting die. It is to our own advantage to believe this, and so we do.

Notes

1. For an account of the difficulties of getting reliable information in this area, see Nick Eberstadt, "Myths of the Food Crisis," *New York Review of Books,* February 19, 1976, 32–37.

2. Richard L. Trammell's "Saving Life and Taking Life," *Journal of Philosophy* 72 (1975): 131–37, is the best defense of this view of which I am aware.

3. This article is a companion to an earlier one, James Rachels, "Active and Passive Euthanasia," *New England Journal of Medicine* 292 (January 9, 1975): 78–80, in which I discuss the (mis)use of the killing/letting die distinction in medical contexts. But nothing in this article depends on the earlier one.

4. Philippa Foot, "The Problem of Abortion and the Doctrine of the Double Effect," *Oxford Review*, no. 5 (1967); reprinted in James Rachels, ed., *Moral Problems*, 2d ed. (New York: Harper and Row, 1975), 66.

5. On this point and more generally on the whole subject of our duty to contribute for famine relief, see Peter Singer, "Famine, Affluence, and Morality," *Philosophy and Public Affairs* 1 (spring 1972), 232.

6. Trammell, "Saving Life," 133.

7. This argument is suggested by Paul Ramsey in *The Patient as Person* (New Haven, Conn.: Yale University Press, 1970), 151.

8. This difference between failing to save and letting die was pointed out by David Sanford in a very helpful paper, "On Killing and Letting Die," read at the Western Division meeting of the American Philosophical Association in New Orleans on April 30, 1976.

9. Trammell, "Saving Life," 133.

10. Ibid., 134.

11. There is also some independent evidence that this prereflective belief is mistaken; see Singer, "Famine, Affluence, and Morality."

12. Grice made this remark several years ago at Oberlin. I do not remember the surrounding details of the discussion, but the remark seems to me an important one that applies to lots of "objections" to various theories. The most famous objections to act-utilitarianism, for example, are little more than descriptions of the theory, with the question-begging addendum, "Because it says *that*, it can't be right."

13. Daniel Dinello, "On Killing and Letting Die," *Analysis* 31, no. 3 (January 1971): 85–86.

14. Trammell, "Saving Life," 131.

15. Dinello, "On Killing," 85.

16. There is another way to meet Dinello's counterexample. A surprisingly strong case can be made that it would *not* be any worse to kill Smith than to "let Jones die." I have in mind adapting John Harris' argument in "The Survival Lottery," *Philosophy* 50 (1975): 81–87.

SIX

LIVES AND LIBERTY

JAMES RACHELS AND WILLIAM RUDDICK

The God who gave us life gave us liberty at the same time;
the hand of force may destroy but cannot disjoin them.

—Thomas Jefferson,
A Summary View of the Rights of British America (1774)

Philosophy ought to help us understand matters that previously were mysterious. But it may first have to teach us what is mysterious, for we take some things so much for granted that it requires an effort to see them as problematic. Liberty is a case in point. We value liberty as much as we value anything. Political thinkers from Locke to Rawls treat liberty, after life itself, as the supreme political value; and the major declarations of human rights take the same view. The problem is to explain *why* liberty is so important to us. What is it about liberty, or freedom, that makes it so valuable?

Our problem is not new. Many philosophers have addressed it, and three main types of explanations have been devised. We will begin by reviewing these traditional accounts. Then we will present our own account, which is based on a new idea, but which we think preserves the elements of the traditional views that are worth preserving.

1. Traditional Explanations

Liberty as Intrinsically Good

Some philosophers have argued that liberty is intrinsically good. On this view, freedom is important simply because of what it is in itself. It is a mistake, these philosophers say, to look for the importance of freedom in its consequences. Free choices do not necessarily have better results, nor are people necessarily better off, on the whole, when they are acting freely. But that does not matter, for freedom has its own intrinsic value that makes it worth having for its own sake.

Gregory Vlastos takes this view in his well-known essay "Justice and Equality."[1] Vlastos relies upon an argument from analogy. His strategy is to compare the value of liberty with the value of enjoyment (which he thinks is clearly intrinsically good) and to suggest that they should be thought of in similar terms. In both cases, he says, it is the nature of the thing and not its uses that make it good. The value of enjoyment is self-evident; it needs no further explanation. And the value of liberty, he adds, is self-evident in the same way.

We believe that the comparison of liberty with enjoyment is illuminating, but for an entirely different reason than Vlastos suggests. A closer comparison of the two does not support Vlastos' conclusion. On the contrary, it suggests just the opposite. In the case of enjoyment, what Vlastos says is plausible enough. We have little difficulty understanding that enjoyment is good simply because of what it is like. Its goodness is transparent. (It is tempting to think that this is because the goodness of enjoyment is guaranteed by its definition, although this is not an easy thought to make out in detail.) But liberty does not seem to be like that. Its value is not similarly transparent (nor does it seem plausible to think that it is good "by definition"). To say that enjoyment is good in itself seems right; to say that liberty is good in itself is merely puzzling. Therefore, we would argue this way: we agree that enjoyment is intrinsically good, if anything is, but the goodness of liberty does not seem to be comparable; hence, it is doubtful that the goodness of liberty should be understood as intrinsic goodness.

We should be careful not to confuse the notion that liberty (or anything else) is intrinsically good with the different notion that its goodness is self-evident. They are different notions, the first having to do with the kind of goodness it has, the second having to do with the manner and ease with which we recognize that goodness. Nevertheless, it may be thought that the two notions are related in this way: if something is intrinsically good, then we should be able to apprehend its goodness just by focusing our minds on its nature. We take it that this is what Vlastos has in mind when he says that the value of liberty is self-evident.

But this is a difficult view to defend, for its plausibility depends entirely on how readily others will agree. If one cannot simply "see" that something is valuable, without need of further explanation, then one can hardly be convinced that the value is self-evident. And in fact critics have often objected that they cannot simply "see" the value of liberty.[2] How can defenders of this view respond? They are in a difficult position because the logic of their view prevents them from offering additional explanations of liberty's value. If, in order to make its value plainer, they explain it in some other terms, they run the risk of abandoning the view they are trying to defend because intrinsic value is by definition not derived from anything else.

Liberty as Instrumentally Good

Rather than having intrinsic worth, liberty may be thought to have "instrumental value"—that is, to be desirable because of the pleasure and other consequences it produces. The classic statement of this view was provided by James Fitzjames Stephen, who suggested that "the question whether liberty is a good or a bad thing appears as irrational as the question of whether fire is a good or bad thing."[3] If one's house is burning, the fire is a bad thing; if the fire is heating one's food, it is a good thing. The fire has no value, positive or negative, apart from the circumstances. Similarly, Stephen argued, liberty has no value apart from its uses. He contended, for example, that if someone freely chooses to do good, then it is good that he was free to choose; but if he chooses evil, it would have been better for him to have been compelled to have acted differently.

This view is also unsatisfying, for it implies that when the consequences of liberty and compulsion are the same, there is nothing to choose between them. This does not seem right. Suppose a person would choose good, if left free to choose, but is compelled to the "right" option without being given a choice. On the face of it, there seems something objectionable here; but the objection cannot be to the consequences, for they are identical. How can Stephen, or anyone taking his general approach, account for this?

It might be thought that free choice of the good will always have one major benefit, namely strengthening the agent's character. By contrast, being forced to the right action would have no effects or would even have deleterious effects on character. (Compelled too often as children to share, we may become misers in later life.) But surely the moral benefits of choice over compulsion are not so general or so evident. Many choices are not choices of the good, but only of the pleasant, the expedient, or the familiar. Do these choices generally build character? (Perhaps they *manifest* character, but why is that desirable—except for the Recording Angel gathering data for God's Final Judgment?) And even in the case of moral good, is every choice character building or preserving? Only perhaps in the early stages of life or in special conditions—emergencies, novel temptations, and the like.

Liberty as Necessary for Self-realization

This concern for character suggests a third, more plausible type of explanation for liberty's value. Liberty may be valued as a *necessary condition* for the existence of something else that is generally and undeniably valuable. (This type of explanation is easily confused with the view that liberty is instrumentally good, but they are importantly different.) The standard version of this view is that liberty is necessary for developing not only moral character, but a whole range of human capacities—it is necessary for developing one's potential as a human being. Joel Feinberg summarizes the argument like this: "The highest good for man is neither enjoyment nor passive contentment but rather a dynamic process of growth and self-realization. Self-realization consists in the actualization of certain uniquely human potentialities, the bringing to full development of certain powers and abilities. This in turn requires constant practice in making difficult choices among alternative hypotheses, policies, and actions."[4] The point is not that such self-development is a *consequence* of being free; it is that freedom is one of the important *conditions* without which this personal growth cannot take place. Freedom makes such growth possible, although it does not make it inevitable.

Mill's View

We believe that each of these three explanations is flawed. However, each has its own special appeal, and it is tempting to affirm that each of them is *in some sense* correct. John Stuart Mill, who was no fool about these matters, did exactly that.

In *On Liberty*, Mill seems, in different places, to endorse all three of these views. In one place, he speaks as though liberty is intrinsically good: "all restraint, *qua* restraint, is an evil.... Leaving people to themselves is always better, *ceteris paribus,* than controlling them."[5] The italicized Latin phrases imply that even if the consequences of freedom and compulsion are the same, freedom is still to be preferred. One would not expect the author of *Utilitarianism* to say such a thing.

In fact, when Mill turns to the discussion of particular freedoms, such as freedom of speech, he reverts to consequentialist arguments: he assumes, compatibly with his general utilitarian approach, that if free speech is to be defended, it must be shown to have desirable consequences. So he argues that without freedom of speech it would be much harder for us to come to know and appreciate the truth.[6]

Finally, in still another place, Mill is at his most eloquent in setting out the self-realization argument:

> He who lets the world, or his own portion of it, choose his plan of life for him has no need of any other faculty than the ape-like one of imitation. He who chooses his plan for himself employs all his faculties. He must use observation to see, reasoning and judgment to foresee, activity to gather materials for decision, discrimination to decide, and when he has decided, firmness and self-control to hold to his deliberate decision.... It is possible that he might be guided in some good path, and kept out of harm's way, without any of these things. But what will be his comparative worth as a human being? It really is of importance, not only what men do, but also what manner of men they are that do it. Among the works of man which human life is rightly employed in perfecting and beautifying, the first in importance is surely man himself.[7]

An adequate theory of the value of liberty should provide some understanding of why these three views, even if they are mistaken, are so appealing. At the end of this essay, after we have presented our own view, we will offer an explanation of their attractiveness.

2. From Persons to Lives

Of the three traditional explanations, the self-realization argument, we think, comes closest to the truth: liberty is important because it is a necessary condition for the development of one's human potentialities or, to use a currently fashionable term, one's personhood. This way of putting the matter, however, invites some awkward questions. If one is supposed to develop "as a person," *which* human potentialities are thereby singled out for cultivation? (Which of our many potentialities are associated with personhood, and why?) Why should these potentialities take priority over others or over indolent self-acceptance of one's undeveloped state? And exactly what kind of folly or confusion do we commit if we do not strive to "perfect and beautify" ourselves through development of these potentialities?

These problems of selection and motivation ("Which are the person-making traits and why should I prize them?") may be awkward because ill-formulated. Personhood, we think, is a notion too *formal* to yield determinate answers to these questions. Person-making traits vary with context. In religious settings, persons are those beings whom God has created or endowed with souls. (*Person* and *soul* are often used as though they were synonymous.) In political discourse, persons are those who possess whatever characteristics are deemed necessary for legal protection and standing. Property, race, gender, and age are the most familiar categories. For Locke, it was personal memory, a prerequisite for legal punishment and reward, that gave one the "forensic" status of personhood. But for most philosophers, it is the more demanding (and self-celebrating) capacity for rationality that makes someone a person.

Despite these contextual variations, there is a common thread—namely, the connection between personhood and equal treatment. By definition, persons are entitled to equal treatment (in context-relevant regards) in virtue of their (context-relative) common features. As besouled children of God, we are equally the objects of divine love and therefore equally entitled to one another's regard. As legal persons, we are entitled equally to the attention of the courts. However striking our differences, we are equal in the eyes of God or of the law or of Kant.

Indeed, the rhetorical and moral point of claiming personhood is to override those striking differences and to challenge the unequal treatment to which they give rise. (Hence, the cry, "They are persons, too!" from advocates of women, blacks, fetuses, or handicapped people.) Accordingly, personhood is a prescriptive or normative notion with pointedly little descriptive content. Attempts to list defining properties[8] are, we think, misguided by the assumption that personhood is a discernible condition, secular or metaphysical. Rather, personhood is a status conferred (on secular or metaphysical grounds) in the interests of equal treatment in some respect or other.

Liberty, by contrast, is not invoked to set aside differences, but to protect and foster them. Although seeming abstract, liberty is an umbrella for a wide variety of specific rights and privileges that determine the texture of daily life. It is the heading under which we strive to bring, with legal aid, our reading, writing, working, childbearing and rearing, social and sexual associations, and so on. Equality is a much more formal, law-theoretical, institutional notion. It is appropriate that immigrants sailed past a Statue of Liberty with a torch to light their way, not a Statue of Equality blindfolded against discriminatory judgments.

In short, personhood is too remote to capture liberty's high value on the third view we are examining. Indeed, the "cultivation and perfection of personhood" has little sense on our account: one cannot cultivate equality or the metaphysical properties that confer religious equality or the secular characteristics that have been deemed to confer political equality (being white, adult, male). What is needed is a notion closer to home and the specific activities liberty protects.

Although closely related to personhood, the familiar notion of *a life* has the right degree of domestic specificity. Only persons have lives, but some persons have several lives, concurrently or serially—and some have none. We'll say more later about persons and lives, but it is the relation between lives and liberty we now wish to foster. The idea we propose is: *without liberty, a person cannot have a life.* We do not mean that a person without liberty cannot have a good life or a productive or satisfying life or anything of that sort. The point is more radical than that. It is that without liberty a person cannot have a life *at all*.

If this initially paradoxical claim can be made out, the importance of liberty should be transparent. If liberty is necessary for having a life, then to question the value of liberty is to question the value of having a life. In dire circumstances, we might become indifferent to life itself. But given our usual attachments and projects, we cannot sensibly or seriously ask, "Why should I care about my life?"

3. Having a Life

To begin to make these claims plausible, we need to distinguish two notions that, in English, are expressed by similar words. We need to distinguish *being alive* from *having a life.*[9] The former is fundamentally a biological notion: to be alive is (roughly) to be a functioning, self-preserving organism. The latter is, by contrast, a notion of biography rather than of biology. The lives we have and lead are constituted by certain kinds of actions, attitudes, emotions, and social relations outside the biologist's ken.

The importance of the distinction may be doubted, for two reasons. First, our biographies are shaped in various ways by our biology. Our life possibilities and the actual course of our lives (our *bios*) are partly defined by our congenital "equipment," our states of health, our age and expected life span, and so on. Biological events (such as puberty and menopause) are crucial in determining life's stages. Second, biological existence is a condition for biography: if you are not alive, you cannot have a life. Stars, nations, concepts, and errors may have histories, but they do not have lives—unless we invest them anthropomorphically with agency and appropriate psychology.

But neither consideration casts real doubt on the distinction. On the contrary, by understanding the *relation* between the two notions, we can explain a number of things. For example, it is precisely this dependence of lives upon life that explains our attitudes in some of the most important areas of morality. Consider the morality of killing. The dependence of lives upon life explains our gradations of attitude about killing. In losing their biological existence, the usual victims of homicide necessarily lose their biographical lives as well. But it is the latter, not the former, that is the morally objectionable loss and is the proper object of moral protection.[10] To the extent that people have ceased to have biographical lives (as, for example, the irreversibly comatose), killing becomes less objectionable. (There may, of course, be other grounds for opposing euthanasia.) And to the degree that animals of other species lack the capacity for lives, to that degree our objections to killing them (painlessly) for food, clothing, and scientific study diminish. (Again, there may be other grounds for opposing these uses of animals.)[11]

It has sometimes been argued (by Tooley, for example) that killing an individual is objectionable only if that individual has a self-conception. We think it is better to say that killing is objectionable just in case the victim is the subject of a life. But the two notions are related. An individual who has a self-conception will have a far richer and more complex life than one who does not. A life consisting only of such activities as can be described without self-reference would be skimpy indeed. Moreover, the subjects of such lives would be incapable of attitudes such as pride, shame, embarrassment, fear, and obligation, for those attitudes and others like them are irreducibly self-referring. *Self-referring* here does not mean only or even primarily egocentric or narcissistic frames of mind, but rather merely those in which one figures in the content of one's own thoughts. Such thoughts may be solely self-directed ("I am proud of what I have accomplished") or other directed ("How may I be of comfort to him?"). Or they may fall in between ("I am embarrassed by the conduct of someone with whom I am closely associated").

These self-referring attitudes presuppose a sense of oneself as having an existence spread over past and future time. In having plans, hopes, and regrets, one considers one's present condition as part of a temporally extended existence. This is obviously true of people with careers or with the "life plans" often invoked in philosophical discussion.[12] But so, too, for people who on epicurean principles "take life one day at a time," as well as for people whose dire circumstances reduce them to living for the next meal. Even if keeping oneself alive is one's sole "project," this struggle involves a conception of an existence to be prolonged or an extinction to be postponed.

For this sense of self over time, we need capacities for memory and anticipation ("I must remember not only that a promise was made that someone would attend next week, but I must remember that I promised to be there"). These very capacities are also cited as necessary conditions of personhood.[13] There is a close connection, as we said, between having a life and being a person: only persons have lives. But the concepts are not paired one to one: a person may have more than one life or none. On certain metaphysical accounts, a person may have several incarnations and hence several lives. Less debatably, a person may lead a double life or a new life, often marked by different names, projects, and styles of dress.

On analysis, perhaps a double life is not two simultaneous lives, but a single life with two aspects; likewise, an old life and a new life may prove to be best counted as two stages or phases of the same life (as, e.g., in the case of religious or political converts). But these questions of individuation or enumeration need not be decided here. Our concern is not with people who have multiple lives (or life stages), but with persons who have none. This may seem impossible: How can someone without a life continue to qualify as a person? The answer lies in the relative abstractness we have noted. A being might retain the capacity for social responses and yet have none of the intentions, plans, and other features of will and action that define a life. The prime candidates for this lamentable condition are people subject to extreme duress, passivity, or restriction. The most obvious cases are victims of dire poverty, illness, and slavery.

Lifeless poverty is that condition of physical need in which even single-minded foraging and fighting for food and shelter have ceased. One becomes wholly and passively dependent on the charity of others. (Victims of war and drought standing silently in relief camp lines are harrowing examples.) Likewise, the seriously ill may be unable to "fight for life" or to manifest the military and athletic virtues expected of hospital patients.[14] Although still capable of socially appropriate expressions of pain, indignation, and gratitude, they may not be able to participate or cooperate in their own care. Again, passive dependence on the decisions and aid of others is their lifeless condition.

4. Can a Slave Have a Biography?

In our society, poverty is not viewed as a deprivation of liberty, nor is hospitalization.[15] Thus, persons whom poverty or illness deprive of any life of their own may not convincingly illustrate our thesis about lives and liberty. Slavery is a clearer test of our slogan "No Liberty, No Life." Does a slave have a life? It might seem so: witness the wealth of slave biographies, especially from the antebellum southern United States.[16] These narratives, first- or secondhand, tell of the slaves' efforts to maintain family ties and community. In one study of American slave communities (significantly entitled *From Sundown to Sunup*), there are scenes such as this: "Cooking was usually done outdoors or in a cooking shed; people sat out in front of the cabins and talked and smoked; children played in front of the huts; young men and women courted wherever they could find privacy; gossip was exchanged while engaging in common chores outdoors."[17] Such scenes were, of course, subject to disruption by rape, whip, forced march, or sale. No slave system, it seems, allows permanent family ties among parents, spouses, and children. This "genealogical isolation" has taken various forms: Turkish sultans recruited slaves from Christian parents and castrated them, thereby ensuring that they would remain perpetual aliens (and objects of fear among Turkish subjects). Just as slaves suffer "natal alienation" from parents and a past, so they are denied a future, living from day to day solely on the whims and mercy of their masters. As such, slaves are made wholly dependent on their masters' definitions of social possibilities and welfare. Slaves have no social existence apart from their masters; they are, accordingly, "socially dead persons," remaining forever "unborn beings (non-né)."[18]

The disappearance of the slave's own life and its replacement by that of the master are remarked upon by Simone Weil in her essay on the *Iliad*. In describing the condition of captives and their radical dependence upon their captors, she writes that

> for those upon whom it [slavery] has fallen, so brutal a destiny wipes out damnations, revolts, comparisons, meditations upon the future and the past, almost memory itself. It does not belong to the slave to be faithful to his city or to his dead.
>
> It is when one of those who made him lose all, who sacked his city, massacred his own under his very eyes, when one of those suffers, then the slave weeps. And why not? Only then are tears permitted him.... On no occasion has the slave a right to express anything if not that which may please the master. That is why, if in so barren a life, a capacity to love should be born, this love could only be for the master. Every other way is barred to the gift of loving, just as for a horse hitched to a wagon, the reins and the bridle bar all directions but one. And if by miracle there should appear the hope of becoming again someone, to what pitch would not that gratitude and that love soar for those very men who must still, because of the recent past, inspire horror?... One cannot lose more than the slave loses, he loses all inner life.[19]

Or, as we would put it, a "barren life" with no "inner life" is no life at all. It is, rather, the condition of a tool, or part of the life of another. Weil argues this is indeed the condition of modern factory work, in which workers are made lifeless parts of the production machine. Only in their nonworking hours can they recover a life of their own. For Weil, workers, like slaves, have biographies only to the extent that they can escape the subordination of will and loss of self-involvement imposed by their overseers.[20]

Few slaves are, however, completely denied ties with the past or hopes for a future free of a master's caprice or anger.[21] For many slaves, a sense of themselves turned on a hope for eventual release, either before or after death. These hopes, however slight, allowed for an imagined life of one's own, free of a master's desires or threat of punishment. The mere possibility of such a distinct life creates a distinction between the slave's will and the master's, and it fosters the self-referring attitudes cited above as life defining.

In most cases, then, slaves do have lives, at least of a minimum kind. Nevertheless, our hypothesis—that liberty is necessary for having a life—is confirmed by the dependence of a slave's having a life, on there being a part of his existence that is under his own control. Suppose this part is eliminated. In imagination, let us call someone for whom *everything* is dictated a *total slave*. The total slave will make no decisions. Every action, from the time he wakes up until he goes to sleep again, will be dictated. Moreover, let us imagine that the master even decrees what the slave thinks as well, so that there is no area of life over which the slave retains control. *This* individual is not the subject of a life. He is like a robot or a tool; we can describe the part he plays in the master's life, but he has no life of his own. Real slaves may have biographies, but only because they are not total slaves.

5. Conclusion

Orlando Patterson claims that slavery is the basic notion from which our very conception of liberty derives.[22] Be that as it may, slavery enables us to see the value of freedom and to understand both the attractions and the deficiencies of the three traditional explanations cited at the outset. Those who argue that liberty is intrinsically good are right to insist that it is better to choose to do something freely than to be compelled to do it, even if the outcome is the same. In general, on our account, freely chosen actions are constitutive elements of one's life, while forced actions are interruptions, limitations, or obstacles in that life. Free actions define and execute our characteristic intentions and projects; coerced actions tend to brook or thwart them. In the rare case in which we are compelled to do what we would otherwise have chosen to do, the action falls outside our life (and within the life of our coercer), and to that extent it is a loss for us.

Consider a young person trying to start or lead the life of a painter. An insensitive teacher might instruct the student to complete the painting in a way the student would have hit upon herself, thereby preventing the work from being wholly hers. (It is, in a way, the instructor's painting now, too.) Even if the student thereby loses no self-respect, adrenalin, or opportunities, the painting does not have the place in her life it otherwise would have had. From a public or third-party point of view, that may not be objectionable. But from "inside" the life, such "biographical losses" are undesirable, even if they involve no specific pains, loss of pleasure, or even loss of pride.

("Biographical losses" may even occur through coercion intended to spare us pain. Consider the case of a woman intent on natural childbirth whose labor is terminated by anesthetics and forceps.) Since our intentional lives are in a sense our closest possessions, losses cannot be a matter of indifference to the livers or leaders of those lives.

Our concern, however, is not to show that lives have intrinsic worth or to argue that liberty makes beneficial contributions to lives. Both claims are either obscure or dubious or both. We have undertaken to explicate a version of the third, "self-realization" argument for liberty. Mill praises freedom because without it we would have no occasion for developing our powers of observation, reasoning, and the like. But why is it important to develop these abilities? It is not that these powers are ends in themselves, and it is not simply, as Mill put it, "to perfect and beautify man." By exercising these capacities in making choices, persons create their lives: liberty makes lives not beautiful, but possible. But this is not to say that liberty is like air, causally necessary for lives. Rather, it is like motion, a component of living. Liberty constitutes our lives through the free choices and actions that embody it.[23]

The quotation from Thomas Jefferson that stands at the beginning of this essay expresses a conviction common among liberal writers: freedom is so important that without it life is not worthwhile. But if our thesis is correct, the connection between life and liberty is even closer than that. Jefferson's words can be understood in a stronger sense: the hand of force may destroy, but it cannot (logically cannot) disjoin them.

Notes

1. Gregory Vlastos, "Justice and Equality," in *Social Justice*, edited by Richard B. Brandt (Englewood Cliffs, N.J.: Prentice-Hall, 1962).

2. See, for example, J. D. Mabbott, *The State and The Citizen* (London: Hutchinson, 1967), chap. 7. In any case, there is ample reason for doubting that the value of liberty is self-evident. Sartre found freedom "dreadful" and expounded upon our desperate desire to escape it; evangelists and dictators speak knowingly, if paradoxically, about the "freedom" of obedience to a "higher will," and, unfortunately, there has been no shortage of people eager to respond to such appeals. This is enough by itself to make us doubt that the value of liberty will be found in a phenomenological analysis of the experience of it, no matter how that analysis is refined.

3. James Fitzjames Stephen, *Liberty, Equality, Fraternity* (London: n.p., 1873), 48.

4. Joel Feinberg, *Social Philosophy* (Englewood Cliffs, N.J.: Prentice-Hall, 1973), 21.

5. John Stuart Mill, *On Liberty*, edited by David Spitz (New York: Norton, 1975), 88.

6. Ibid., chap. 2.

7. Ibid., 56.

8. See Michael Tooley's analysis in "Abortion and Infanticide," *Philosophy and Public Affairs* 2, no. 1 (1972): 37–65, and Joseph Fletcher's longer list of person-making characteristics in *Humanhood* (Buffalo: Prometheus, 1979). Tooley's more detailed account is given in his book *Abortion and Infanticide* (Oxford: Clarendon Press, 1983). Mary Anne Warren's defense of abortion in her article "Abortion and the Concept of a Person," *The Monist* 57 (1973): 43–61, also proceeds from a list of characteristics that she takes to be definitive of personhood.

9. Ancient Greek distinguishes *zoe*, animal life, from *bios*, the course of life. Similar possible distinctions may be found in German, French, and Hindi. In English, we have to resort to grammatical devices: *life*, for the biological, and *a life* for the biographical.

10. This idea is elaborated in James Rachels, *The End of Life: Euthanasia and Morality* (New York: Oxford University Press, 1986).

11. See, for example, James Rachels, "Vegetarianism and 'the Other Weight Problem,'" in *World Hunger and Moral Obligation*, edited by William Aiken and Hugh LaFollette, 180–93 (Englewood Cliffs, N.J.: Prentice-Hall, 1977).

12. The notion of a life plan occurs (with increasing, but still sketchy analysis) in the writings of Mill, Sidgwick, Royce, Rawls, Fried, and Nozick. Richard Wollheim has offered a detailed account of what it means to *lead* a life in his *The Thread of Life* (Cambridge, Mass.: Harvard University Press, 1984). A somewhat different account in a different context is sketched in William Ruddick's "Parents and Life Prospects," in *Having Children*, edited by Onora O'Neill and William Ruddick, 123–37 (New York: Oxford University Press, 1979). Also see Rachels, *The End of Life*, chap. 3.

13. Locke, for example, apparently believed that the connections of memory are what make one the "same person" at different times. The Lockean account of personal identity is familiar. Suppose we let X and Y name persons existing at different times, X being the earlier. On this view, X and Y are the same person if and only if Y remembers doing what X did, thinking what X thought, and so on. (See John Locke, *An Essay Concerning Human Understanding* [1690], book 2, sec. 27.) This account has been criticized on various grounds, but its most basic flaw can be exposed by considering the case of total amnesia. If someone loses his memory, does he

thereby become a different person? No, for there are too many other connections that remain intact. So Locke seems to have been wrong.

Nevertheless, there is *something* tempting in the idea that the amnesiac has become a "different person," and this temptation is worth analyzing. How is the amnesiac's plight to be understood? We believe the amnesiac's plight is not that he has become a different person, but that he is alienated from his life. He is (temporarily) without a life, forced to "start over." Even if he takes up the same projects he formerly pursued—the same job, the same family, and so on—he adopts them as one might try to fit oneself into someone else's life. He can feel pride in past accomplishments or regret over past misdeeds only by the effort of reminding himself, "they were mine," and not in the natural way provided by unprompted memory. Locke was right to think that the connections of memory are crucial to our existence, but he gave a wrong account of why they are crucial. Memory is important not so much to our continuing existence as persons, as to our continuing ability to lead our lives.

14. See William Ruddick, "Patient Morality: Compliance, Perseverance, and Other Athletic Virtues," *Philosophic Exchange* 4 (1983): 87–96.

15. Socialist analyses often employ the notion of "economic liberty" in discussing the poverty that, on those analyses, capitalism allows or requires. There is a similar suggestion in Franklin Roosevelt's phrase "freedom from want." Hospitals, as much as prisons and army camps, are examples of what Erving Goffman called "total institutions." See his *Asylums* (Garden City, N.Y.: Aldine, 1962).

16. See, for example, Arna Bontemps, *Great Slave Narratives* (Boston: Beacon Press, 1969). Also Erlene Stetson, "Studying Slavery: Some Literary and Pedagogical Considerations on the Black Female Slave," in *All the Women Are White, All the Blacks Are Men, but Some of Us Are Brave,* edited by Gloria T. Hull, Patricia Bell Scott, and Barbara Smith, 61–84 (Old Westbury, N.Y.: Feminist Press, 1982).

17. George P. Rawick, *From Sundown to Sunup: The Making of the Black Community* (Westport, Conn.: Greenwood, 1972), 77.

18. Orlando Patterson, *Slavery and Social Death* (Cambridge, Mass.: Harvard University Press, 1983), 38.

19. Simone Weil, "The *Iliad,* Poem of Might," reprinted in *The Simone Weil Reader,* edited by George A. Panichas (Mt. Kisco, N.Y.: McKay, 1977), 158–59. Tolstoy gives a strikingly similar account of the emotions of a young woman in love with an older man in "Happily Ever After." Some feminist critics take such feelings to be the ideal of all traditional marriage.

20. Simone Weil, "Factory Work," in *The Simone Weil Reader,* 53–72. For American analogues, see Studs Terkel, *Working* (New York: Pantheon, 1972).

21. R. M. Hare distinguishes prisoners of war from slaves on the grounds that the former know that their condition is not permanent. "What Is Wrong with Slavery," *Philosophy and Public Affairs* 8, no. 2 (1979), 120.

22. Patterson, *Slavery and Social Death*, 341–42.

98

23. Our remarks may suggest a kind of individualism we do not embrace. A life may be associated with public, social, collective purposes as well as with the narrower goals of "private" life. A life of one's own need not be a life defined by egoistic or narcissistic projects. But it does require that associations or identifications with the good of others be in some sense chosen or freely and reflectively endorsed by the liver of that more generous life.

SEVEN

POLITICAL ASSASSINATION

I want to discuss some conditions under which political assassination might be justified. At the present time, it may seem idle or even irresponsible to speak of justifying political assassination since there have been so many tragic and senseless political killings in recent years. Yet it is precisely these recent tragic events that make the subject worth discussing, for a study of the moral basis of political assassination should give us not only some understanding of the conditions under which it is justified, but also some insight into the much more frequent sorts of cases in which it is not justified at all.

I

First, I will say something about two preliminary matters.

1. There is something especially awful about political assassination, above and beyond the awfulness of ordinary murder, that any adequate account of the subject must be able to explain. This special awfulness is not due merely to the fame of the victim: movie stars are famous, yet people do not react to the killing of a movie star in the same way. Nor is it a matter of the personal popularity of the victim or of the esteem or affection that people have for him: people who thought very badly of George Wallace, for example, were nevertheless horrified by the attempt on his life.

I believe that the special horror that attends acts of political assassination is due to the system of social relationships that is created by the political organization of a society. We generally have this sort of heightened reaction to a killing when there are special social relationships between the killer and his victim or between the victim and ourselves. In the former case, we even have special words to denote the type of killing in question, such as *fratricide* and *patricide*. Thus, it is bad enough to kill any human being, but when someone kills his own brother, there is an additional element of horror about it. And when someone kills one's own brother, the tragedy involves oneself in a very intimate way.

Now, the system of social relationships created by the political organization of a society typically includes everyone in the society, or virtually everyone; thus, Richard Nixon is *our* president, for better or worse. For this reason, a political killing can be and often is an act that touches not only the victim and his personal associates, but the society as a whole. It is not merely that the assassination has repercussions that affect everyone, although that is often so. More fundamentally, in any society in which people are not totally alienated from their political system, the act of assassination will arouse the citizen's feelings of identification with his country and its political processes: if it is the president who is attacked, then the act will be felt by the citizen as an attack on *his* president, just as the killing of a brother will be experienced as an attack on a member of *his* family. So when John Kennedy was killed, *our president* was killed; and it was not inappropriate or melodramatic even for people who had never met him to take it as a personal blow, any more than it would be inappropriate or melodramatic for someone to take his brother's death as a personal blow. In each case, what makes this sort of reaction appropriate is that the individual is linked to the victim by a definite and important social relationship. "The nation mourns the President's death"—and rightly so, for the nation is precisely the natural and appropriate unit here, just as family and friends form the appropriate group to mourn the death of an ordinary person.

2. In a great many historically noteworthy cases of political assassination, there has been a common pattern: the members of a political faction assassinate their opponents in order to seize power or to consolidate the power they already have, or at least with the intention of having some substantial effect on government policy. In 133 B.C., for example, the Roman aristocrat Tiberius Gracchus was assassinated by his political enemies because he favored curtailing certain privileges of the rich in order to benefit

the masses of poor people. This touched off a bloody feud between the rival factions that lasted for many years and in the course of which there were many further killings.

If the received account of Gracchus' murder is correct, then his assassins certainly were not justified in what they did. Gracchus appears to have been a good man working in a good cause, who was killed by bad men in a bad cause. And this, unfortunately, has often been the case. More recent examples are provided by Hitler, whose rise to power was marked by countless political killings, and by the Japanese military officers whose political power was multiplied several times over when they assassinated Prime Minister Inukai in 1932. Of course, there is no question of justifying this sort of murder. In other instances, assassination has been merely one of the weapons used by corrupt groups struggling against one another, where neither side can claim any sort of moral justification for its activities. The assassination of Ngo Dinh Diem in South Vietnam in 1963, for example, seems to me to have been simply an exercise in power politics having no basis in morality at all.

Not all assassinations have followed these historic patterns; most notably, none of the assassinations or attempted assassinations of American presidents has involved attempts to seize power or to perpetuate persons or parties in power or to bring about major social changes.[1] In all, eight presidents (out of a total of thirty-six) have been assassins' targets. Of these, Lincoln, Garfield, McKinley, and Kennedy were killed, but Jackson, the two Roosevelts, and Truman escaped. (Theodore Roosevelt was shot four years after he had left the White House, while campaigning unsuccessfully to return to office; and Franklin Roosevelt was attacked two weeks before his inauguration, but the five bullets missed him and struck bystanders instead.) These assassins were, by and large, mentally unbalanced people with obscure or ludicrous motivations. Garfield was killed by a man who wrote, a few days before the assassination, "I am clear in my purpose to remove the President. Two points will be accomplished. It will save the Republic, and it will create a demand for my book." Only the attempted assassination of Harry Truman, by a group seeking independence for Puerto Rico, was motivated by anything like an ordinary political goal; but even here it is very obscure just how Truman's death was supposed to contribute to the realization of that goal. Again, these assassinations and assassination attempts are so far from being justified that they provide little material for serious reflection on the subject.

We might begin to approximate the conditions under which assassination would be justified if we think of a case in which the death of a political figure is necessary to achieve some political or social end that is of overriding importance. The famous attempts to assassinate Hitler in March 1943 and July 1944 might be examples of such cases. It is reasonable to think that if either of these attempts had succeeded, the Second World War would have ended much sooner, and a great deal of death and suffering would have been prevented. If so, then that assassination would have been justified.

Here the justification is in essentially utilitarian terms: the act is justified by reference to *what will happen* as a result. But if this sort of justification is to succeed, several conditions have to be satisfied. The first condition is this. Assassination is a species of killing, and killing a person is itself objectionable simply because it means destroying a human life. Therefore, if an act of assassination is to be justified by the good results it produces, those results must be *good enough* to outweigh the evil involved in the killing itself. For example, shortening a global war by a year may have been a great enough good to justify killing Hitler, but securing a minor improvement in a tax law would not be a great enough good to justify killing anyone.

A second condition is that there must be no alternative strategy that would achieve the same results but by a less objectionable method. For example, if it were possible to end an unjust war simply by capturing and imprisoning a tyrant, then there would be no need to assassinate him.

These two conditions seem self-evident to me, and they are strong enough so that they are only rarely satisfied in practice. Yet even these conditions are not nearly strong enough, for they both could be satisfied and the assassination still not be justified. For suppose that even though the same superlative results could not be achieved in any other way, some results only slightly less good could be brought about by means considerably less objectionable than killing. Suppose that by assassinating a group of wicked leaders, revolutionaries could radically transform a society for the better, and all the wicked leaders' bad influence would die with them. (This will almost never be so, but suppose it anyway.) Let us further assume that such a good result could not be achieved in any other way and that the good to be accomplished here far outweighs the undesirability of the killing. However, what if simply by imprisoning the old leaders, the revolutionaries could bring about the same transformation of the society for the better, the only difference being that now the old leaders will retain some slight influence? The results would not be quite so good, but the method used to achieve them would be very much less objectionable.

The general point is that even if the two previously stated conditions are satisfied—even if the same superlatively good results could not be achieved by any less objectionable method than killing—it still may be that only slightly inferior results can be brought about by considerably less bad means. In that case, assassination would not be a justifiable course of action simply because, although it would maximize good results, it would not strike the best overall balance between maximizing good and minimizing evil.

Therefore, whenever we think that an assassination may be justified because of the results it would produce, we should ask:

(a) Would these results be good *enough* to outweigh the evil involved in destroying a human life?

(b) Is assassination the only or least objectionable means of achieving these results?

(c) Of all the possible actions available in the situation, does this one strike the best overall balance of maximizing good and minimizing evil?

The assassination will be justified only if the answer to all three questions is "Yes."

At this point, I want to anticipate a certain objection: it may be said that such matters as I have been discussing mean very little in actual practice. A situation has to be fairly desperate before assassination becomes a morally tempting option, and it is not likely that people in such desperate circumstances will have a wide variety of appealing strategies from which to choose. They will most likely be politically powerless, without access to a fair and impartial legal system sympathetic to their cause, and without the resources necessary to implement other, less drastic plans of action. Moreover, it may be extremely difficult, if not impossible, to know for certain what the exact effects of such action will be, much less whether any alternative plan would come anywhere near having the same effects.

This is fair enough; however, none of it reveals any gap between theory and practice that is unique to the sort of theory I am discussing. These observations only bring out how hard it is, in some cases, to decide what to do because in those cases our options are limited and distasteful, and we do not have the information that would be needed to make a fully rational choice even from among the few alternatives that are open to us. If it is sometimes impossible to know what the effects of one's action will be or whether any alternative plan would work as well, then it is impossible in those cases to know what is the right thing to do. What I have said so far merely underscores this fact. The world is a hard place, and any account of moral reasoning that said or implied otherwise would be a bad account. All that should be expected from moral theory is an account of the sorts of considerations that would be important if they could be known. Whether they can be known is another matter; and when we are condemned to ignorance, we just have to do the best we can.

But matters are still more complicated than anything that I have said so far would indicate. These further complications arise because our moral thinking does not proceed along strictly utilitarian lines. Thus, even if an act of political assassination did bring about the best possible balance of good over evil results and so could not be faulted on utilitarian grounds, it might still be faulted on other grounds. For it is not true, in general, that it is morally permissible to kill someone any time doing so would have better results than not doing so. The following case shows this.

Suppose we have three men, each of whom needs an organ transplant to live: one needs a heart, another a lung, and the third a kidney. All three men have socially important jobs that no one else can do as well, and all three have families dependent on them, so their deaths will be bad not only for them but for others as well. But since there are no donated organs available for transplant, all three are going to die. However, we can seize some strong, healthy man who has no family or anything else of the sort, kill him, and divide his organs among our patients; and as a result of this one man's dying, the three will be saved.

Almost all of us would agree that it would be wrong to kill this man for his organs, even if doing so would have the best balance of good-over-evil results. We might express this judgment by saying that we have no *right* to kill him. Each person has the right to the protection of the moral rule against killing, and in this case it does not seem that we are justified in setting aside that rule, even though on purely utilitarian grounds it may seem that we should.

The same may be true in a case of political assassination. Politicians, too, have a right to live, and we cannot assume that we have the right to kill them merely because we foresee favorable results, any more than we could make such an assumption in the case of the organ transplants.

This difficulty may be gotten around in either of two ways.

1. First, it may be that the evil to be removed by the assassination is so enormous that the victim's rights simply must be set aside. People's rights cannot be thought of as inviolable in all circumstances, although perhaps they should be respected in all but the gravest circumstances. Yet if the circumstances are sufficiently serious—if the evil to be eliminated is great enough—then it may be required that we override some people's rights. The example of the organ transplants indicates just how serious the situation must be before we may override someone's right not to be killed: not even the need to save several *more* lives is serious enough.

There is a curious asymmetry here between our duties to do good and our duties to prevent or eliminate evil. In a way, the two may be regarded as equivalent since in preventing or correcting a bad situation we are doing something good and in doing something good we are "preventing" at least one thing worse, namely the nonexistence of the good thing we are doing. But there is an important difference that can be brought out by considering the difference between causing someone pleasure or happiness (a good thing) and preventing him from suffering pain (a bad thing). The asymmetry is that our duty *not* to cause suffering or our duty to relieve it where it exists is greater than our duty to make people happy or give them pleasure. Compare a man who refuses to do something that would relieve someone in great agony, although he could do it easily, with a man who declines to do something that would make someone (who is not already unhappy, but in an indifferent state) very happy. We might think badly of both men, but I believe that we would think much worse of the first man. The man who will not bother to make others happy certainly is not very generous, but the man who won't relieve another person's agony is simply wicked.

A similar point may be made about political assassination. It might be possible to justify assassination as part of a strategy to correct a very bad condition of society, where there is a lot of injustice, oppression, and suffering, but it would be much harder—in fact, I think impossible—to justify political killing as part of a strategy designed to make an already tolerable society even better. This is because while it may be permissible for us to override our victim's rights if it were necessary to eliminate great suffering, it would not be permissible to override his rights merely to increase the happiness of an already minimally contented population—even though the net gain, according to some sort of utilitarian calculus, is the same in both cases.

The practical point about when assassination is permissible is, I hope, obvious. But for all its obviousness, the point has considerable significance for our understanding of the relation between human rights and social utility. The situation seems to be this. The achievement of a minimally decent society, where human suffering and pain have been reduced to a tolerable level, is such an important business that it may justify overriding people's rights in some circumstances. Respecting people's rights is not more important than bringing about this minimally decent sort of society. However, once this has been achieved, it is no longer permissible to flout people's rights simply to make things still better. This is why in a minimally well-off society human rights have primary importance. Thus, while it may be all right for a revolutionary temporarily to set aside the rule against killing in order to eliminate a great evil from a society, after the revolution the rule must be restored to its full force.

2. The second way of getting around the difficulty about the assassination victim's rights has to do with his possible complicity in causing or perpetuating the bad situation that his death is supposed to help correct. If the political figure is himself responsible for the injustice or suffering that we are concerned to eliminate, then his "rights" are not nearly so important as they otherwise would be. This explains why we would not worry about Hitler's rights if, in 1943 or 1944, he were to have been an assassin's victim. Hitler had so much blood on his hands that his "rights" need give us no pause at all.

In fact, I would argue that Hitler literally had no rights for the assassin to violate, for he had forfeited them long before by the acts of murder and violence that had led to his attaining power and that he perpetrated in the aggressions leading to World War II. To recognize that people have rights is, in part, to recognize that they have justifiable claims against other people. However, one may forfeit one's claims against other people by refusing to recognize that they have similar claims against oneself; and if a person is himself responsible for bringing upon others a great evil or injustice, then we may regard ourselves as released from any obligations that we might have had toward him in virtue of his "rights" when it is necessary to treat him badly in order to eliminate that evil or injustice.

The concept of *forfeiting one's rights* is helpful in understanding various sorts of cases in ethics. Consider the example of killing in self-defense. Self-defense is a justification, and not merely an excuse, for killing; but looked at in a certain way it is hard to see why this should be so. If A attacks B with deadly force, and B must kill A to save himself (there is no other way), then in a sense the outcome is the same no matter who wins the fight: in either case, one person lives and one dies. Why, then, do we think it better that A, rather than B, ends up dead? What's the difference? Surely B's life is not more "valuable" than A's?

To understand what is going on here we need to think not about utilities, but about rights and how people may forfeit their own rights by not respect-ing the rights of others. Each person has a general right not to be harmed by others. Throughout the episode we are imagining, B retained this right without doing anything to compromise it. However, when A attacked B, he forfeited his rights in the matter. We might sum up the situation by saying that A had no right to attack B, but B did have the right to defend himself. So the difference between A's dying and B's dying as a result of this alterca-tion is that A's death involved no violation of his rights, whereas if B had died, his rights would have been violated.

In any actual case where a political assassination would help to remove a great social evil, it is very likely that the indicated victim would be at least partly responsible—and be morally culpable—for the bad situation and so would have forfeited his normal claim on our consideration. Only in the most extraordinary case would the assassination of an innocent man do any good, for the continued existence of an innocent person, who himself did nothing to perpetuate the evil or injustice, would not ordinarily be an obstacle to its removal.

So far I have been speaking as though the guilt of the politician freed us to assassinate him *only if* doing so would bring about a clear balance of good results over evil results. But this may not be so; it is arguable that it is morally permissible to assassinate a really guilty culprit even if the evil to be corrected by doing so is relatively small. Consider the following sort of case. A government official of great power has knowingly imprisoned an innocent man simply because of a personal grudge. The innocent man will remain imprisoned for five years if nothing is done. However, if the official dies, the prisoner will be released, for no one else much cares about the prisoner. Now one of the prisoner's friends is in a position to kill the politician and tells him, "I don't want to kill you, but if it's the only way I can get my friend out of prison, I will." In spite of this warning, the official continues to refuse to release the prisoner.

I have presented this case to several people, with mixed results. Some feel that it would be wrong for the prisoner's friend to shoot the official on the grounds that this one offense is not enough to justify his being shot. It is sometimes suggested that if the official were guilty of even further injustices, as would seem likely in any real case of this sort, and if he could reasonably be expected to continue such behavior in the future, then perhaps such strong action would be permissible. But if we are asked to consider only this one offense, it is not enough to justify killing him. Against this, it may be argued that it would be all right for the friend to shoot him for no more reason than that it is necessary to correct this one injustice. In the first place, it is not as though we were trying to decide how much *punishment* the official deserves. If we were, then it would be relevant to insist that death is too harsh a penalty for his crime. But punishment is not the issue here. Rather, the issue is this: If someone must suffer, which is better, that the official should suffer the consequences of his own injustice or that the innocent prisoner should suffer for nothing? I think the former, even though the evil that would be suffered by the prisoner is less than that which would be suffered by the official. To be sure, the official would normally have the right to the protection of the moral rule against killing; however, in perpetrating and then refusing to correct the injustice, he has forfeited his claim to the protection of that rule, insofar as it is necessary to break the rule in his case in order to right the wrong that he has done. Bluntly, he has brought it on himself and has no one but himself to blame.

At any rate, this is a case where disagreement in concrete moral judgment will be reflected by a disagreement in moral theory. Those who think that the shooting is not justified will tend to be content with a utilitarian appraisal of the situation, while those who think that it may be justified will tend to find fault with pure utilitarianism and look about for an alternative theory, perhaps still containing utilitarian elements, which places some emphasis on people's rights and how they can forfeit them by doing injustice.

III

It is never an attractive proposition to defend the use of violence, especially deadly violence, against human beings. The idea of deliberately hurting someone, even for the best of reasons, goes against one's deepest moral instincts. So it is tempting to say simply that one shouldn't do it and to condemn the use of violence as such. If one took such a pacifist view, then of course political assassination would simply be out as a moral option.

Nonpacifists sometimes try to embarrass those who hold this view by asking them something like whether they would be willing to use violence against a mugger if it was required to keep him from beating up three little old ladies. When the pacifist replies that he would not, it is said that he prefers for three people to be beaten instead of only one. And it is then charged that he is inconsistent, for while he claims to abhor violence, he prefers that more of it exist rather than less.

Now a pacifist *could* defend his position on some sort of utilitarian grounds; that is, he could hold that we should never resort to violence because nonviolent conduct has the best results. Martin Luther King Jr. did argue for nonviolence in the civil rights movement on these grounds; he thought that violent tactics would hinder, rather than help promote, the wider recognition of black people's rights. If one did argue for a general pacifism along this sort of line, then pacifism would be open to the sort of objection that I just mentioned. For now the viability of the position depends on the facts about what actions produce what results, and it may be that in some cases, such as the case of the three little old ladies, violent behavior has the best results.

However, a pacifist need not be motivated by the belief that nonviolent behavior *always* has the best consequences. He may admit that violent conduct will sometimes produce better results, but hold that such circumstances are so rare that it would be better on the whole if we were to forswear violence altogether. This view—which is a kind of rule-utilitarian pacifism—seems to me to be simply irrational. For if a certain act would bring about the best results in a given set of circumstances, it is absurd not to do that act merely because *other* actions, in *other* circumstances, would not have such good results.

It may be replied that people cannot be trusted to accurately distinguish the few cases in which violence would have good results from the great majority in which it would not; and if so, it would be better simply to prohibit violence altogether. Or, it may be argued that if we condone any acts of violence at all, we will be creating a social climate in which violence will become a more acceptable form of behavior; and this, of course, is highly undesirable. These arguments, however, seem to involve the admission that in some cases violence *is* justified—it is not the wrongness of violence itself, but the ignorance, bad judgment, and irrationality of people that according to these arguments make it necessary to forbid every act of violence. If people weren't so ignorant or had better judgment, then they could tell the difference between cases in which violence would have good results and those in which it wouldn't; and if people were not so irrational, they would not become more prone to violence in general by a few cases of *justifiable* violence in regrettably difficult circumstances. And if so, then it wouldn't be necessary to forbid actions that would otherwise be morally permissible. At least, that is all that follows from these arguments.

However, I do not think that most pacifists hold their views on account of any beliefs about the *consequences* of violent behavior at all. I believe that most pacifists hold the views they do simply because they find violent behavior so deeply offensive *in itself*, quite apart from its consequences, that they cannot condone it no matter what results it has. So, for them, violence is a type of action that is absolutely forbidden just on account of the kind of action it is. It is important to be clear about the exact nature of this absolutist form of pacifism. It is an ethic that stresses the *kinds of actions* that people perform rather than what comes of those actions. It says that the rule against violence may never be broken, and the rationale of the rule is understood to be simply that violence is, in itself, *such a bad sort of thing to do* that it must never be done.

I want to give one argument against this form of pacifism. This form of pacifism rests, as I said, on the view that doing violence is such a bad thing in itself that the rule against it may never be broken. Utilitarians would contest whether any sort of action can be good or bad in itself; they would insist that actions are made good or bad only by their consequences. However, I do not want to claim this, for I think that lots of things are good or bad in themselves, including actions, states of affairs, feelings, human relationships, and so on. But my argument does not require the acknowledgment of so large a list of intrinsic goods and evils as this. It only requires that we admit that even if violence is a bad thing in itself, there are other things that are also bad—for example, human suffering. The argument is that an absolute prohibition on violence in all circumstances is justified only if violent behavior is the *worst* thing possible. And I do not think that anyone could reasonably maintain that it is the worst thing, even if it is agreed on all hands to be a very bad thing. For even if violent action, such as the assassination of a dictator, is in itself a bad thing, the suffering of an entire nation may be even worse. And in that case, if the greater evil can be eliminated only at the cost of incurring the lesser evil, it is only rational to prefer the lesser evil to the greater.

But even if one were not a pacifist, it is easy to be skeptical about attempts to justify actual instances of political assassination. Certainly the vast majority of political killings are tawdry, shameful affairs from which no good at all comes. In this paper, I have sketched out some conditions under which I think political assassination might be justified, but perhaps the moral to be drawn from the exercise is just that these conditions are so rarely satisfied in practice. The sort of reasonably clear case provided by the attempts to assassinate Hitler will occur infrequently in real life. The tragedy is that although injustice and suffering do exist in great abundance, it is usually not possible for individuals or small groups to eliminate them even by such desperate acts as killing.

Notes

1. For a readable account of the circumstances surrounding the assassinations and attempted assassinations of American presidents before Kennedy, see Robert J. Donovan, *The Assassins* (London: Elek Books, 1956). The literature on the Kennedy assassination is, of course, enormous.

THEORIES

EIGHT

THE LEGACY OF SOCRATES

THE IRELAND LECTURE

Birmingham, Alabama
May 22, 1992

My subject is moral philosophy. I pursue it in the belief that a better understanding of what morality is and what it requires of us can contribute to the
improvement of our common life. At times, of course, this can seem unlikely—human beings are an ornery lot whose improvement does not come
easily. Nevertheless, the subject always seems worthwhile, if only because
understanding is itself a worthy goal. Aristotle said that it is our capacity for
understanding that separates us from the other animals and that if we abandon the search for understanding, we abandon what is most distinctively
human in us. I believe he was right. At any rate, on this occasion I would
like to offer some reflections about the nature of my subject by considering
the legacy of its founder.

Socrates

Socrates wrote nothing, but he was lucky to have among his pupils a match-
less literary artist who would record his life and teachings for posterity. In
Plato's dialogues, we see Socrates discussing the great questions of truth
and justice with the young men of Athens; we see him being charged in the
Assembly with corrupting those young men by teaching them impious doctrines; and finally we watch as he is put on trial and sentenced to death.

The Athenians were democrats, and we admire them for that—it is one of the reasons we count them as our spiritual ancestors. Of course, their system was not perfect. They held slaves, and women were excluded from political participation, to name but two failings that are notable from our present perspective. But even on their own terms, the condemnation of Socrates was a great blot on Athenian democracy. Why it happened is something of a mystery. Why would the Athenians, who prided themselves on their intellectual accomplishments and on their respect for freedom of speech, condemn a philosopher to death for his teachings? The answer is not at all clear. According to Plato, Socrates was charged with teaching "impiety toward the gods." The Greeks did take their gods seriously. Yet Socrates does not seem to have been much of a religious skeptic—at least we have no record of his having been particularly scornful of religion—and at his trial he protested his innocence of the charge. So it is hard to believe he would have been put to death for *that*. To understand what happened, then, we have to look deeper.

We should remember that although Socrates has been revered by subsequent generations, he was not a popular figure in his own time. The Oracle at Delphi had said that he was the wisest of men, and Socrates accepted the accolade, but with a peculiar qualification. Socrates agreed that he was wiser than others, but only because he alone realized how *ignorant* he was. And he took it as his mission to demonstrate to others—particularly to the high and mighty—that they were ignorant also. His persistent questioning and his insistence that the most prominent people of the day did not know nearly as much as they thought they knew made him a contentious and nettlesome sort of man.

It seems unlikely, however, that this alone would have resulted in a judicial condemnation. The more serious problem was that Socrates was the severest critic of Athenian democracy at a time when the future of that democracy was uncertain. The Athenians were proud of their democratic institutions, but Socrates did not share their pride. Democracy, he said, elevates men to positions of authority not as a result of their wisdom or their ability to govern, but as a result of their being able to sway their fellow citizens with empty rhetoric. In a democracy, the people and policies that come out on top are not the best ones but are merely the ones that are promoted most effectively. It is not truth that matters; it is public relations. There were already specialists in this appearing in Athens. The most influential teachers of the time were the Sophists, who taught the art of persuasion and who were openly skeptical of such notions as "truth." Had they lived 2,400 years later, they would have been "media consultants." Socrates despised them.

If the Athenian democracy had been secure, Socrates' hostility could have been taken in stride, much as we in the Western democracies today tolerate criticism of even our most basic institutions. But the Athenian democracy was not stable; it had suffered a series of traumatic disruptions. The most recent had occurred only five years before Socrates' trial, when a group known as the Thirty Tyrants had staged a bloody coup. Among the leaders of this group was Socrates' friend Critias. During the reign of the Thirty Tyrants, many of the respected figures of Athens had fled the city. Socrates, however, had remained.

It is understandable, then, that after the democracy was restored, the leaders of Athens would want to get rid of Socrates. So he was duly charged, tried, and sentenced to death. But it does not appear that anyone expected him actually to die. The death sentence was intended merely as a device for forcing him into exile. While Socrates was in prison, awaiting execution, means were provided for him to escape: a chariot was brought to take him away. Plato lets us understand that no one would have prevented his going, and indeed, Socrates' friends gathered around to bid him good-bye.

But instead of fleeing, Socrates did a remarkable thing. He began to discuss with his friends the reasons for and against fleeing.[1] He had always maintained that one's conduct should be guided by reason: his idea was that what we ought to do, in any situation, is what there are the best reasons for doing. Here, then, was the ultimate test of his commitment to that idea. If the best arguments were for going, he would go; but if the best arguments were for staying, he would stay. After looking at the matter from all sides, Socrates concluded that he could not justify disobeying the court's order. And so he drank the hemlock, as the court had prescribed, and he died. Perhaps he had some inkling that this would make him a memorable figure for future generations. He warned the Athenians that it would not be his reputation, but theirs, that would be tarnished by his death.

Morality and Reason

There are a number of Socratic ideas that we might focus upon in examining his legacy, but here I want to fix attention on the central idea just mentioned: namely, the idea that our conduct—our decisions about what to do—should be under the control of reason. Socrates believed that ethics, no less than natural science, is a domain in which there are *truths* accessible to human understanding. Ethics is not just a matter of private opinion. There are some forms of conduct that really are better than others. We may discover what they are by rational assessment: when we are faced with choices about what to do, we may assess the reasons that can be given for and against the various alternatives; and the right thing to do will be whatever course of action has the weight of reason on its side.

This is a simple idea that has fundamental importance for understanding human life. I believe it is *the* key idea for understanding ethics. But it is not universally accepted. There are other, competing ways of understanding ethics, and Socrates was well aware of them. The rival doctrines that were advanced in his time are very much like ones that we encounter today. Let us look briefly at three of them.

Relativism

First, there is the relativist idea that ethics just consists in the customs of one's society. Every society has its conventions—its policies regarding acceptable and unacceptable conduct. A society's ethical code is the summation of such policies, and the various social codes, according to the relativist, are all that exist. There is nothing more, and it is a mistake to go looking for "absolute" or "universal" values because there aren't any.

This view is taken by many social scientists today, who regard ethics as a social product and who think it is naive to believe it can be anything more. Herodotus, who lived at about the same time as Socrates, had already advanced the principal argument in favor of this view. Herodotus recounts the story of Darius, a king of ancient Persia, who had traveled the known world and was much impressed by the differences among people that he had observed. One day, to illustrate the point, Darius called some Greeks into his court and asked them what they would take to eat the bodies of their dead fathers. The Greeks, who practiced cremation, were shocked by the suggestion, as Darius knew they would be, and said that no amount of money could induce them to do such a thing. Then Darius called in some Callatians—"men who eat their fathers," as Herodotus puts it—and, while the Greeks listened, asked them what *they* would take to burn the bodies of their fathers. The Callatians were equally shocked and replied that Darius should not even mention such a dreadful thing. Reflecting on this story, Herodotus concludes that "custom is king o'er all."[2]

To this way of thinking there is a simple reply. Some social customs are, indeed, merely arbitrary, and when these customs are at issue, it is fruitless to insist that one society's practices are better than another's. Funerary practices are a good example. It is neither better nor worse to bury the dead than to burn them. Even the Callatians' practice of eating the dead might be seen to make a certain sort of sense—it might be a ritualized way of honoring the dead, by saying, in effect, that we wish their spirits to live on in us.

But it does not follow from this that *all* social practices are arbitrary in the same way. Some are, and some are not. The Greeks and the Callatians were free to accept whatever funerary practices they liked because no objective reason could be given why one practice was superior to the other. In the case of other practices, however, there may *be* good reasons why some are superior. It is not hard, for example, to explain why honesty and respect for human life are socially desirable, and similarly it is not hard to explain why slavery and racism are undesirable. Because we can support our judgments about these matters with rational arguments, we do not have to regard those judgments as "merely" the expression of our particular society's moral code. Relativists like to say that there is no transcultural standard that can be used to compare the different codes. But, as Socrates realized, rational argument provides just such a standard: it is a method that can be used to assess the various codes as better or worse. Considered in the light of reason, some social practices come out looking good; others do not. But in any case, the social codes themselves are not "all that exist."

To give this point substance, we may consider one pertinent example in some detail. Can we construct a general argument to show that slavery is unjust—an argument that does not appeal merely to the values of our society, but that appeals instead to considerations that any reasonable person must accept?

Such an argument might go as follows. All forms of slavery (and it must be remembered that *slavery* is a general name for a fairly wide range of historical practices that have differed significantly from one another) involve setting apart a class of humans for treatment that is systematically different from that accorded other members of the community. Deprivation of liberty is the feature that these various practices have most in common, although slaves have also been subject to a variety of other unwelcome treatments. Now the argument is that it is unjust to set some people apart for different treatment *unless there is a relevant difference between them that justifies the difference in treatment*—that is to say, if we treat one person differently than another, we must be able to point to some difference between them that justifies it. This is a principle, not just of modern liberal thought, but of rationality itself. But it follows from this that slavery is unjust, for there is no general difference between humans that would justify setting some of them apart as slaves: those who have been enslaved are not less worthy or less deserving than those who have been their "masters." They have the same desires, the same abilities, and the same human nature. Therefore, slavery is unjust.

Should this argument be compelling even to those who live in different sorts of societies, with different sorts of traditions? To test this, we might consider a slave society such as ancient Athens—the society of which Socrates himself was a member. According to one estimate, there were as many slaves in Socrates' Athens, in proportion to the population, as there were in the slave states of America before the Civil War. Socrates never condemned slavery, and Aristotle defended it explicitly. Yet the rational resources available within their tradition seem to have been sufficient for an appreciation of its injustice. Aristotle reports that "Some regard the control of a slave by a master as contrary to nature. In their view the distinction of master and slave is due to law or convention; there is no natural difference between them: the relation of master and slave is based on force, and being so based has no warrant in justice."[3]

But, as is well known, Aristotle did not share this enlightened view. A slave owner himself, he held that slavery is justified by the inferior rationality of the slave. Because slaves are not so rational as other humans, they are fitted by nature to be ruled rather than to rule. Aristotle knew that slaves are inclined to revolt, but he attributed this not to any sense they might have of the injustice of their position, but to an excess of "spiritedness." In his sketch of the ideal state, near the end of the *Politics*, he suggests that farm labor should be provided by slaves, "but slaves not drawn from a single stock, or from stocks of a spirited temper. This will at once secure the advantage of a good supply of labour and eliminate any danger of revolutionary designs."[4] But Aristotle was not of a single mind about this, for he also supported provisions for manumission. After recommending that farm labor be performed by slaves, he adds that "It is wise to offer all slaves the eventual reward of emancipation." In his will, Aristotle provided for the emancipation of his own slaves. This is an unexpected and puzzling concession from someone who held that slaves are fitted for their station by nature itself.

Plainly, Aristotle accepted the principle that differences in treatment are unjustified unless they are correlated with differences between individuals that justify those differences in treatment. In fact, this is just a modern version of an idea he advances in the *Nicomachean Ethics,* namely that like cases should be treated alike and different cases differently. That is why he felt it necessary to defend slavery by contending that slaves possess an inferior degree of rationality. But this is a claim that can be shown to be false by evidence that should be counted as evidence as much by Aristotle as by us. Therefore, even on Aristotle's own terms, slavery should be recognizable as unjust. In arguing this, we are not simply transporting our standards of rationality back into a culture that was "different," although in developing the argument we might well cite information about the nature of human beings that we have now, but that was unavailable to Aristotle.

Morality and Self-interest

The second alternative to Socrates' view is that ethics consists entirely in self-interest: each person should "look out for number one" and leave everyone else to do likewise. This view—which is as much a denial of ethics as it is anything else—evidently has many adherents today. The chief executive officer (CEO) of one American corporation, for example, recently paid himself $12.7 million in a single year for his accomplishments in "streamlining" his company by, among other things, firing scores of clerks and other low-level employees whose income was thus reduced to zero. The greed of the 1980s and 1990s is real, and it is not limited to Ivan Boesky and Michael Milken. Unlike Boesky and Milken, this CEO did not go to jail; on the contrary, he acted within the rules of the prevailing economic game, and his performance was regarded as a great success. And if we think that ethics is nothing but the pursuit of self-interest, we should agree.

The idea that ethics can be reduced to self-interest was also well known to Socrates. In Book I of the *Republic,* a character named Glaucon challenges Socrates to explain how it can be otherwise. Glaucon begins his argument by relating the legend of Gyges, a poor shepherd who was said to have found a magic ring in a fissure opened by an earthquake. Gyges discovered that when he twisted the ring on his finger, he would become invisible, and so he could go anywhere and do anything undetected. He could "go into any house, and take anything he desired." As a result, Gyges became rich. And more than that: we are told he used the power of the ring to go into the Royal Palace, where he seduced the queen, murdered the king, and seized the throne, thus ending his days as the monarch of his country.

Having recalled this story, Glaucon challenges Socrates to explain why any man should keep to the moral rules if he could violate them without fear of reprisal. Glaucon's assumption is that the fear of reprisal is the *only* thing that deters us from harming others when it would be to our own benefit. A man who does not enrich himself when he could safely do so, Glaucon intimates, is a fool—What principle of "reason" can prove otherwise?

Socrates' reply is, essentially, an appeal to human nature. He assumes that, at the most basic level, *what counts as a reason for us depends on the kinds of creatures we are.* So what are we? We are social beings, wanting and needing the company and affection of others, living together with them in communities, benefiting from their presence and unable to flourish without them. Therefore, we must, necessarily, take the good of others as a reason for moderating our pursuit of self-interest. To consider people as solitary individuals interested only in themselves misunderstands the nature of human beings. Naked egoism is not a realistic philosophy; it is *un*realistic because it misrepresents the kinds of creatures we are and our place in the social world.

Of course, this view of human nature has often been disputed, and when we remember Ivan Boesky, Michael Milken, and the CEO, it might appear to be only a wishful fantasy. Yet I believe that Socrates has in the end been vindicated from a direction he could not have foreseen. It was Charles Darwin who set the stage for egoism's final refutation when he discovered that morality is grounded in "social instincts" produced by natural selection.[5] These instincts have the power to make us set aside narrow self-interest and act for the good of others. They have been fashioned and preserved through the course of our development, as have so many of our characteristics, because they have conferred an advantage in what Darwin calls the "struggle for life." The social instincts are manifested not only in human conduct, but in the behavior of other animals as well. The existence of such instincts has now been amply confirmed by psychologists investigating animal behavior, and the evolutionary reason for their existence has been elaborated in great detail by contemporary sociobiologists. Thus, Darwin, who is so often regarded as having undermined the conception of man as a moral being, in reality made an important contribution to our understanding of morality's basis.[6]

Therefore, the egoistic theory of human nature and human morality, which was thought so plausible by a long parade of Western thinkers, no longer seems to be a viable option. This does not mean, of course, that all people are saints or that selfishness and mean-spiritedness are not a part of human life. But it does mean that such tendencies must be understood in the context of a larger picture of human nature that provides reason for optimism where morality is concerned. Whatever else we say about them, the Boeskys and the Milkens may no longer be understood simply as representative human beings.

Morality and Religion

We come now to the third and perhaps most important alternative way of understanding ethics: ethics may seem to be, simply, an adjunct of religion. This is probably the most commonly held view today, at least in the United States. Consider, for example, who is thought to "speak" for ethics. When ethical controversies are in the news and political leaders want guidance, they turn more often than not to the representatives of organized religion. In the mid-1970s, when the prestigious National Commission for the Protection of Human Subjects of Biomedical and Behavioral Research was formed, two seats on the commission were reserved for "ethicists"; those seats went to a Jesuit priest and a professor at the Pacific School of Religion. And in the mid-1980s, when Governor Mario Cuomo of New York organized his own advisory group on ethical issues, he carefully explained to the *New York Times* that he would invite "Roman Catholic, Protestant, and Jewish leaders" to serve.[7]

This, of course, is no more than we might expect. But what accounts for it? It is not that priests and rabbis are better people than the rest of us. On the contrary, as a group they seem to be no better and no worse than the rest of humankind—they share the same virtues and vices as other people. The explanation is, rather, that the identification of ethics with religion is mandated by a general picture of the world that many people accept. According to this picture, God created the world and laid down the laws that govern its operation. He also created human beings and laid down laws to govern how they should behave. The natural conclusion is, therefore, that living rightly is simply living in accordance with these divine commandments.

Socrates was, once again, familiar with this way of thinking. In Plato's *Euthyphro*, he is shown considering at some length whether "right" can be the same as "what the gods command." Now we may notice, to begin with, that there are considerable practical difficulties with this as a general theory of ethics. How, for example, are we supposed to *know* what the gods command? There are, of course, those who claim to have spoken with God about the matter and who therefore claim to be in a position to pass on his instructions to the rest of us. But people who claim to speak for God are not the most trustworthy folks—hearing voices can be a sign of schizophrenia or of megalomania just as easily as an instance of divine communication. Others, more modestly, rely on scripture or church tradition for guidance. But those sources are notoriously ambiguous—they give vague and often contradictory instructions—and so, when people consult these authorities, they typically rely on whatever elements of scripture or church tradition that support the moral views they already happen to think are right. Moreover, because scripture and church tradition have been handed down from earlier times, they provide little direct help in addressing distinctively contemporary problems: the problem of environmental preservation, for example, or the problem of how much of our resources should be allocated to AIDS research as opposed to other worthy endeavors.

Still, it may be thought that God's commands provide the ultimate *authority* for ethics, and this is the issue that Socrates addressed. Despite being charged with impiety, Socrates did not deny that the gods exist. He accepted that the gods exist and that they may issue instructions. But he argued that this cannot be the ultimate basis of ethics. He pointed out that we have to distinguish two possibilities: either the gods have some *reason* for the instructions they issue, or they do not. If they do not, then their commands are merely arbitrary—the gods are like petty tyrants who demand that we act in this way and that even though there is no good reason for it. But this is an impious view of the gods that religious people themselves will not want to accept. On the other hand, if we say that the gods *do* issue their instructions for good reasons, then we have admitted that there is a standard of rightness independent of their commands—namely, the standard to which the gods themselves refer in deciding what to require of us. It follows, then, that even if one accepts the theological picture of the world, the rightness or wrongness of actions cannot be understood *merely* in terms of their conformity to divine prescriptions. We may always ask *why* the gods command what they do, and the answer to *that* question will reveal why right actions are right and why wrong actions are wrong.

Socrates' argument on this point is a paradigm of good reasoning—it is an example of how even the most abstract and apparently "subjective" questions can be resolved by rational analysis. And this argument has been tremendously influential among subsequent thinkers—so influential, in fact, that the divine-command theory of right and wrong has been rejected even by Christian theologians such as St. Thomas Aquinas. People who are not familiar with the history of Christian thought often assume that the divine-command theory must be the dominant Christian theory of ethics. But that is not so. The dominant theory of the Church has been the theory of natural law, according to which moral precepts are precepts of reason accessible to any rational person. God is viewed as the creator of the rational order in which we all participate, but the source of our knowledge of that order is in the operation of our individual rational faculties.

Thus, the believer and the nonbeliever are in exactly the same position, where morality is concerned. The religious believer has access to no special knowledge that is not available to the rest of us. We must all try to figure out what to do by examining the reasons that support our choices, without anyone being able to claim special privilege. Again, as Socrates stressed, this conclusion is not reached by denying the truth of religion. For the believer, religious ideas may still fit into the overall picture because the believer will think that God has provided the rationality that we all share. Yet this additional belief does not enter into moral calculations as such: moral calculations are, simply, the products of reason. Socrates' central idea about ethics is, therefore, vindicated once again from a direction that he could not have foreseen.

Ethics in a Democratic Society

Ethical thinking, on Socrates' view, is a matter of trying to figure out what there are the best reasons for doing; and I should like now to offer some comments about our present situation in light of this conception.

Our present situation is quite different from what has been the norm throughout most of human history. Most human societies have been characterized by a kind of homogeneity: people living together within a single community have generally shared a common worldview, a common set of beliefs, and a common set of ideals. In such social settings, morality is not considered to be something private to the individual; it is more like a public institution in which all participate. Moreover, in such settings, disagreements about values are relatively rare and do not present a significant social problem. And because there is so little disagreement, public policy can be based on the commonly accepted values—they can, in other words, be incorporated into the law—without causing excessive controversy.

But our own situation is not like this. A distinctive feature of modern democratic society is its pluralism: in our society, people lead very different kinds of lives, animated by very different systems of beliefs and values. This is a relatively new type of cultural configuration, and it makes a great deal of difference to how we conceive ethics and to the types of ethical problems we encounter. In our kind of society, morality is more likely to be considered a highly personal, individualized affair, with each person claiming the right to live as he or she thinks best. Moreover, in such a social setting the formulation of public policy becomes much more difficult. If public policy favors the views of one segment of the society over those of other segments, it cannot be stable—it will be inherently controversial—and it cannot provide a framework suitable for everyday life.

But how can a social system accommodate such diversity? That is the central theoretical problem of ethics in our kind of society. As people have tried to deal with this problem, some elements of a solution have begun to emerge. In particular, the distinction between *private life* and *public life* has taken on great importance, and the value of *freedom* has come to play a central role. Thus, we respect people's right to disagree about right and wrong, especially when it is *their* lives and interests that are affected by what they believe and what they do—where private life is concerned, private ideals and private standards are to be tolerated. This, we have come to think, is the very essence of a society in which freedom is respected. Public policy, on the other hand, remains a difficult matter, as it must be formulated in such a way as to provide for a stable social order while at the same time permitting such private diversity.

Reason and Private Moral Judgment

Private moral judgment, however, is not *merely* a matter of personal opinion because even in the most personal areas of life a Socratic commitment to reason will have significant implications. Not every personal belief is equally reasonable. Consider, for example, sexual relations between people, which is often taken to be the single most personal area of moral judgment. Many people believe that only heterosexual relations between married couples is morally acceptable (although this belief is not nearly so widespread or firmly held as it used to be) and that other types of sexual relations—homosexuality, for example—are to be condemned as wrong and even as perverse. Believing this, those people may favor social policies that make it difficult for homosexuals to lead satisfying lives. Meanwhile, others have very different beliefs about the matter and think that homosexuals are morally blameless—homosexuality being just another human possibility—and that, therefore, social policies discriminating against them are wrong.

Now we might easily regard this situation as just another instance in which the conflicting views of various groups must be accommodated within the democratic process: each group can maintain its private view, with the social policies adopted depending on the outcome of the political give-and-take, probably with some sort of compromise eventually emerging. That is the model of democratic reconciliation usually adopted. Looked at in this way, however, the "private" beliefs are taken simply as given, as brute data to be incorporated into the political equation. But before making that assumption, we may ask whether either point of view is *correct*, in Socrates' sense—whether, in other words, either view is more reasonable than the other.

This is a complicated matter, but I want to mention two recent developments in science that seem relevant. First, some investigators believe they have now identified the feature of the brain that accounts for sexual orientation: there appears to be a difference in the structure of the hypothalamus between heterosexual and homosexual individuals. It may be too early to know whether this is correct, but if it is true, it strongly suggests that sexual orientation is determined from birth by something over which individuals have no control. The idea that homosexuality results from some sort of moral failing, then, will have to be rejected.

Second, sociobiologists have recently argued that homosexuality can be accounted for as an evolutionary adaptation that confers a benefit in Darwin's sense—if this is correct, it would explain *why* the different sorts of hypothalamuses, with their differing implications for sexual behavior, are preserved by natural selection. This, too, will make a difference to moral assessment. Proponents of the theory of natural law have often taken homosexual conduct to be a paradigm case of conduct that is contrary to nature; but if these findings are borne out, that judgment will have been shown to be mistaken. People may continue to say, of course, that in their private views homosexuality is evil; but the facts are increasingly against them, and the facts are what they are regardless of what moral view one might have wanted to hold. A respect for the facts, and a willingness to accommodate one's moral view to them, is the first requirement of Socratic reasonableness.

It may seem strange that I refer to scientific results in a discussion of ethics. Especially to those of us in the universities, the division of intellectual labor into different departments seems natural and right; and we may easily assume that those divisions reflect basic cleavages in reality itself. Thus, the concerns of the sciences may seem fundamentally different from the concerns of ethics, and we might conclude that one has nothing to do with the other. But this, I think, would be a mistake. In reality, all sorts of connections exist between the concerns of philosophers, physicists, biologists, psychologists, anthropologists, and historians. That is because the world we study does not split up neatly into isolated, independent parts that match our academic structure. As W. V. O. Quine once put it, the universe is not the university.

For the study of ethics, to think otherwise is an especially pernicious mistake, for it encourages the belief that all ethical views are equally valid. If your view of affirmative action does not have to be judged against the facts of recent history, for example, then you can believe anything you like. If your view of women's issues does not have to take account of facts about their needs and aspirations and the history of their functioning in society, not to mention the best studies concerning similarities and differences between the sexes—well, then, you can think what you want. And, more generally, if your understanding of "human dignity" does not have to reflect a realistic appraisal of what human beings are really like—an appraisal to which the findings of evolutionary biology, psychology, and anthropology are plainly relevant—then anything goes. The connections between all these matters are so plain and so evident that it is amazing that academic thinkers could ever have accepted the old saw that science and ethics are unrelated. On the contrary, ethics cannot be investigated in a responsible manner without taking a very wide range of "other" studies into account.

Private Ethics and Public Policy

Even if ethics is considered as a private matter for individual judgment, then there are standards of reasonableness that will determine which views will be acceptable to thoughtful people. But ethics is also a public affair, or at least it has a public dimension. Ethical standards govern our behavior as a community, the way we commit our resources, and what we permit individuals acting in the social setting to do. A central problem of ethics, therefore, is whether it is possible to formulate standards that *all* can acknowledge as binding, despite individual differences. This is an especially critical problem in a pluralistic society in which the differences between individual ethical outlooks are large and substantial. Because individuals have differing personal ideals, and because we want to respect those differences as much as possible, the formulation of common public standards requires a much greater willingness to compromise than would be necessary in a more homogeneous society. I should like to suggest three criteria that may be invoked in establishing such standards.

First, public policies cannot favor the interests of some members of the community over others. In setting public policy, the interests of blacks must count equally with the interests of whites; the interests of women must count as much as those of men; and the same goes for working people and rich people, Christian Scientists and Catholics, and homosexuals and heterosexuals. It does not matter if some whites privately hold racist views regarding blacks, or vice versa; or if Catholics think Christian Scientists are wrong; or if heterosexuals think homosexuals are disgusting. Public policy cannot reflect any of this. Such privately held views may not be allowed to stand as a barrier to any segment of the society living and flourishing as best they can. Otherwise, a fundamental condition of social living is violated.

Second, the standards of public life must be permissive in that they allow individuals to follow their own consciences, at least insofar as this is compatible with the public good. When it is stated in this abstract way, few people would argue with this idea—freedom of conscience is one of those fundamental values that most of us endorse reflexively. Yet taking this principle seriously can be a hard business, for it may require us to tolerate conduct that we personally think is unwise or even wrong. Let me give an example.

In March 1991, Dr. Timothy Quill of Rochester, New York, published an article in the *New England Journal of Medicine* describing how he had helped one of his patients commit suicide.[8] Dr. Quill had advised a woman with leukemia, whom he called "Diane," that she would have a 25 percent chance of prolonging her life if she underwent an arduous program of chemotherapy and bone-marrow transplantation. Diane rejected this possibility, saying that she wanted to live a normal life for as long as possible and then kill herself when her condition became intolerable. She did some research, discovered what drugs she would need, and asked her physician to prescribe them. He did as she requested; and eventually she used the drugs, and as a result she died. Dr. Quill's thoughtful account of all this elicited considerable sympathy. The fact that he decided to "go public" about what he had done made some people consider him a moral hero.[9]

Others, however, felt that both Diane and Dr. Quill had acted impermissibly. According to a long tradition in our culture, suicide, in any circumstances whatever, is wrong. When one takes this sort of view, it is natural to start looking for reasons to justify *forbidding* people like Diane and Dr. Quill from acting as they did. Yet obviously Diane and Dr. Quill did not share this moral view, and the principle we are considering says that they must be permitted to act on *their* view of the matter, so long as other people's interests are not affected. This is why I said that respecting the principle of individual freedom can be a hard business. We cannot *both* claim to respect freedom of conscience *and* at the same time demand that others conform to *our* notions of right and wrong. A respect for freedom necessarily means tolerating in others conduct that we would not approve of in ourselves. Those who believe in personal freedom just have to live with this hard fact.

Third, the standards of public life cannot depend for their validity on contentious doctrines that are accepted by only some of the community's members. The current debate over abortion is a case in point. Sometimes politicians who happen to be Roman Catholics, such as Governor Cuomo, say that while they are personally opposed to abortion, they support the right of other citizens to choose for themselves. (Some polls indicate that a majority of Americans hold just this combination of beliefs.) But for taking this stance they are accused of inconsistency. However, there is nothing *inconsistent* about this, for there is nothing inconsistent in holding private religious views while at the same time believing that public policy should not be based on such views, whether one's own or those of others. In this connection, it is important to understand that "democracy" is not the same as "majority rule" in any crude sense. It does not matter whether a majority of people hold the private views in question: the principle is that in a free society *not even a majority* may compel others to conform to doctrines that they do not accept.

Of course, this does not mean that there are *no* moral values that may be publicly enforced. Some moral values will be common to the community as a whole; and they are properly expressed in such laws as the laws against murder, theft, and the violation of privacy. But such laws do not depend on contentious doctrines for their validity; each of them is justifiable, in the manner of Socrates, by reference to considerations that all reasonable people must accept. Where such considerations are available, a case can legitimately be made for social policy. The reason why Governor Cuomo and others regard abortion as something that should *not* be socially prohibited is that, on their view, considerations of this more general type are not available. On the contrary, the case for condemning abortion seems to be essentially religious in nature.

Abortion, Ethics, and Religion

What I have just said about the abortion controversy is liable to seem altogether too quick and simpleminded. So let me elaborate the point just a bit.

Is it true that the case against abortion is essentially religious? This is a difficult issue, with much to be said on both sides. Some people who oppose abortion argue that their opposition can be justified entirely on secular grounds. Abortion, they say, is simply the murder of an innocent human being, and the murder of innocent humans is something that is rightly condemned by secular law. There are, to be sure, religious reasons for condemning murder, but there are good nonreligious reasons as well (if there are *not*, then secular ethics is bankrupt), and those secular reasons, whatever they may be, are all that are needed for the condemnation of abortion. This is a powerful line of argument that has persuaded many thoughtful people.

Nevertheless, this line of reasoning seems to be defective. It assumes that *the same nonreligious considerations that justify prohibiting the murder of children and adults also justify prohibiting the killing of fetuses.* This assumption is needed to reach the conclusion that there is no distinction between abortion and murder in the normal sense. Yet this assumption does not seem to be correct. Let me explain why it seems incorrect.

It is crucial to notice that human beings—both children and adults—have two very different kinds of characteristics. First, they have *physical* characteristics—that is, they have certain kinds of *bodies*. They have fingers and toes and kidneys and spleens and bones and muscles. These physical characteristics, along with the genetic material that produces them, distinguish humans from the members of other species. But they also have *psychological* characteristics as well: they have thoughts, emotions, desires, aspirations, hopes, fears, and much more of a similar kind.

With this in mind, suppose we ask why it is wrong to kill people—what is it about people that makes their protection morally important? The answer seems obvious. It is *not* merely the fact that people have certain sorts of bodies. The fact that you have a heart and a liver and kidneys is not, in and of itself, what makes your life morally precious. Your physical attributes are important only because they make possible your psychological existence— they make it possible for you to think and feel and hope and all the rest. *These* are what give your individual existence its value and worth. If you did not have such psychological capacities, your mere physical existence would be as insignificant, from a moral point of view, as that of a slug. Once this point is understood, I do not believe it can reasonably be denied.

Now we can understand why some people say that an unborn baby is not a "human being" in the same sense as you and me. Fetuses have some of the characteristics of human beings, but they lack others. They do have human bodies. But the fetus does not have a *personality*—it lacks a distinctively human consciousness. It cannot think or reason or feel, and it is these qualities, as we have seen, that make human beings the kinds of creatures whose protection is morally important. As gestation progresses, of course, the fetus may begin to acquire psychological attributes, but early on they are entirely absent. Thus, if one bases one's moral assessment on these facts, a position not unlike that taken in *Roe v. Wade* might seem appropriate, with abortion permitted in the early stages of pregnancy, but forbidden in the later stages.

This is how the matter looks if we do not resort to religious doctrines. There is one other aspect of the problem, however, that requires comment. It will be noted, quite properly, that even if a fetus lacks psychological capacities, it nevertheless has the potential to *develop* such capacities. If its development is not thwarted, it will eventually become a full human being in exactly the same sense that you and I are full human beings. And this is undoubtedly important. Indeed, this is *the* crucial fact about fetuses that gives them whatever moral importance they have.

But exactly how much importance is that? We are brought to an enormously difficult issue of moral theory: Even assuming that the protection of *actual* human beings is morally important, of what importance is the protection of *potential* human beings? Or to put the question more perspicuously, if a bit more abstractly: Does the fact that a being has the potential to *develop into* something of moral worth constitute a reason for thinking that it *already has* moral worth?

This is a vexing question. One might try to answer it by appealing to religious doctrines, by saying for example that in the case of unborn babies, they are precious to God from the very beginning. But without recourse to religious doctrines, it is not at all clear what the answer will turn out to be. It might just turn out to be that the protection of potential Xs is important only to the extent that more Xs are needed in the world—in other words, that the protection of potential humans is important only if there is a shortage of people. And, of course, there is no shortage of people; on the contrary, overpopulation is a serious problem that has led us to mount birth-control campaigns aimed at reducing their number. But contraception, like abortion, stops potential people from developing into full-fledged people, for a spermatozoon and an ovum that are prevented from combining represent a specific potential person just as surely as a newly fertilized ovum represents a specific potential person. So to the extent that one regards abortion as evil, perhaps one should regard contraception as evil also. And the corollary would be that if contraception is *not* evil, then neither would abortion be evil.

My purpose in making these points is not to argue for a specific conclusion regarding the morality of abortion. My aim is only to show that the same secular considerations that justify prohibiting murder do not lead straightaway to the conclusion that abortion is also wrong. Thus, the idea that one can argue against abortion simply by appealing to those considerations is misguided. Whatever else may be said about it, abortion is not, *in the normal, secular sense,* murder.

One could resist such a conclusion, of course, by appealing to religious ideas: one could say that the protection of *all* genetically human life is mandated by God, regardless of its level of development and regardless of whether the individuals in question have only potential psychological lives rather than actual ones. But that would be to abandon the thought that the prohibition of abortion can be justified by nonreligious considerations, and it would land us back where we started. The reason Governor Cuomo's position seems reasonable is that, absent such religious considerations, the case for an absolute prohibition of abortion seems quite difficult to make out; and so the enforcement of a stringent social policy prohibiting it would stand as a clear example of forcing religious ideas on segments of the community that do not accept them.

Conclusion

Socrates was not part of any school. Soon after his death, however, Plato founded the Academy, and, not long after that, Plato's pupil Aristotle started still another school. Thus began the tradition of education and research that we continue today in modern universities. In those early schools, it was common for the curriculum to be divided into three parts: ethics, physics, and logic.[10] An understanding of ethics—of how we ought to live—was considered to be the ultimate goal. But, it was said, we cannot discover the best way to live unless we first know how the world is, so physics is necessary; and we cannot discover anything at all unless we can reason effectively, so logic is needed. There was wisdom in this scheme, at least as far as ethics is concerned. The truth about ethics cannot be known apart from reasoning, and ethical reasoning cannot proceed in ignorance of facts about human nature, social reality, and the world, as revealed by the sciences.

As we continue the Socratic tradition, there are grounds for both optimism and despair—despair because after two and a half millennia there is still so much work to be done; and optimism because there is reason to hope that the work will ultimately pay off. Although we are certainly not smarter than Socrates and his followers, we have the great advantage of knowing much more than they knew about the nature of human beings and the way the world is. At least as regards the last two parts of that ancient curriculum, much progress has been made. And we might hope that, as they believed, progress in logic and science will lead finally to progress in ethics as well.

I like to believe that if Socrates were alive today, he would think us lucky, and he would find our present situation enviable and exciting. One of the reasons death is a misfortune is that it deprives us of the chance to see what will happen next; and Socrates was never able to learn even the little that we now know about the matters that intrigued him. Yet there are basic truths that have not changed. He would continue to insist that in trying to discover the best way to live, we cannot ultimately rely on our emotions or our self-interest. Nor can we simply trust the traditions of our society; nor can we just go by what our parents and teachers and priests have told us.

As Socrates realized, none of this is a satisfactory substitute for trying to reason out the truth. But this is just to say that being autonomous, reasonable human beings remains hard work, now as then.

Notes

1. This discussion may be found in Plato's *Crito*, which is available in several translations, including a useful one by Hugh Tredennick in *The Last Days of Socrates* (Harmondsworth: Penguin, 1969).

2. Herodotus, *The Histories*, translated by Aubrey de Selincourt, revised by A. R. Burn (Harmondsworth: Penguin, 1972), 219–20.

3. Aristotle, *The Politics of Aristotle*, translated by Ernest Barker (London: Oxford University Press, 1946), 9.

4. Ibid., 306.

5. Charles Darwin, *The Descent of Man, and Selection in Relation to Sex* (London: John Murray, 1871), chap. 3.

6. For an extended discussion of this, see James Rachels, *Created from Animals: The Moral Implications of Darwinism* (Oxford: Oxford University Press, 1990).

7. *New York Times*, October 4, 1984, 1.

8. Timothy E. Quill, "Death and Dignity—A Case of Individualized Decision Making," *New England Journal of Medicine* 324 (March 7, 1991): 691–94.

9. Those who approve of Dr. Quill's conduct may find some support in the view of a panel of twelve physicians, chaired by Dr. Daniel D. Federman of the Harvard Medical School, which issued a report in 1989 concluding that physician-assisted suicide is "morally correct" in some circumstances. See Sidney H. Wanzer et al., "The Physician's Responsibility Toward the Hopelessly Ill: A Second Look," *New England Journal of Medicine* 320 (March 30, 1989): 844–49.

10. About one hundred years after the death of Socrates, Zeno of Citium founded a school in Athens in which the curriculum was explicitly conceived in this way; this school, teaching the doctrine known as Stoicism, would last for five hundred years and would become the leading intellectual influence in the Roman Empire.

NINE

NIETZSCHE AND THE OBJECTIVITY OF MORALS

> I understand the philosopher as a terrible explosive, endangering everything.
> —Friedrich Nietzsche, *Ecce Homo*

1. Nietzsche's Rejection of Traditional Morality

Few philosophers are as infuriating as Friedrich Nietzsche. Today he enjoys great popularity. His haunted-looking face adorns T-shirts and coffee mugs, and his writings can be found in any shopping-mall bookstore. Yet for a half-century after his death in 1900, Nietzsche was a disreputable figure who seemed destined to be remembered as one of the preeminent villains of modern thought. It is not hard to understand why. His views were often outrageous, and he expressed himself in angry, belligerent prose. The combination could be stunning.

What he wrote about women, for example, seemed to flow from some deep personal bitterness: "What is truth to woman? From the beginning, nothing has been more alien, repugnant, and hostile to woman than truth—her great art is the lie, her highest concern is mere appearance and beauty" (BG 232). And if women care nothing about truth, why do some of them pursue scholarly careers? Nietzsche's explanation is that "When a woman has scholarly inclinations, there is usually something wrong with her sexually" (BG 144). Even the worst misogynists will usually concede women *something*—if they are no good as intellectuals, perhaps they are at least fit to be cooks. But Nietzsche does not even leave them that: "Stupidity in the kitchen; woman as cook: the gruesome thoughtlessness to which the feeding of the family and of the master of the house is abandoned! Woman does not understand what food *means*—and wants to be cook" (BG 234).

As if this weren't bad enough, there was an even more serious charge against Nietzsche. He was taken as a prophet by the Nazis, and it is easy to see why. Read superficially, his writings seemed to blame the Jews for the worst turns of history and to call for a new race of supermen to dominate the world. Hitler's apologists quoted with relish such lines as "The young stock-exchange Jew is altogether the most disgusting invention of mankind" (HA 475). Hitler himself visited the Nietzsche Archive in Weimar and was photographed contemplating a bust of the philosopher. Near the end of World War II, Bertrand Russell wrote: "[Nietzsche's] followers have had their innings, but we may hope that it is coming rapidly to an end" (HP 773). Considering all this, one might well wonder why Nietzsche is regarded today as a great moral philosopher.

How Nietzsche Got Such a Bad Reputation

Nietzsche's remarks about women can hardly be defended. But he was neither an anti-Semite nor a nationalist, and it was only by distorting his thought that the Nazis could claim him. Nietzsche was particularly unfortunate in the events that made their distortions possible.

Nietzsche was born in 1844 in Röcken, Germany. His father, a Lutheran pastor, died when Friedrich was four years old, leaving the boy to be raised in a household consisting of five women—his mother, his sister, his grandmother, and two maiden aunts. Some commentators have linked Nietzsche's later misogyny to this circumstance. Be that as it may, Nietzsche was a brilliant student and became a university professor in Basel, Switzerland, when he was only twenty-five years old. After one year in the job, however, he volunteered as a medical orderly in the Franco-Prussian War, and when he returned to Basel a few months later, his health was ruined. For a time, he was enthusiastic about the music of Richard Wagner. He became friends with the celebrated composer, but eventually Nietzsche broke off the relationship, at least in part because he was disgusted with the mindless nationalism and anti-Semitism of the Wagner clique. At age thirty-five, he quit teaching to devote himself completely to writing. During the next decade, he produced a book a year. Then in 1889, when Nietzsche was forty-five, everything went tragically wrong. He went insane, and eleven years later he was dead. Although it is not certain what was wrong with him, syphilis is a strong possibility.

At the time he went insane, Nietzsche did not have much of a reputation. Although he had published a number of books, they were not widely read. But his reputation grew during the next decade, and by the time he died he had become famous. Mercifully, Nietzsche never knew the kind of reputation he was to acquire: he would become known as the champion of doctrines that, in fact, he detested. This was largely due to his sister Elisabeth.

When Nietzsche had been a part of the Wagner circle, Elisabeth had also become involved with it. It was a glamorous crowd, and she loved the excitement. In 1885, she married a fringe member of the group, a professional anti-Semitic agitator named Bernhard Förster, and together they embarked on a monumentally harebrained adventure: they set out to found a racially pure, Aryan colony in the jungles of South America. They raised enough money to take fourteen families to Paraguay, where they founded "Nueva Germania"—New Germany—in an isolated spot 150 miles upriver from Asunción. Things went badly from the beginning. The land was unsuitable for farming, the climate was stifling, there were insects everywhere, and the Europeans had no idea how to manage living in the jungle. Förster committed suicide. Elisabeth's way out of the mess was provided by her brother's collapse: she could return to Germany to take care of Friedrich, leaving the hapless settlers to fend for themselves.

Back in Germany, Elisabeth turned out to have a genius for promoting her brother—or herself, which came to the same thing. She arranged for publication of cheap editions of Nietzsche's books. She collected and edited his unpublished papers. She established the "Nietzsche Archive." She wrote a three-volume biography of her brother, featuring herself as his dearest friend. In short, she set herself up as the chief guardian of the Nietzsche heritage. As Nietzsche's reputation grew, she became an important person in German cultural life. Three times she was nominated for the Nobel Prize in literature (although there is no reason to think the Nobel Committee took the nomination seriously). She cultivated the friendship of Mussolini and Hitler, encouraging them to believe that her brother's thinking went along with theirs. On the occasion of one meeting between the two leaders, she sent them a telegram declaring that "the spirit of Nietzsche hovers over this meeting of the two greatest statesmen of Europe" (MF 194). When Elisabeth died in 1935, the leading figures of the Third Reich, including the führer himself, attended her funeral.

Some of Nietzsche's ideas, such as his notion of the *Übermensch*, may have possessed a natural appeal for the Nazis. But Nietzsche was no anti-Semite, and he could be made to appear so only by taking his words out of context. The remark about the "young stock-exchange Jew," for example, is a half-sentence from a passage in which Nietzsche is praising the Jews and condemning bigotry. It is worth quoting this passage at length because it shows what a vast gulf separated the real Nietzsche from the hate-mongers:

> [T]he whole problem of the Jews exists only in nation-states, for here their energy and higher intelligence, their accumulated capital of spirit and will, gathered from generation to generation through a long schooling in suffering, must become so preponderant as to arouse mass envy and hatred. In almost all contemporary nations, therefore—in direct proportion to the degree to which they act up nationalistically—the literary obscenity is spreading of leading the Jews to slaughter as scapegoats of every conceivable public and internal misfortune.... Unpleasant, even dangerous qualities can be found in every nation and every individual: it is cruel to demand that the Jew be an exception. In him, these qualities may even be dangerous and revolting to an unusual degree; and perhaps the young stock-exchange Jew is altogether the most disgusting invention of mankind. In spite of that, I should like to know how much one must forgive a people in a total accounting when they have had the most painful history of all peoples.... In the darkest times of the Middle Ages, when the Asiatic cloud masses had gathered heavily over Europe, it was Jewish free-thinkers, scholars, and physicians who clung to the banner of enlightenment and spiritual independence in the face of the harshest personal pressures and defended Europe against Asia. We owe it to their exertions, not least of all, that a more natural, more rational, and certainly unmythical explanation of the world was eventually able to triumph again, and that the bond of culture which now links us with the enlightenment of Greco-Roman antiquity remained unbroken. (HA 475)

Anti-Semites, Nietzsche says, are "people whose nature is still feeble and uncertain," who could "easily be wiped out" by the Jews, "the strongest, toughest, and purest race at present living in Europe" (BG 251). The anti-Semites "are all men of *ressentiment*, physiologically unfortunate and worm-eaten" (GM 3.14). Nietzsche said of those who went to Paraguay with Elisabeth, "I am so happy that they voluntarily exile themselves from Europe" (quoted in YN 219).

Why did Nietzsche take such pains to denounce anti-Semitism? Partly, it was because hatred of the Jews was a potent force in Europe at that time, and so it was important, on general grounds, to declare where one stood. But Nietzsche had a more specific reason to distance himself from the anti-Semites. In his writings, he sometimes said harsh things about historical Judaism, and he did not want these remarks to be misunderstood.

Nietzsche believed that the Western moral tradition was rotten to the core, and this tradition, in his view, originated with the ancient Israelites. The Israelites were an enslaved people. As a result, they developed an ethic tailored to the needs of slaves: "Suppose the violated, oppressed, suffering, unfree, who are uncertain of themselves and weary, moralize: what will their moral valuations have in common?...Those qualities are brought out and flooded with light which serve to ease existence for those who suffer: here pity, the complaisant and obliging hand, the warm heart, patience, industry, humility, and friendliness are honored—for here these are the most useful qualities and almost the only means for enduring the pressure of existence" (BG 260). Nietzsche says of the Jews: "They mark the beginning of the slave rebellion in morals" (BG 195). But if the Jews originated this way of thinking, the Christians took it over, and Nietzsche is no less harsh in his comments about them: "Christianity," he said, is "a form of mortal hostility to reality as yet unsurpassed" (AC 27). The Christians proclaimed that the meek shall inherit the earth; they preached humility and self-denial; they regarded pride as a sin. Nietzsche saw this as the dominant ethic of Western culture, and he hated it.

Slave morality glorifies the wrong kind of man, but that is not the whole problem. At a deeper level, it is the mark of an unhealthy mind, a mind in which hatred and resentment have taken control.

They walk among us as embodied reproaches, as warnings to us—as if health, well-constitutedness, strength, pride, and the sense of power were in themselves necessarily vicious things for which one must pay some day, and pay bitterly: how ready they themselves are at bottom to *make* one pay: how ready they crave to be *hangmen*. There is among them an abundance of the vengeful disguised as judges, who constantly bear the word "justice" in their mouths like poisonous spittle.... Nor is there lacking among them that most disgusting species of the vain, the mendacious failures whose aim is to appear as "beautiful souls" and who bring to market their deformed sensuality, wrapped up in verses and other swaddling clothes, as "purity of heart": the species of moral masturbators and "self-gratifiers." (GM 3.14)

And eventually the sickness spreads: "Undoubtedly if they succeeded in poisoning the consciences of the fortunate with their own misery, with all misery, so that one day the fortunate began to be ashamed of their good fortune and perhaps said one to another: 'it is disgraceful to be fortunate: *there is too much misery!*'" (GM 3.14). And thus the ethic of "compassion" is born.

Nietzsche contrasts slave morality with an outlook that idealizes a different sort of person. "The noble type of man" is the opposite of the slave. He is strong rather than weak, proud rather than humble, and self-affirming rather than self-denying. He is "the ideal of the most high-spirited, alive, and world-affirming human being" (BG 56). A man endowed with such qualities will live his life boldly, making his own rules, confident of himself and of his own value. "The herd," Nietzsche said, will envy and despise such self-sufficient men. Incapable of looking beyond traditional values, they will call such men "immoral." But that does not matter; the new man will not care what the herd thinks. He will have only contempt for their morality, which is at bottom nothing more than an expression of their fear and resentment of his superiority.

Nietzsche referred to such men as *Übermenschen;* and it was this notion that the Nazis cited to support their idea of an Aryan "superman." One of the most striking things about this superior man is that he creates his own values: "The noble type of man experiences *himself* as determining values; it does not need approval; it judges, 'What is harmful to me is harmful in itself'; it knows itself to be that which first accords honor on things'; it is *value-creating*" (BG 260). How can someone create his own values? It is possible because the noble man realizes something important about morality: not only does he realize that the old morality is a sham; even more importantly, he realizes that there is nothing about the nature of the world that requires him to accept *any* predetermined moral code. He knows, as Nietzsche put it, that *"there are altogether no moral facts"* (TI 7.1).

2. Are There Any Moral Facts?

Ethics, in Nietzsche's view, is a deeply problematic subject. The problem is not merely that we sometimes make mistakes in our moral thinking or that we need to adopt a different moral outlook than the one we have customarily chosen. Nietzsche's diagnosis was more radical than that. He insisted that no moral outlook, regardless of its content, has any basis in reality. The world does not contain anything that could make moral judgments true or false. "There are no moral phenomena at all," he wrote, "but only moral interpretations of phenomena" (BG 108).

This would not be so disturbing if there were a God to issue instructions about how we should live—then, even in the absence of "moral phenomena," the divine commandments could still form the basis of ethics. But the difficulty for ethics is deepened because, on Nietzsche's view, there is no God—or, in his more colorful phrase, "God is dead" (GS 125). Indeed, those who believe in God suffer from the same delusion as those who believe in objective morality: "Moral judgement has this in common with religious judgement, that it believes in realities which do not exist.... Moral judgement belongs, as does religious judgement, to a level of ignorance at which even the concept of the real, the distinction between the real and the imaginary, is lacking.... To this extent moral judgement is never to be taken literally: as such it never contains anything but nonsense" (TI 7.1). Thus, Nietzsche considered himself to have been announcing a crisis in Western history: we have reached a point at which ethics has lost its foundations, and it is not clear how—or if—they can be rebuilt.

*The Relation Between Ethics and Our Overall View of
What the World Is Like*

Nietzsche was not the first to be troubled about ethics or to be skeptical about "moral facts." Philosophers have been worried about those problems since the beginning of the seventeenth century. To see why, we must understand the difference modern science has made to our way of understanding the world. Before the rise of modern science, people could reasonably believe that their moral judgments were warranted by the facts of nature. Their view of what the world was like supported such a belief. But from the point of view of modern science, the world looks very different. The world as described by Galileo, Newton, and Darwin has no place for "facts" about right and wrong.

THE ARISTOTELIAN WORLDVIEW

The Greeks developed a way of understanding the world that dominated Western thinking for more than 1,700 years. They conceived the world to be an orderly system in which everything has its proper place and function. A central feature of this conception was the idea that *everything in nature exists for a purpose.*

Aristotle incorporated this idea into his system of thought around 350 B.C. when he said that in order to understand anything four questions must be asked: What is it? What is it made of? How did it come to exist? And what is it for? (The answers might be: this is a knife, it is made of metal, it was made by a craftsman, and it is used for cutting.) Aristotle assumed that the last question—What is it for?—could sensibly be asked of anything whatever. "Nature," he said, "belongs to the class of causes which act for the sake of something" (BW 249).

It seems obvious that artifacts such as knives have purposes because we have a purpose in mind when we make them. But what about natural objects that we do not make? Do they have purposes, too? Aristotle thought so. One of his examples was that we have teeth so that we can chew. Such biological examples are quite persuasive; the parts of our bodies do seem, intuitively, to have particular purposes—eyes are for seeing, the heart is for pumping blood, and so on. But Aristotle's thesis was not limited to organic beings. According to him, *everything* in nature has a purpose. He also thought, to take a different sort of example, that rain falls so that plants can grow. As odd as it may seem to a modern reader, Aristotle was perfectly serious about this. He considered other alternatives, such as that the rain falls "of necessity" and that this helps the plants only by "coincidence," and rejected them. He even considered a hypothesis strikingly like Darwinian natural selection: "Wherever then all the parts [of plants and animals] came about just what they would have been if they had come to be for an end, such things survived, being organized spontaneously in a fitting way; whereas those which grew otherwise perished and continue to perish, as Empedocles says his 'man-faced ox-progeny' did" (BW 249). But Aristotle rejected this, too. His considered view was that plants and animals are what they are and that the rain falls as it does "because it is better so."

The world, therefore, is an orderly, rational system, with each thing having its own proper place and serving its own special purpose. There is a neat hierarchy: the rain exists for the sake of the plants, the plants exist for the sake of the animals, and the animals exist—of course—for the sake of people, whose well-being is the point of the whole arrangement. "[W]e must believe, first that plants exist for the sake of animals, second that all other animals exist for the sake of man, tame animals for the use he can make of them as well as for the food they provide; and as for wild animals, most though not all of these can be used for food or are useful in other ways; clothing and instruments can be made out of them. If then we are right in believing that nature makes nothing without some end in view, nothing to no purpose, it must be that nature has made all things specifically for the sake of man" (AP 40). It was a stunningly anthropocentric view. Aristotle may be forgiven, however, when we consider that virtually every important thinker in our history has entertained some such thought. Humans are a remarkably vain species.

The Christian thinkers who came later found this view of the world to be perfectly congenial. There was only one thing missing: God needed to be added to make the picture complete. (Aristotle had denied that God was a necessary part of the picture. For him, the worldview we have outlined was not religious; it was simply a description of how things are.) Thus, the Christian thinkers said that the rain falls to help the plants *because that is what the Creator intended,* and the animals are for human use *because that is what God made them for.* Values and purposes were, therefore, conceived to be a fundamental part of the nature of things because the world was believed to have been created according to a divine plan.

THE IMPLICATIONS OF THE ARISTOTELIAN WORLDVIEW FOR ETHICS

This view of the world had a number of consequences for ethics. On the most general level, it affirmed the supreme value of human life, and it explained why humans are entitled to do whatever they please with the rest of nature. The basic moral arrangement—human beings, whose lives are sacred, dominating a world made for their benefit—was enshrined as the Natural Order of Things.

At a more detailed level, a corollary of this outlook was that the "laws of nature" specify how things ought to be as well as describing how things are. In turn, knowing how things ought to be enables us to evaluate states of affairs as objectively good or bad. Things are as they ought to be when they are serving their natural purposes; when they do not or cannot serve those purposes, things have gone wrong. Thus, teeth that have decayed and cannot be used for chewing are defective; and drought, which deprives plants of the rain they need, is a natural, objective evil.

There are also implications for human action: moral rules are now viewed as one type of law of nature. The key idea here is that some forms of human behavior are "natural," while others are not, and "unnatural" acts are said to be wrong. Beneficence, for example, is natural for us because God has made us as social creatures. We want and need the friendship of other people, and we have natural affections for them; hence, behaving brutishly toward them is unnatural. Or to take a different sort of example, the purpose of the sex organs is procreation. Thus, any use of them for other purposes is "contrary to nature"—and that is why the Christian Church has traditionally regarded any form of sexual activity that does not result in procreation, such as masturbation, gay sex, or the use of contraceptives, as impermissible.

This combination of ideas, together with others like them, formed the core of an ethical outlook known as natural-law ethics. The theory of natural law was adumbrated most fully by St. Thomas Aquinas (1225–74), who lived at a time when the Aristotelian worldview was unchallenged. St. Thomas was the foremost thinker among traditional Catholic theologians. Today natural-law theory still has adherents inside the Catholic Church, but few outside. The reason is that the Aristotelian worldview, on which natural-law ethics depended, has been replaced by the outlook of modern science.

THE WORLDVIEW OF MODERN SCIENCE

The Aristotelian worldview began to break up in the sixteenth century when it was discovered that the earth orbits the sun, rather than the other way around. This was an alarming development because the earth's being at the center of things was an important symbol of mankind's central place in the divine plan. The Church responded by declaring the Copernican cosmology to be heresy and persecuting those who taught it, forcing some to recant and putting others to death.

But the heliocentric solar system was by no means the most subversive aspect of the emerging new science. Galileo, Newton, and others developed ways of understanding natural phenomena that made no use of evaluative notions. On their way of thinking, the rain has no purpose. It does not fall in order to help the plants grow. Instead, it falls as a result of physical causes. Is it, then, a mere coincidence that there happen to be plants growing beneath the rain to benefit from it? The Aristotelians and the Christians had found this too far-fetched to believe: How can the wonderful arrangement of nature, with each part supplementing and benefiting the other, be mere coincidence? But the modern thinkers eventually found a way to explain the whole setup: the plants are there because they have evolved, by natural selection, in the rainy climate. Natural selection produces an orderly arrangement that appears to have been designed, but, as Darwin emphasized, that is only an illusion. To explain nature there is no need to assume teleological principles, neither Aristotle's "final causes" nor the Christians' God. This was by far the more insidious feature of the new science.

This style of explanation—appealing only to physical laws devoid of any evaluative content—was developed in such great and persuasive detail, in connection with so many natural phenomena, that educated people universally gravitated to it. With its superior predictive and explanatory power, this way of thinking transformed people's view of what the world is like. But part of the transformation, inseparable from the rest, was an altered view of the nature of ethics. Right and wrong could no longer be deduced from the nature of things in themselves, for on the new view the natural world does not in and of itself manifest value and purpose. The inhabitants of the world may have needs and desires that generate values special to them, but that is all. The world apart from those inhabitants knows and cares nothing for their values, and it has no values of its own. One hundred and fifty years before Nietzsche declared that "There are no moral facts," the Scottish philosopher David Hume had come to the same conclusion. Hume summed up the moral implications of the new worldview when he wrote: "Take any action allow'd to be vicious: Wilful murder, for instance. Examine it in all lights, and see if you can find that matter of fact, or real existence, which you call *vice*. In which-ever way you take it, you find only certain passions, motives, volitions and thoughts. There is no other matter of fact in the case" (TH 468). To the old idea that "nature has made all things for the sake of man," Hume replied: "The life of a man is of no greater importance to the universe than that of an oyster" (EM 590).

3. Nietzsche's Perspectivism

We have been considering one possible basis for denying that there are moral facts—namely, the appeal to the worldview of modern science. But Nietzsche's rejection of moral facts was based on a much more radical idea. His skepticism about moral facts was part of a larger skepticism about all facts, including those of science. "Against positivism, which halts at phenomena—'There are only *facts*'—I would say: No, facts is precisely what there is not, only interpretations. We cannot establish any fact 'in itself': perhaps it is folly to want to do such a thing" (WP 481). It is a mistake, he thought, to believe that we can know what the world is "really" like. We view the world from a limited perspective and interpret it according to our needs and desires. That is all we can do. To demand more—to demand that we see things as they really are, independent of any interpretation, is like asking that we see with "an eye turned in no particular direction." "There is *only* a perspective seeing," says Nietzsche, "*only* a perspective 'knowing'" (GM 3.12). "It is our needs that interpret the world; our drives and their For and Against" (WP 481).

All our knowing is *human* knowing. We are one particular species, occupying one particular position in the universe, and we inevitably interpret things from our own limited point of view. But it is easy to forget this. We commonly assume the world simply is the way it appears to us. We call the view from our own vantage point "knowledge," as though our standpoint has some special, privileged status. Nietzsche writes:

> In some remote corner of the universe, poured out and glittering in innumerable solar systems, there once was a star on which clever animals invented knowledge. That was the haughtiest and most mendacious minute of "world history"—and yet only a minute. After nature had drawn a few breaths the star grew cold, and the clever animals had to die.
>
> One might invent such a fable and still not have illustrated sufficiently how wretched, how shadowy and flighty, how aimless and arbitrary, the human intellect appears in nature.... Only its owner gives it such importance, as if the world pivoted around it. But if we could communicate with the mosquito, then we would learn that it floats through the air with the same self-importance, feeling within itself the flying center of the world. (TL 42)

Nietzsche was reacting against a cluster of ideas that has become known as *modernity*. Modernity is an outlook that embraces the worldview of modern science, but it includes more than just science. It includes such conceptions as these:

- that the world consists of facts that exist independently of human beliefs and desires;
- that human beings have capacities of reason and perception that enable them to discover what those facts are;

- that there is one objectively correct way of understanding what the world is like, and human reason is capable of attaining such an understanding;
- that there is one logic, one scientific method, one set of rational principles that are independent of historical and cultural context; and
- that rational thought will show us the one correct way we should live and how an enlightened society should be structured and governed.

If you reject all this and look for an alternative—especially an alternative that involves some form of relativism—then you are *postmodern*. Accepting Nietzsche's perspectivism is one way of being postmodern. Some commentators believe that Nietzsche's primary importance is that he was an early and trenchant critic of modernity. Today one often hears this opinion in literary circles, where being "postmodern" is equated with being in the know.

A Limited Objectivity

The idea that "there are no facts, only interpretations" is disturbing, as Nietzsche knew it would be. What, exactly, are its implications? There are two obvious questions that need to be addressed:

1. Does this mean we are free to believe whatever we like because any interpretation of the world is as good as any other? And,
2. Does this mean that objectivity is impossible—that we can never achieve an objective understanding of what the world is like?

Let us consider these one at a time.

ARE WE FREE TO INTERPRET THE WORLD IN
ANY WAY WE CHOOSE?

Nietzsche does not think so. Not all interpretations are equal; some are better than others. In this respect, interpreting the world is like interpreting a work of art. There are no "facts" about what a work of art really means—there may be many legitimate ways to view a work of art, and many different meanings that may legitimately be attached to it. In fact, the richer the artwork, the greater are the possibilities for alternative interpretation. Moreover, our interpretations of an artwork will inevitably be colored by our particular backgrounds and experience. *But this does not mean that there aren't better and worse interpretations.* Obviously, some interpretations of art can still be insightful, while others are silly.

The same is true of interpreting the world: even though there is no single "correct" way of viewing the world, some viewings are reasonable, while others are preposterous. Christianity is Nietzsche's favorite example of a preposterous interpretation. Christianity, he says, is nothing but a blatant projection of how some people would like for things to be. Christians have the astonishing arrogance to imagine that the entire universe was made for their benefit. They have persuaded themselves that they were created in the image of God, who loves them above all others and who made the world as a home for them. They believe in addition that they will never perish because God will keep them eternally in heaven. The self-aggrandizement and wish fulfillment of such a view is evident. Therefore, even though Nietzsche rejects "facts" and insists that all knowledge is a matter of interpretation, he does not hesitate to denounce "the falseness and mendaciousness of all Christian interpretations of the world" (WP 1).

This, however, only raises a further question. What makes one interpretation better than another? It is difficult to give a general answer because there are a variety of ways in which an interpretation might be assessed. Christianity, on Nietzsche's view, involves crude projections of human wishes and assumes the existence of a divine being when there is no good reason to think such a being actually exists. The worldview of science, on the other hand, does not involve such blatant wish fulfillment and does not assume the existence of supernatural beings. Unlike Christianity, science is not a "lie." Rather than being mendacious, science merely abstracts and oversimplifies. But science is also an interpretation motivated by our needs—in particular, our need for order and our need to control and exploit events. If we understand that science is essentially a tool we have developed to serve these needs, we will understand both its strength and its limitations. Its strength is that it serves these needs very well. Its limitations are its perspective character and its essential connection with these needs—which means that it is not and cannot be a source of "absolute truth" about the way things are. Unlike Christianity, science can be embraced for what it is by reasonable people.

Other interpretations might have different sorts of virtues and vices. The important thing is to cultivate what Nietzsche calls an "intellectual conscience," the habit of critically assessing rival interpretations and seeing them for what they are. Nietzsche laments that most people lack such a conscience: "The great majority of people do not consider it contemptible to believe this or that and to live accordingly, without first having given themselves an account of the final and most certain reasons pro and con, and without even troubling themselves about such reasons afterward: the most gifted men and noblest women still belong to this 'great majority'" (GS 2).

IS OBJECTIVITY POSSIBLE?

Even if every set of beliefs expresses some particular interpretation of the world, it is still possible, on Nietzsche's view, to achieve a kind of objectivity. There are at least three things one can do to accomplish this.

The first step toward being objective is simply to realize that the world cannot be comprehended within a single point of view. We will continue to form beliefs and act on them—we can hardly do otherwise if we go on living as human beings—but we will be appropriately modest in what we claim for our outlook. We will not make the mistake of identifying "truth" with any one point of view.

The second step is the cultivation of an intellectual conscience. We can learn to "give ourselves an account of the reasons pro and con" before crediting any particular interpretation of the world; and when we adopt an interpretation, we can do so without having any illusions about its nature and purpose.

Finally, we can learn to look at things from different perspectives and take them all into account when we form our conceptions. Objectivity, says Nietzsche, may be understood as "the ability *to control* one's Pro and Con and to dispose of them, so that one knows how to employ a *variety* of perspectives and affective interpretations in the service of knowledge.... The *more* affects we allow to speak about one thing, the *more* eyes, different eyes, we can use to observe one thing, the more complete will our 'concept' of this thing, our 'objectivity,' be" (GM 3.12). Our understanding of morality can especially benefit from this sort of approach. The more we can control our emotions and examine morals from a variety of perspectives, "the more complete will our 'objectivity' be."

Moralities

Rather than speaking of "morality," which suggests a single universal system of right and wrong, Nietzsche often prefers to focus on *moralities*, using a term that emphasizes the multitude of outlooks that actually exist. But although they may differ in important ways, all moralities have certain things in common. They are all rival perspectives invented by humans to serve human purposes. At the most general level, they are social products that arise within communities, and their function is to protect the community and to ensure its preservation. Moral values are, in Nietzsche's words, "always expressions of the needs of a community and herd: whatever benefits it most—and second most, and third most—that is also considered the first standard of value of all individuals.... The conditions for the preservation of different communities were very different; hence there were very different moralities" (GS 116). Like all interpretations, rival moralities may be subjected to the scrutiny of the "intellectual conscience." We can ask about any particular morality:

- What is its historical origin?
- Whose interests does it serve?
- What motivates people to accept it? What deep human needs and drives give it life?
- What are its psychological effects on the people who live under its sway? What sort of people do they become?

Although Nietzsche repeatedly says that there are "many moralities," the only one he discusses at length is the slave morality of Western culture—an understandable choice, perhaps, considering that this is the morality of Nietzsche's own culture (and ours). As we have seen, slave morality originated with the Jews, whose experience of bondage led them to develop an ethic that glorified such traits as humility, obedience, and self-denial. What deep human feelings are being expressed here? Nietzsche's answer is *fear*— fear of failure, fear of being hurt, fear of one's own insufficiencies, and, above all else, fear of people superior to oneself. Superior people are, after all, stronger and more capable, and so they pose a threat. They can win the competition for life's goods, and in furthering their own interests they can hurt those more vulnerable than themselves. So, to be safe, one needs some way of controlling them and neutralizing their great natural advantage. A code of conduct that limits what they may do accomplishes this. "Fear," Nietzsche says, "is the mother of morals" (BG 201).

Slave morality also emphasizes such values as pity and compassion, and we may profitably ask whose interests are served by such an ethic. Who benefits from an ethic that requires us to take pity on those worse off than ourselves, to share what we have with others, to feed the hungry? In short, who benefits from an ethic of self-sacrificial altruism? The answer, plainly, is that such an ethic serves the interests of the weak and the poor. It is not the strong, self-sufficient man who benefits from charity—on the contrary, an ethic that requires self-sacrificial altruism imposes burdens on him to benefit someone else. Indeed, so long as slave morality prevails in a society, it will be hard for strong, self-sufficient people to arise and flourish—slave morality is not an ethic designed with *their* needs in mind.

All this, Nietzsche thinks, provides the "intellectual conscience" with ample grounds for rejecting slave morality. There is, then, a limited sense in which ethics can be objective. The old distinction between "objective" and "subjective" morality becomes, in Nietzsche's hands, the distinction between views that survive scrutiny by the intellectual conscience and those that do not. If we can look into the origins of an ethical view, examine its psychological and social functions, consider from various perspectives its effects on different types of people, with different interests—if we can do all this and still find it agreeable to adopt this outlook, or some modified part of it, then it has all the objective validity that such a perspective could ever have. (Conversely, if no moral view survives this kind of scrutiny—that is a possibility Nietzsche took very seriously—then it might turn out that morality must be rejected altogether.) This may not be "objective" in the robust sense of corresponding to "moral facts," but it is a very long way from believing whatever we choose.

4. Morality Without Illusions

If there are no moral facts and no God, what becomes of morality? This had been one of the primary questions of philosophy from the seventeenth century on. And many thinkers had concurred with Nietzsche's general answer: ethics, they said, must be understood as a purely human phenomenon—as the product of human needs, interests, and desires—and nothing else.

Thomas Hobbes, the foremost English philosopher of the seventeenth century, suggested one way in which ethics might be understood in purely human terms. Hobbes assumed that "good" and "bad" are just names we give to things we like and dislike. Thus, when we like different things, we may disagree about what is good or bad. However, Hobbes said, in our fundamental psychological makeup we are all very much alike. We are all basically self-interested creatures who want to live and to live as well as possible. This is the key to understanding ethics. Ethics arises when people realize what they must do to live well.

The Social Contract

Hobbes was the first important modern thinker to provide a secular, naturalistic basis for ethics. He pointed out that each of us is enormously better off living in a mutually cooperative society than we would be if we tried to make it on our own. The benefits of social living go far beyond companionship: social cooperation makes possible schools, hospitals, and highways; houses with electricity and central heating; airplanes and telephones; newspapers and books; movies, opera, and football; science and agriculture. Without social cooperation, we would lose all of this. Therefore, it is to the advantage of each of us to do whatever is necessary to establish and maintain a cooperative society.

But it turns out that a mutually cooperative society can exist only if we adopt certain rules of behavior—rules that require telling the truth, keeping our promises, respecting one another's lives and property, and so on:

• Without the presumption that people will tell the truth, there would be no reason for people to pay any attention to what other people say. Communication would be impossible. And without communication among its members, society would collapse.

• Without the requirement that people keep their promises, there could be no division of labor—workers could not count on getting paid, retailers could not rely on their agreements with suppliers, and so on—and the economy would collapse. There could be no business, no building, no agriculture, no medicine.

• Without assurances against assault, murder, and theft, no one could feel secure; everyone would have to be constantly on guard against everyone else, and social cooperation would be impossible.

Thus, to obtain the benefits of social living, we must strike a bargain with one another, with each of us agreeing to obey these rules, provided others do likewise. (We must also establish mechanisms for enforcing these rules—such as legal sanctions and other, less formal methods of enforcement—so that we can count on one another to obey them.) This "social contract" is the basis of morality. Indeed, morality can be defined as nothing more or less than *the set of rules that rational people will agree to obey, for their mutual benefit, provided that other people will obey them as well.*

This way of understanding morality has a number of appealing features. First, it takes the mystery out of ethics and makes it a practical, down-to-earth business. Living morally is not a matter of blind obedience to the mysterious dictates of a supernatural being, nor is it a matter of fidelity to lofty but pointless abstract rules. Instead, it is a matter of doing what it takes to make social living possible.

Second, this theory makes it clear how morality can be rational and objective even if there are no moral facts. It is not merely a matter of opinion that the rule against murder must be a part of any workable social scheme or that rational people, to secure their own welfare, must agree to adopt such a rule. Nor is it merely a matter of opinion that rules requiring truthfulness and promise keeping are needed for people to flourish in a social setting. Even if there are no moral facts, the reasoning that leads to such conclusions is perfectly objective. In this sense, Hobbes did "want to supply a rational foundation for morality," as Nietzsche puts it—but he did not simply "accept morality as 'given,'" as Nietzsche charges. Instead, he accepted the same limitations as Nietzsche—no God and no moral facts—and worked within those limits to construct a positive account of moral obligation.

Third, the Social Contract Theory explains why we should care about ethics. If there is no God to punish us, why should we bother to do what is "right," especially when it is not to our advantage? The answer is that it is to our advantage to live in a society where people behave morally—thus, it is rational for us to accept moral restrictions on our conduct as part of a bargain we make with other people. We benefit directly from the ethical conduct of others, and our own compliance with the moral rules is the price we pay to secure their compliance.

Fourth, the social contract approach gives us a sensible and mature way of determining what our ethical duties really are. When "morality" is mentioned, the first thing that pops into many people's minds is an attempt to restrict their sex lives. It is unfortunate that *morals* has come to have such a connotation. The whole purpose of having a system of morality, according to Social Contract Theory, is to make it possible for people to live their individual lives in a setting of social cooperation—its purpose is not to tell people what kinds of lives they should live (except insofar as it is necessary to restrict conduct in the interests of maintaining social cooperation). Therefore, an ethic based on the social contract would have little interest in what people do in their bedrooms.

Finally, we may note again that Social Contract Theory assumes relatively little about human nature. It treats human beings as self-interested creatures and does not assume that they are naturally altruistic, even to the slightest degree. One of the theory's charms is that it can reach the conclusion that we ought, often, to behave altruistically, without assuming that we are naturally altruistic. We want to live as well as possible, and moral obligations are created as we band together with other people to form the cooperative societies that are necessary for us to achieve this fundamentally self-interested goal.

ALTRUISM AND SELF-INTEREST

Are people essentially self-interested? Although the Social Contract Theory continues to attract supporters, not many philosophers and psychologists today would accept Hobbes' egoistic view of human nature. It seems evident that humans have at least some altruistic feelings, if only for their family and friends. We have evolved as social creatures just as surely as we have evolved as creatures with legs—thus, caring for our kin and members of our local group is as natural for us as walking.

If humans do have some degree of natural altruism, does this have any significance for morals? David Hume thought so. Hume agreed with Hobbes that our moral opinions are expressions of our feelings. In 1740, when he invited his readers to consider "willful murder" and see if they could find that "matter of fact" called "vice," Hume concluded that: "You can never find it, till you turn your reflexion into your own breast, and find a sentiment of disapprobation, which arises in you, towards this action. Here is a matter of fact; but 'tis the object of feeling…. It lies in yourself, not in the object. So that when you pronounce any action or character to be vicious, you mean nothing, but that from the constitution of your nature you have a feeling or sentiment of blame from the contemplation of it" (TH 468–69). And what, exactly, is "the constitution of our nature"? Of course, it is part of our nature to care about ourselves and our own welfare. But Hume added that we also have "social sentiments"—feelings that connect us with other people and make us concerned about their welfare. That is why, Hume said, we measure right and wrong by "the true interests of mankind": "In all determinations of morality, this circumstance of public utility is ever principally in view; and wherever disputes arise, either in philosophy or common life, concerning the bounds of duty, the question cannot, by any means, be decided with greater certainty than by ascertaining, on any side, the true interests of mankind" (IP 12–13). This view came to be known as Utilitarianism. In modern moral philosophy it is the chief alternative to the theory of the social contract.

Utilitarianism

Utilitarians hold that there is one principle that sums up all our moral duties. The ultimate moral principle is that *we should always do whatever will produce the greatest possible balance of happiness over unhappiness for everyone who will be affected by our action*. This "principle of utility" is deceptively simple. It is actually a combination of three ideas. First, in determining what to do, we should be guided by the expected consequences of our actions—we should do whatever will have the best consequences. Second, in determining which consequences are best, we should give the greatest possible weight to the happiness or unhappiness that would be caused—we should do whatever will cause the most happiness or the least unhappiness. And finally, the principle of utility assumes that each individual's happiness is equally as important as anyone else's.

Although Hume proposed this theory, two other philosophers elaborated it in greater detail. Jeremy Bentham, an Englishman whose life spanned the eighteenth and nineteenth centuries, was the leader of a group of philosophical radicals who aimed to reform the laws of Britain along utilitarian lines. They were remarkably successful in advancing such causes as prison reform and restrictions on the use of child labor. John Stuart Mill, the son of one of Bentham's original followers, gave the theory its most popular and influential defense in his book *Utilitarianism*, published in 1861.

The utilitarian movement attracted critics from the outset. It was an easy target because it ignored conventional religious notions. The point of morality, according to the utilitarians, had nothing to do with obedience to God or gaining credit in heaven. Rather, the point was just to make life in this world as comfortable and happy as possible. So some critics condemned Utilitarianism as a godless doctrine. To this Mill replied: "the question depends upon what idea we have formed of the moral character of the Deity. If it be a true belief that God desires, above all things, the happiness of his creatures, and that this was his purpose in their creation, utility is not only not a godless doctrine, but more profoundly religious than any other" (MU 28).

Utilitarianism was also an easy target because it was (and still is) a *subversive* theory in that it turned many traditional moral ideas upside down. Bentham argued, for example, that the purpose of the criminal justice system cannot be understood in the traditional way as "paying back" miscreants for their wicked deeds—that only piles misery upon misery. Instead, the social response to crime should be threefold: to identify and deal with the causes of criminal behavior; where possible, to reform individual lawbreakers and make them into productive citizens; and to "punish" people only insofar as it is necessary to deter others from committing similar crimes. (Today, of course, these are familiar ideas, but only because the utilitarians' victory was so sweeping.) Or, to take a different example: by insisting that everyone's happiness is equally important, the utilitarians offended various elitist notions of group superiority. According to the utilitarian standard, neither race nor sex nor social class makes a difference to one's moral status. Mill himself wrote a book called *The Subjection of Women,* which became a classic of the nineteenth-century suffragist movement.

Finally, Utilitarianism was controversial because it had no use for "absolute" moral rules. The utilitarians regarded the traditional rules—against killing, lying, breaking one's promises, and so on—as "rules of thumb," useful because following them will generally be for the best. But they are not absolute—whenever breaking such a rule will have better results for everyone concerned, the rule should be broken. The rule against killing, for example, might be suspended in the case of voluntary euthanasia for someone dying of a painful illness. Moreover, the utilitarians regarded some traditional rules as dubious, even as rules of thumb. For example, Christian moralists had traditionally said that masturbation is evil; but from the point of view of the Principle of Utility, it appears to be perfectly harmless. A more serious matter is the traditional religious condemnation of homosexuality, which has resulted in misery for countless people. Utilitarianism implies that if an activity makes people happy, without anyone being harmed, it cannot be wrong.

But it is one thing to describe a moral view; it is another thing to justify it. Utilitarianism says that our moral duty is to "promote the general happiness." Why should we do that? This is the key question. As Mill puts it,

"I feel that I am bound not to rob or murder, betray or deceive; but why am I bound to promote the general happiness? If my own happiness lies in something else, why may I not give that the preference?" (MU 34). Aside from the "external sanctions" of law and public opinion, Mill thinks there is only one possible reason for accepting this or any other moral standard. The "internal sanction" of morality must always be "a feeling in our minds," regardless of what sort of ethic this feeling endorses: "The ultimate sanction, therefore, of all morality (external motives apart) being a subjective feeling in our own minds, I see nothing embarrassing to those whose standard is utility in the question, What is the sanction of that particular standard? We may answer, the same as all other moral standards—the conscientious feelings of mankind. Undoubtedly this sanction has no binding efficacy on those who do not possess the feelings it appeals to; but neither will these persons be more obedient to any other moral principle than the utilitarian one" (MU 37). The kind of morality we accept will, therefore, depend on the nature of our feelings: if human beings have "social feelings," then Mill says that utilitarian morality will be the natural standard for them. "The firm foundation [of utilitarian morality] is that of the social feelings of mankind—the desire to be in unity with our fellow creatures, which is already a powerful principle in human nature, and happily one of those which tend to become stronger, even without express inculcation, from the influences of advancing civilization" (MU 40).

Impartiality

Utilitarianism, as we have seen, has implications that are at odds with traditional morality. Much the same could be said about Social Contract Theory. In most of the practical matters that have been mentioned—punishment, racial discrimination, women's rights, euthanasia, homosexuality—the two theories have similar implications. But there is one matter on which they differ dramatically. Utilitarians believe that we have a very extensive moral duty to help other people. Social contract theorists deny this.

Suppose, for example, you are thinking of spending one thousand dollars for a new living-room carpet. Should you do this? What are the alternatives? One alternative is to give the money to an agency such as the United Nations Children's Fund. Each year between ten and twenty million third-world children die of easily preventable diseases because there isn't enough money to provide the vitamin A capsules, antibiotics, and oral rehydration treatments they need. By giving the money to UNICEF and making do a while longer with your old carpet, you could provide much-needed medical care for dozens of children. From the point of view of utility—seeking the best overall outcome for everyone concerned—there is no doubt you should give the money to UNICEF. Obviously, the medicine will help the kids a lot more than the new rug will help you.

But from the point of view of the social contract, things look very different. If morality rests on an agreement between people—remember, an agreement they enter into to promote their own interests—what would the agreement say about helping other people? Certainly, we would want the contract to impose a duty not to harm other people, even strangers. Each of us would obviously benefit from that. And it might be in our best interests to accept a mutual obligation to provide aid to others when it is easy and convenient to do so. But would rational people accept a general duty to provide virtually unlimited aid to strangers, even at great cost to themselves? From the standpoint of self-interest, that sounds crazy. Jan Narveson, a contract theorist who teaches philosophy at the University of Waterloo in Canada, writes:

> morals, if they are to be rational, must amount to agreements among people—people of all kinds, each pursuing his or her own interests, which are various and do not necessarily include much concern for others and their interests. But people have minds, and apply information gleaned from observing the world around them to the task of promoting their interests, and they have a broad repertoire of powers including some that can make them exceedingly dangerous, as well as others that can make them very helpful. This gives us reason to agree with each other that we will refrain from harming others in the pursuit of our interests, to respect each other's property and grant extensive civil rights, but not necessarily to go very far out of our way to be very helpful to those we don't know and may not particularly care for....
>
> ...It is reasonable, then, to arrive at a general understanding that we shall be ready to help when help is urgent and when giving it is not very onerous to us. But a general understanding that we shall help everyone as if they were our spouses or dearest friends is quite another matter. (MM 130–31, 146)

Unlike many philosophers who prefer to keep things abstract, Narveson is good about spelling out the implications of his view in a way that leaves no room for misunderstanding: "What about parting with the means for making your sweet little daughter's birthday party a memorable one, in order to keep a dozen strangers alive on the other side of the world? Is this something you are morally required to do? Indeed not. She may well *matter* to you more than they. This illustrates again the fact that people do *not* 'count equally' for most of us. Normal people care more about some people than others, and build their very lives around those carings" (MM 145).

Which view is correct? Do we have a moral duty to provide extensive aid to strangers, or not? Both views appeal ultimately to our emotions. A striking feature of Narveson's contractarian argument is its appeal to the fact that we care more for some people than others. This is certainly true: as he says, we care more for our own children than for "strangers on the other side of the world." But does this really mean that I may choose some trivial benefit for my children over the very lives of the strangers? Suppose there were two buttons on my desk at this moment: by pressing button A, I can provide my son with a nice party; by pressing B, I can save the lives of a dozen strangers. Is it really all right for me to press A just because I "care more" for my son? Mill agrees that the issue must be decided on the basis of feelings (how else could it be?), but for him it is not these small-scale personal feelings that have the final say. Instead, it is one's "conscientious feelings"—the feelings that prevail after everything has been thought through—that finally determine one's obligations. Mill assumes that we cannot, when we are thoughtful and reflective, approve of ourselves' pushing button A.

However, some contemporary utilitarians have argued that the matter need not be left to the vicissitudes of individual feeling. It may be true, they say, that we all care more for ourselves, our family, and our friends than we care for strangers. But we have rational capacities as well as feelings, and if we think objectively about the matter, we will realize that other people are no different. Others, even strangers, also care about themselves, their families, and their friends, in the same way that we do. Their needs and interests are comparable to our own. In fact, *there is nothing of this general sort that makes anyone different from anyone else*—and if we are in all relevant respects similar to one another, then there is no justification for anyone's taking his or her own interests to be more important. Peter Singer, a utilitarian philosopher, writes:

> Reason makes it possible for us to see ourselves in this way ... I am able to see that I am just one being among others, with interests and desires like others. I have a personal perspective on the world, from which my interests are at the front and centre of the stage, the interests of my family and friends are close behind, and

the interests of strangers are pushed to the back and sides. But reason enables me to see that others have similarly subjective perspectives, and that from "the point of view of the universe" my perspective is no more privileged than theirs. Thus my ability to reason shows me the possibility of detaching myself from my own perspective, and shows me what the universe might look like if I had no personal perspective. (HL 229)

So, from an objective viewpoint, each of us must acknowledge that our own perspective—our own particular set of needs, interests, likes, and dislikes—is only one among many and has no special status. This thought is not unlike Nietzsche's idea that each of us looks at things from a particular perspective and that in order to think objectively we must realize this and consider how things look from other perspectives as well. As Nietzsche put it, "the *more* affects we allow to speak about one thing, the *more* eyes, different eyes, we can use to observe one thing, the more complete will our 'concept' of this thing, our 'objectivity,' be" (GM 3.12). But the utilitarians draw a very un-Nietzschean conclusion from this: namely, that from a moral point of view, everyone counts equally.

5. Nietzsche's Noble Man

Near the end of his career, Nietzsche described his moral philosophy as a form of naturalism. "I might designate the tendency of these reflections," he said, "as moralistic naturalism: my task is to translate the apparently emancipated and denatured moral values back into their nature—i.e., into their natural 'immorality.'" By a "denatured" ethics, he meant an ethic that associates morality with "the antithesis of life, with 'God'—also as the revelation of a higher world which here and there looks down upon us through them." A naturalistic ethics, on the other hand, would see morality as having "the aim of enhancing life" (WP 298–99).

Considering this, we might expect Nietzsche to find Utilitarianism congenial. But when he speaks of morality's "enhancing life," Nietzsche does not mean enhancing the lives of everyone alike. On his view, not everyone's life is worthy of being enhanced. Rather, he means enhancing the life of a particular kind of person—his noble man. Utilitarianism would require the noble man to make sacrifices to benefit the less worthy; thus, it is a variation of the slave morality that Nietzsche rejects. After his initial description of slave morality as an ethic of "the obliging hand, the warm heart," Nietzsche adds: "Slave morality is essentially a morality of utility" (BG 260).

Equally, remembering Nietzsche's remarks about morality being a social product, we might expect him to be sympathetic to the idea of a social contract. But neither will he have any part of this conception. In *Beyond Good and Evil*, he gives a clear statement of the basic idea of the social contract and rejects it emphatically:

> Refraining mutually from injury, violence, and exploitation and placing one's will on a par with that of someone else—this may become, in a certain rough sense, good manners among individuals if the appropriate conditions are present (namely, if these men are actually similar in strength and value standards and belong together in *one* body). But as soon as this principle is extended [to include everyone], and possibly even accepted as the *fundamental principle of society*, it immediately proves to be what it really is—a will to the *denial* of life, a principle of disintegration and decay. (BG 259)

The problem, once again, is Nietzsche's conviction that not all human beings are equally worthy of respect. Who will be included in the social contract? So long as the noble man is dealing with men similar to himself, all is well. Then the contract amounts to little more than "good manners" between them. But when "the herd" is allowed into the arrangement, there is trouble. The "noble man" does not belong in "one body" with "the cowardly, the petty...those who humble themselves, the doglike people who allow themselves to be maltreated, the begging flatterers, above all the liars." For him, "the exalted, proud states of the soul are experienced as conferring distinction and determining the order of rank. The noble human being separates from himself those in whom the opposite of such exalted, proud states finds expression: he despises them" (BG 260). To lower himself to a position of "equality" with them, subjecting himself to a contract in which all are equal partners, is beneath him—his life will "disintegrate and decay" in such a degrading arrangement.

The Noble Man's Virtues

If Nietzsche rejects these options, what does he offer in their place? What positive understanding of morality does he finally endorse? How, when all is said and done, does Nietzsche think we ought to live?

In keeping with his "amoralism," Nietzsche never says we *ought* to live one way rather than another—he had nothing but contempt for that sort of pious pronouncement. (Besides, the noble man creates his own values; he does not take instructions from anyone, not even Nietzsche.) Yet Nietzsche says enough to make it clear what sort of people he thinks are worthy of respect and what sort of ethical theory would be appropriate to describing them.

Nietzsche's ethical theory—insofar as we may shoe-horn his various remarks into the confines of a conventional theory—is a type of Virtue Theory. Virtue Theory is an approach to ethics that begins by describing the traits of character (the "virtues") that make a person admirable. This was the approach taken by Socrates, Plato, and Aristotle; indeed, in the ancient world this way of understanding morality was more or less taken for granted. The virtues were regarded as fundamental, and the notion of right action came into play only derivatively, as the notion of what a virtuous person would do. Modern theories such as Social Contract Theory and Utilitarianism take things the other way around: they take the notion of right action as primary, concentrating on the nature and justification of the rules that determine what we should do. The two approaches lead to strikingly different pictures of the moral life. Nietzsche was clear in his preference for the former: "It is obvious," he said, "that moral designations were everywhere first applied to *human beings* and only later, derivatively, to actions" (BG 260).

Nietzsche's description of the "noble man" may be understood in this context, as an account of the qualities of character that make a person admirable. What sort of person would that be? And should we agree that Nietzsche's noble man really is admirable?

PRIDE AND SELF-DIRECTION

As we have already observed, Nietzsche sometimes presents the noble man as the antithesis of the "slave" of traditional ethics—rather than being humble, obedient, and self-denying, the noble man is proud, self-directing, and self-affirming. This is probably the most attractive aspect of Nietzsche's description of him. The reader is apt to think that Nietzsche is on to something important: Should we embrace the "slave morality" of humility and obedience, or should we choose instead a life of pride and self-direction? When the options are put like this, the answer may seem obvious. Certainly, as Nietzsche describes the alternatives, pride and self-direction seem like easy winners. But a little thought shows that things are not so simple. The truth probably lies somewhere in between the extremes that Nietzsche presents.

First, it is too simple to say that we should be proud rather than humble (or, for that matter, the other way around). Pride is justified in some circumstances, but not in others. Modesty is appropriate when we reflect on our limitations and on the difference between what we could accomplish and what we actually have accomplished. Modesty is also called for when we think about the greater achievements of others. Pride, on the other hand, is justified when we have done our best, and the result has been of value. In general, our attitude toward ourselves should reflect the truth. This isn't very exciting—it certainly isn't as exciting as Nietzsche's bold declarations—but it does seem to be correct. As for humility, if we mean by this a habitual groveling self-deprecation, then Nietzsche was certainly right.

Similarly, while self-direction is no doubt a great good, there are obviously times when a wise person will take his cue from others. It is easy to think of examples: we follow instructions when working at a job under another person's direction, when submitting to the authority of a police officer or a judge, or when we are ignorant about a situation and have available the advice of someone who is more knowledgeable and experienced. As Aristotle observed, it is a matter of practical wisdom to recognize when it is best to defer to someone else. If Nietzsche's criticism of the traditional virtue of obedience seems to hit the mark, it may be only because some traditional moralists got the nature of this virtue wrong. But Nietzsche's alternative is not altogether satisfactory either. There is a difference between confident self-direction and arrogance, and Nietzsche's flamboyant way of writing often blurs that difference. One is a virtue; the other is not.

We may also note that although Nietzsche predicted he would be condemned by "the herd," most people today would find at least part of his view quite congenial. Many of the "traditional" virtues that he criticized so harshly were in fact the monkish virtues of medieval Europe. While the priest's vows of "poverty, chastity, and obedience" remain familiar, they no longer express an ideal that many people would willingly embrace. They belong, at best, to a very particular way of life, and today even priests sometimes rebel against them.

Nietzsche does not describe the noble man merely as proud and self-directing. If that were all there were to him, the noble man could be a pretty
ordinary kind of person, with a conventional moral outlook. He could even
be a utilitarian. After all, a proud, self-directing man *could* devote his life
to helping the poor: when he "creates his own values," he could choose the
values of kindness and compassion.

165

But Nietzsche rejects this possibility. The noble man, he says, disdains
"compassionate feelings and a 'warm heart'" (BG 260). He may sometimes
help the poor—although he certainly would not devote his life to them—but
not because he cares anything about their welfare. Instead, he may help them
as a way of displaying his own power: "[T]he noble human being, too, helps
the unfortunate, but not, or almost not, from pity, but prompted more by an
urge begotten by an excess of power. The noble human being honors himself
as one who is powerful" (BG 260). What Nietzsche says here is strongly remi-
niscent of Hobbes' definition of charity: "There can be no greater argument
to a man, of his own power," said Hobbes, "than to find himself able not only
to accomplish his own desires, but also to assist other men in theirs: and this
is that conception wherein consisteth *charity*" (HN 221). Like Hobbes' every-
man, Nietzsche's noble man may sometimes seem selfless, but in reality his
motive is "self-glorification" (BG 260). Thus, Nietzsche sides with those who
believe "altruism" is just a myth. "Selfless" and "unegoistic" actions, he says,
are "all unreal, imaginary" (WP 786).

The noble man is therefore amoral in two senses. First, he knows that
there are no moral facts and that "moralities" are only devices by which the
herd attempts to control and limit him. He finds this knowledge deeply
liberating. He is freed to assert his own will, rejecting all constraints except those he chooses to impose on himself. And second, when he chooses
which constraints to impose on himself, "compassionate feelings and a
'warm heart'" are permitted no influence. The noble man does not pretend
otherwise. He says, without qualm, "What is harmful to me is harmful in
itself" (BG 260).

It is a nice question whether the noble man simply has a different morality than other people or rejects morality altogether. The noble man has
his standards—he admires some things and detests others; he behaves in
some ways and considers other forms of behavior beneath him. We might
call this his morality. (Writing about himself, Nietzsche once declared that

rather than lacking a morality, he had "a more severe morality than any-body" [DL 102].) Nevertheless, if we conceive of morality in the usual way, as a set of constraints limiting what one may do in the pursuit of self-interest, it might be more perspicuous to say that the noble man rejects morality altogether. This description of him seems even more apt when we consider some further aspects of the noble man's character.

The Dark Side of Nietzsche's Noble Man

Nietzsche does what we should expect a great philosopher to do: he identifies and challenges assumptions that others unthinkingly take for granted. There is something enormously appealing about his iconoclastic spirit. Yet at the same time there is a side to Nietzsche's thought that is deeply troubling. He seriously believed that there is an "order of rank" among people, and that superior people are free to use "inferior" people as means to their own ends. This was not a racial or nationalist doctrine—he did not identify the noble men with Aryans or Germans or anything like that. Nevertheless, in describing the character of his noble man, Nietzsche permits him options that no other major moral philosopher would countenance. No one but Nietzsche could have written that "The essential characteristic of a good and healthy aristocracy, however, is that it...accepts with a good conscience the sacrifice of untold human beings who, *for its sake,* must be reduced and lowered to incomplete human beings, to slaves, to instruments. The fundamental faith simply has to be that society must *not* exist for society's sake but only as the foundation and scaffolding on which a choice type of being is able to raise itself to its higher task and to a higher state of being" (BG 258). When we read such words, we may naturally assume that they are not to be taken at face value, and we may search for an interpretation that removes the sting. There is, in fact, a serious point here with which one might have some sympathy. One might think of the "choice type of being" as Beethoven or Newton or Churchill—men whose creative achievements set them apart. It is not hard to understand the special value of such individuals and to see the point of making special provisions for them. Thus, if we want to maximize the best things in a culture, we must create conditions in which such people can flourish; and that will be a very different sort of project than seeking to promote everyone's welfare equally. This, one might think, is the real and defensible point of Nietzsche's elitism.

But Nietzsche's harsh words can be softened only up to a point. He mentions "sympathy, the kind, helping hand, the warm heart, patience, diligence, and friendliness" only to sneer at them. We must, he says, "resist all sentimental weakness" and realize that "life itself is *essentially* appropriation, injury, overpowering of what is alien and weaker, suppression, hardness, imposition of one's own forms, incorporation, and at least, at its mildest, exploitation"— and so, he insists, it is pointless to object to such things (BG 259). He is too insistent, too explicit, and goes on at too great a length to permit a reading that would make him into some sort of misunderstood nice guy.

Thus, Nietzsche's call for a "new kind of man," expressed in such compelling prose—"Behold, I teach you the overman. The overman is the meaning of the earth. Let your will say: the overman *shall be* the meaning of the earth!" (TZ 1.3)—which seemed at first to be the most exciting and interesting part of his moral philosophy, turns out on closer inspection to be at the same time its most disappointing aspect. Perhaps an even harsher appraisal might be justified. One does not have to be a profound thinker to realize that there is not enough sympathy, kindness, and helpfulness in the world, and that injury, suppression, and exploitation are great evils. If that is right, then even though Nietzsche was no Nazi, and even though he might be admired for fifteen volumes of brilliant writing, he was, in the end, a philosophical villain after all.

References

Most of Nietzsche's writings are divided into sections, and for ease of reference it is customary to refer to section numbers rather than to page numbers of particular editions. I have used the following editions, giving page numbers only when there are no section numbers available. The citation for the quotation at the beginning of the essay ("I understand the philosopher as a terrible explosive") would be EH 5.3, meaning the third section of the fifth part of Nietzsche's *Ecce Homo*.

Nietzsche's Works

AC   *The Anti-Christ*. In *Twilight of the Idols; and The Anti-Christ*, translated by R. J. Hollingdale, 113–87. Harmondsworth: Penguin Books, 1968; written in 1888.

BG   *Beyond Good and Evil.* Translated by Walter Kaufmann. New York: Vintage Books, 1966; first published in 1886.

DL   *Draft of a Letter to Paul Ree.* In *The Portable Nietzsche,* translated and edited by Walter Kaufmann, 102. New York: Viking Press, 1954; written in 1882.

EH   *Ecce Homo.* In *Basic Writings of Nietzsche,* translated and edited by Walter Kaufmann, 657–60. New York: Modern Library, 1966; written in 1888.

GM   *On the Genealogy of Morals.* Translated by Walter Kaufmann and R.J. Hollingdale. New York: Vintage Books, 1967; first published in 1887.

GS   *The Gay Science.* Translated by Walter Kaufmann. New York: Vintage Books, 1974; first published in 1882.

HA   *Human, All-Too-Human.* In *The Portable Nietzsche,* translated and edited by Walter Kaufmann, 51–64. New York: Viking Press, 1954; first published in 1878.

TI   *Twilight of the Idols.* In *Twilight of the Idols; and The Anti-Christ,* translated by R.J. Hollingdale, 19–112. Harmondsworth: Penguin Books, 1968; written in 1888.

TL   *On Truth and Lie in an Extra-Moral Sense.* In *The Portable Nietzsche,* translated and edited by Walter Kaufmann, 42–47. New York: Viking Press, 1954; written in 1873.

TZ   *Thus Spoke Zarathustra.* In *The Portable Nietzsche,* translated and edited by Walter Kaufmann, 103–439. New York: Viking Press, 1954; first published in 1883.

WP   *The Will to Power.* Translated by Walter Kaufmann. New York: Random House, 1967; notes written in 1883–88.

Other Works Cited

BW   Aristotle. *The Basic Works of Aristotle.* Edited by Richard McKeon. New York: Random House, 1941.

AP   ———. *The Politics.* Translated by T.A. Sinclair. Harmondsworth: Penguin, 1962.

HN   Hobbes, Thomas. *Human Nature.* In *Body, Man, and Citizen: Selections from Thomas Hobbes,* edited by Richard S. Peters. New York: Collier Books, 1962; first published in 1650.

TH   Hume, David. *A Treatise of Human Nature.* Oxford: Oxford University Press, 1988; originally published in 1739.

EM   ———. *Essays Moral, Political, and Literary.* Oxford: Oxford University Press, 1963; originally published in 1741–42.

IP   ———. *An Inquiry Concerning the Principles of Morals.* Indianapolis, Ind.: Bobbs-Merrill, 1957; originally published in 1752.

MF   Macintyre, Ben. *Forgotten Fatherland: The Search for Elisabeth Nietzsche.* New York: Farrar Straus Giroux, 1992; paperback published by Harper-Collins.

MU   Mill, John Stuart. *Utilitarianism.* Indianapolis, Ind.: Bobbs-Merrill, 1967; originally published in 1861.

MM   Narveson, Jan. *Moral Matters.* Peterborough, Ontario: Broadview Press, 1993.

HP   Russell, Bertrand. *A History of Western Philosophy.* New York: Simon and Schuster, 1945.

HL   Singer, Peter. *How Are We to Live?* Amherst, N.Y.: Prometheus Books, 1995.

YN   Yovel, Yirmiyahu. "Nietzsche, the Jews, and *Ressentiment*." In *Nietzsche, Genealogy, Morality,* edited by Richard Schacht, 214–36. Berkeley: University of California Press, 1994.

TEN

TWO ARGUMENTS AGAINST ETHICAL EGOISM

The form of ethical egoism that I shall discuss is the view that the right thing for anyone to do, on any occasion, is whatever would best promote his own interests, no matter how other people's interests would be affected. Very few philosophers who write books or publish articles in journals believe in this doctrine, although many are at pains to refute it. There are at least three interconnected reasons for wanting to refute this view: first, it is a pernicious doctrine that goes against some of our most central moral beliefs. According to ethical egoism, each of us should take the attitude that other people simply don't matter, except insofar as they are useful to us; and that is a wicked attitude. Second, even though few philosophers accept the doctrine, many people are tempted by it. Moreover—and this is perhaps the most important reason, from a philosophical point of view—the refutation is bound to shed some light on the rationale behind the alternative view that other people's interests should be respected for their own sakes.

Some philosophers have argued that ethical egoism is unacceptable because it violates principles of logic that every rational person must accept.[1] I am going to present two arguments against ethical egoism, but neither of them is of this type. I will not try to show that egoism is self-contradictory. Rather, I will argue that even if ethical egoism is a logically consistent doctrine, it is unacceptable on other grounds. My first argument will be that ethical egoism is incompatible with a principle that expresses the social-political ideal of human freedom, so that anyone who accepts ethical egoism will be forced to abandon that principle. The second argument is based on the idea that ethical egoism is simply a wicked view.

Before giving these arguments, I need to say something about my defi- anyone to do, on any occasion, is whatever would best promote his own interests, no matter how other people's interests would be affected. (Readers familiar with the relevant philosophical literature will recognize this as a form of what is known as "universal" or "impersonal" ethical egoism; thus, what I have to say will not be directed to "individual" or "personal" versions of the doctrine.) This definition allows for the fact that satisfying some of a person's interests may conflict with satisfying other of his interests. What would *best* promote his interests is what would lead to the satisfaction of most of them or of those that are most important. The definition also takes into account the possibility of someone's being mistaken about what is in his own interests: it says that it is right for anyone to do what *will* promote his interests and not merely what he thinks will promote them. Finally, the definition does not preclude the possibility that in some cases what is in one's own interests also benefits others. It is merely that, in such a case, the benefit to others is not what makes the act right: what makes the act right is, rather, the fact that it is to one's own advantage.

1. Why an Egoist Must Renounce Liberty as a Social Ideal

I am going to formulate a principle that I believe expresses what is at the heart of a commitment to personal liberty as a social or political ideal and then use that principle as a premise in an argument to the conclusion that ethical egoism is false. It might be said, with justice, that an egoist could maintain his position in the face of this argument simply by renouncing the principle in question. But that is the way it is with any argument of this type: one can always escape the conclusion by rejecting one or more of the premises. However, if I am right about this, and the egoist does have to reject this principle to maintain his position, then we will have exposed a bit more that is questionable in that position, and we will have shed a little more light on the rationale behind the alternative view that we do have other-regarding obligations.

The principle is:

(1) It is not permissible for one person to interfere with another person's freedom of action unless there is a specific justification for doing so.

The idea behind this principle is that people should be allowed as much freedom as possible. But this is not to say that interference with people's freedom is never justified. There is no problem with our right to interfere with the activities of murderers, thieves, and rapists. A commitment to freedom merely commits one to the view that such interference *requires justification;* and in the case of murderers and thieves and rapists, the justification is easy to give. The important point, though, is that in the *absence* of such a justification, interference is not permitted.

In this respect, interfering with other people's conduct differs from other sorts of actions that one might perform, such as taking a bath or going to the movies. In most ordinary circumstances, there is no objection to anyone's taking a bath or going to the movies, so such things do not require any justification. A person is, morally speaking, free to do or not do them as he pleases. But it is different when the act in question is interfering with another person's freedom of action: there is a presumption against this that must be overcome by a specific justification before it will be permissible.

Now the presumption of noninterference with other people's conduct may be suspended in certain special contexts. The rules of competitive games, for example, may permit interference with the activities of one's opponent. Moreover, the presumption of noninterference may be suspended within the framework of social institutions that give some individuals special authority over others. In the army, for example, an officer may have the right to interfere with a private's activities by issuing him a quite arbitrary command, without needing any special justification for doing so. Similar examples could be drawn from parent-child relations in the context of the family and from employer-employee relations in the context of a business organization. However, in a society in which freedom is valued, these institutions themselves will require justification before they are admitted as a desirable part of the social structure, precisely because of the curtailment of personal liberty that they involve. Moreover, insofar as it is possible, individual participation in such institutions will be on a voluntary basis—military conscription, for example, may not be thought desirable except as an emergency measure. And finally, in such a society our lives will never be so completely organized along institutional lines that at every point there is someone with the authority to tell us what to do. The ideal will be that, wherever possible, people will be left free to make their own decisions and to live their own lives accordingly. At any rate, I am going to assume that for the purposes of this argument we are talking about actions that take place outside any such special contexts as these.

If we need a justification for interfering with other people's freedom of action, we need to know what would count as such a justification. Under what conditions would we be justified in interfering with someone? I think we can say this small amount with some confidence: a justification would have to show that there is something *wrong* or *objectionable* in what the other person is doing. Suppose I am about to board a train that I think is the train to Amagansett, when you grab my arm and stop me. To explain, you might say that you had suddenly noticed that this was not the train to Amagansett at all, but the train to Baltimore. I was about to make a mistake and end up in the wrong place. Or you might tell me that my child has just been hurt, and I must not catch the train because I am needed at the hospital. In either case, if you are telling the truth, you have produced a justification for your action. But notice that each justification succeeds only by putting my action of boarding the train in a bad light: I shouldn't be getting on the train to Baltimore because that's not where I want to go; and I shouldn't be getting on any train at all if I am needed at the hospital. On the other hand, if I was not doing anything wrong—if I was getting on the right train at the right time, and so on, and if there were no good reason why I shouldn't be doing this—then you could not produce any justification for stopping me. In line with this, the second premise of our argument[2] is:

(2) If a certain act is the right thing for someone to do, then there can be no justification for anyone to interfere with his doing it.

The example of the train makes this claim plausible; but in addition here are two general arguments in support of it. First, if there is a reason sufficient to justify us in stopping someone from doing something, then that same reason would also serve to show that he shouldn't be doing it in the first place—that is, that it isn't the right thing for him to do. If so, then it will be impossible for there to be a counterexample to (2), and so (2) must be true. Second, if an act A is the right thing for someone to do, then it must also be the very *best* thing for him to do. For if there were an alternative action B such that it would be better for him to do B than A, then B and not A would be the right thing for him to do. And if there were other actions available to the agent that would be equally as good as A, then A would not be *the* right thing for him to do, but only one among many things that he could do, any of which would be right, but none of which would be *the* right thing for him to do. (I take it that expressions of the form "*the* so-and-so" imply uniqueness: thus, *Vertigo* is not *the* movie directed by Alfred Hitchcock, but only *one of* the movies, or a movie, directed by Alfred Hitchcock; and Noam Chomsky is not *the* critic of American foreign policy, but only *one of* the critics, or a critic, of American foreign policy. Here I am following Russell.) But now it seems clear that there can be no justification for interfering with someone who is doing *the very best thing that he can possibly be doing;* and if not, then there can be no justification for interfering with someone who is doing what is the *right thing* for him to be doing. Therefore, (2) must be true.

We may be tempted to doubt the truth of premise (2) if we forget the difference between there being a *justification* for doing something and someone's *wanting* to do it. We can certainly want to do things for which there is no justification, and there can be a justification for things which we don't want to do. We also need to remember the difference between having a justification and having a *reason.* Murderers, for example, often have reasons for their crimes, even when there is no justification for what they do. The man who assassinated President Garfield had a reason for killing him: he said that he did it in order to create a demand for a book he had written. But of course this was no justification. Bearing these differences in mind, premise (2) only says that we can have no justification for interfering with right actions; it does not deny that we may have a reason for doing so or that we might sometimes want to do so. Moreover, premise (2) does not even say that we *ought not* to interfere with right actions: for it does not follow from the fact that there is no justification for doing something that we ought not to do it. (Remember that in many cases it is all right to do things without a justification simply because no justification is needed—think again of going to the movies or taking a bath.)

The preceding two premises have to do with the ideal of freedom and with when we are justified in interfering with people's freedom. The next one concerns a different matter; it expresses a necessary connection between the concepts of rightness and permissibility.

(3) If a certain act is the right thing for someone to do, then it is permissible for him to do it.

This seems to me self-evident on its face; and it is taken as a necessary truth in standard systems of deontic logic. However, if a rationale for it is needed, one may be provided very easily: any act is permissible just in case it is not wrong; it is never wrong for someone to do the right thing; therefore, if an act is the right thing for someone to do, it is permissible for him to do it.

The final premise of this argument has to do with situations in which people's interests are in conflict. It sometimes happens that it is in one person's interests to do a certain act, while it is in another person's interests to stop him. That is to say:

(4) There are situations in which it would best promote the interests of one person, X, to do a certain act A, while it would best promote the interests of another person, Y, to stop X from doing A.

Situations of this sort are common. For example, Jones is expecting an inheritance from his wealthy aunt, but she is considering changing her will to exclude him. If he could get away with it, it would be to Jones' advantage to poison her; but of course it would be to her advantage to stop him.

People have tried in various ways to show that such conflicts of interest cannot occur. Traditional Christian theology, for example, provides a hell for Jones to roast in for all eternity if he should do such a thing; so, on this familiar view, it can never really be in his interests to do it. For all its implausibility and objectionableness on other grounds, the doctrine of hell at least has the advantage of eliminating the need for any further explanation as to why one shouldn't cut one's brother's throat for personal gain. The threat of hell-for-the-wicked, together with the identification of wickedness with harming others, keeps people's interests nicely in harmony. Someone who believes in hell could reject premise (4) on these grounds. I will not discuss whether such a belief is defensible; rather, I will address my argument only to those who do not find such a way out satisfactory.

The most widely discussed nontheistic argument that conflicts of interest cannot occur derives from chapters 13–15 of Hobbes' Leviathan. Since this is the only plausible argument of its kind that I know of, I will conclude, if it fails, that we have no good reason to deny that such conflicts can occur. Hobbes argued that it is in each person's own interests to do whatever is necessary to secure and maintain a peaceable society in which he can live safe from the threat of harm by his fellows and in which he can enjoy the advantages that come from a division of labor and from mutually cooperative enterprises. But in order for anyone to secure these goods, Hobbes said, there must be certain rules in force in this society: among these are rules directing one to keep one's contracts, to respect the rights of others and not harm them, to tell the truth, and so forth—in short, all the rules that are summed up in the commandment to treat others as you want them to treat you. Therefore, it is to one's advantage to agree to obey these rules, provided that others will obey them, too; and in any reasonably well-ordered society this is just the sort of arrangement that is already in force. The upshot is that in obeying the ordinary rules of morality, a person is merely doing his part to maintain the sort of social environment that it is to his own advantage to have. So, appearances to the contrary, self-interest requires conformity to other-regarding principles and does not conflict with them.

The problem with this argument is that while it surely is to the individual's own advantage to live in a society in which the ordinary moral rules are obeyed, he does not have to obey them himself all the time in order to live in such a society. If the Hobbesian argument were to be taken seriously on this point, we would have to believe that society is such a fragile thing that it could be brought down by a few selfish people pursuing their own interests without regard for the good of others. But of course this is not so. Most people will go on behaving as they usually do, regardless of what any odd individual here or there does; so no one need fear that if he does not himself conform to the moral rules on every occasion, he will lose the advantages of living in a decent society. Of course, if *everyone* were to make it his policy to deviate from the rules of social morality whenever it is to his own advantage to do so, then a tolerable social order might be impossible. However, in estimating the likely consequences of his *own* actions, an egoist may take into account the fact that everyone will *not* do this and that his own actions will not bring about any such results. So the careful fellow can, after all, have it both ways.

The considerations advanced by Hobbes do show something, even though they do not show that conflicts of interest are impossible. What they do show is that it is in each person's interests to work for and promote social arrangements that would make it very *hard* for him to advance his own interests at the expense of others. It is in each person's interests, for example, for there to be an efficient and well-run police force and judicial system so that people cannot hope to gain from hurting him or cheating him or breaking their agreements with him. Hobbes was right to observe that not even the cleverest and strongest man can expect to have a decent life apart from the protection of such institutions. But in promoting these institutions that would make it harder for other people to benefit from harming us, we are at the same time decreasing the chances of our benefiting from harming them.

The importance of Hobbes' argument is that it points up the way in which our major social and political institutions force the interests of individuals into a rough but imperfect harmony and how such institutions are vital to the welfare of each person. Taken this way, the argument is a brilliant success (and I think that this is the way Hobbes himself intended the argument to be taken). But taken as a proof that people's interests are in fact always in harmony, it fails. So I can see no good reason to doubt what is in any case plain on the face of it: that people's interests can and do conflict in the manner spelled out in premise (4) of our argument.

Now, given these four premises, we can easily deduce the conclusion that ethical egoism is an incorrect view. According to ethical egoism, the right thing for X to do is A, while the right thing for Y to do is to stop X from doing A. But from this it follows both that there is a justification for Y's preventing X from doing A and that there can be no justification for Y's preventing X from doing A. Therefore, ethical egoism must be incorrect. The details of the derivation are obvious, but I will give them anyway:

(5) If ethical egoism is correct, then the right thing for X to do is A.

This follows from the definition of ethical egoism together with (4).

(6) If ethical egoism is correct, then the right thing for Y to do is to stop X from doing A.

This follows from the definition of ethical egoism together with (4).

(7) If the right thing for X to do is A, then there can be no justification for Y's stopping him from doing it.

This follows from (2).

(8) If the right thing for Y to do is to stop X from doing A, then it is permissible for Y to stop X from doing A.

This follows from (3).

(9) If it is permissible for Y to stop X   This follows from (1).
    from doing A, then there is a
    justification for Y's stopping X
    from doing A.

(10) If ethical egoism is correct, then   This follows from (5) and (7).
     there can be no justification for Y's
     stopping X from doing A.

(11) If ethical egoism is correct, then   This follows from (6), (8), and (9).
     there is a justification for Y's
     stopping X from doing A.

(12) Therefore, ethical egoism is   This follows from (10) and (11).
     not correct.

Now as I said before, one can always escape the conclusion of an argument by rejecting one or more of the premises. Of the four premises of
this argument, it seems to me that the last two must be accepted, for the
reasons that I have given. As for the second premise, it places only the
most minimum sort of restriction on what can count as a justification for
interfering with another person's freedom of action. Of course, if anyone
thinks that such interference does not *need* justifying, then he will not have
to accept or reject any view about what counts as a justification. For him,
the latter question simply will not arise. But for anyone who *does* think that
interference requires justification—that is, for anyone who accepts premise
(1)—the minimum restriction expressed in (2) seems unavoidable. Therefore, it seems that in order to avoid the conclusion that ethical egoism is an
incorrect view, premise (1) must be rejected.

And this could be done. It could be said that we do not need to justify interference with other people. It could be said that limiting another
person's liberty is no different from going to the movies or taking a bath,
in this respect; it is one of the things that we are free to do or not do, as
we please. And if my argument has been correct, the ethical egoist is in
the position of having to say this. But those of us who are unwilling to say
such things will draw a different conclusion. For us, the fact that ethical
egoism lands one in such a position provides a compelling reason for
rejecting that doctrine.

2. The Wickedness of Ethical Egoism

The most obvious objection to ethical egoism is that it is a *morally pernicious* doctrine. One aspect of this perniciousness is that it is incompatible with the social ideal of freedom, as I have just argued. But on an even more obvious level, ethical egoism says straight-out that we need never be concerned with the needs or interests of other people, except insofar as they are useful to us; and this seems, on its face, an encouragement to wickedness. However, not many philosophers have pressed this point as a serious objection to egoism. The reason, I think, is that most philosophers feel that such an objection merely begs the question. To say that this view is wicked—or, more precisely, that many actions endorsed by it are wicked—is to express a moral judgment that the egoist himself would not accept. The essence of his theory is that those actions are *right,* and if we deny this, then we are disagreeing with his theory, but we are not refuting it. We are merely substituting abuse for argument.

I believe that this way of thinking is mistaken and that the wickedness of ethical egoism is a decisive objection against it. In what follows, I will present an argument based on this idea, and I will defend the argument against the charge of question begging.

A friend of mine who lives in a very small town in south Georgia told me about the following incident that occurred within the past year. The town is so small that there is only one doctor, and he is, as one might expect, one of the town's more affluent citizens. One day the doctor was visited by a poor, uneducated black woman with a variety of minor complaints. A brief examination showed that she was suffering from malnutrition. The problem was that the woman did not have enough money to buy food for herself and her several small children. She worked, whenever she could, as a cleaning woman in the homes of the better-off people in the town, but she was able to earn only a few dollars a month in this way. All this was known to the doctor. After spending no more than five minutes with the woman and having done absolutely nothing for her, the doctor told her that the charge would be twenty-five dollars. The woman had only twelve dollars—this was, literally, all the money she had in the world—so the doctor took that.

It was to the doctor's own advantage to take the woman's money simply because it made him twelve dollars richer. This was not much of an improvement in his financial position, but it was some improvement. Moreover, as far as anyone can tell, this slight financial gain was the only effect that his action had on his own interests. There were no harmful reactions toward him from the black community or from any other quarter, and none were expected. The doctor himself had no guilty conscience about the matter, for he never gave it another thought.

Now the argument I want to propose is this:

(1) If ethical egoism is correct, then the doctor did the right thing.

(2) The doctor did not do the right thing.

(3) Therefore, ethical egoism is not correct.

This argument, although it is rather obvious, has all the virtues that a good argument should have. The premises are true, and the conclusion follows logically from them. Each of the premises is independently plausible; the argument does not try to settle the truth of a controversial matter by appealing to considerations that are themselves equally controversial. Finally, this argument goes to the heart of the matter: it points out that ethical egoism leads to the conclusion that certain acts are right when those actions in fact are not right; and since ethical egoism is a theory about right and wrong, I do not see what could be a more serious difficulty for it.

Does this argument beg the question against ethical egoism? I think not, although accusations of "begging the question" are notoriously hard to answer. Arguments must clearly beg the question when one of the premises states the conclusion in a disguised form. But neither of the premises of this argument does that. Neither of the premises alone entails the conclusion, although of course taken together they do entail it. Moreover, the argument is a simple *modus tollens,* which is a form of argument not usually thought to be fallacious in any sense.

But still the feeling may persist that this argument somehow begs the question at issue. There are several things that might be said in an attempt to bring out exactly how the argument begs the question. I will consider them one at a time:

"The argument begs the question because it has a premise that the ethical egoist would not accept. The egoist would not accept premise (2). If it *was* in the doctor's own interests to take the money, then the egoist would say that the doctor did the right thing. Premise (2) says that the doctor did *not* do the right thing, so obviously the egoist would not agree."

The problem with this, as it stands, is that it doesn't matter at all what some real or imaginary defender of egoism would *say* about premise (2). All that matters is whether premise (2) is true. Premise (2) happens to be true, so if someone denies it, he is saying something false.

> "But that is mere dogmatism; it presupposes that ethical egoism is wrong. The point is that if ethical egoism *is* correct, as the egoist believes it to be, then the doctor was right to take the money. Again, to say otherwise assumes that ethical egoism is not correct, and so begs the question at issue."

This sort of thing is often said in discussions of egoism, but it seems to me nothing but a string of confusions. In the first place, the conditional statement that *"if ethical egoism is correct, then the doctor was right to take the money"* is certainly true; but it is nothing more than a restatement of premise (1) of our argument! And as for the claim that premise (2) presupposes the falsity of ethical egoism, clearly that is not so. Taken by itself, the simple statement that *"the doctor did not do the right thing"* does not presuppose the truth or falsity of any ethical theory whatever. Of course, when taken together with premise (1), premise (2) *entails* that ethical egoism is incorrect—but that is not a defect of the argument; it is the argument's whole point.

> "Let's start again. Let's just say that premise (2) is *controversial;* nonegoists would accept it, but egoists would deny it. And any argument that depends on that sort of premise cannot help us to decide the truth or falsity of the view in question."

The suggestion that premise (2) is controversial may be taken in several ways. It may just be a reminder that it has been, or may be, controverted, that is, that some people may deny it. But again, this by itself is not impressive. People have denied all sorts of true things, and what of it?

Or, in saying that (2) is controversial, it might be meant that its truth is questionable, uncertain, or doubtful. But this does not seem to be so. Premise (2) is as obviously and clearly true as anything could be. What originally struck me about my friend's story was that the doctor's action was so *plainly* reprehensible.

Finally, in saying that (2) is controversial, it may be meant that there is no more reason to believe it than to deny it because the evidence in its favor is not conclusive; and so anyone who insists that (2) is true is merely being dogmatic. But this is false. The evidence that the doctor did the wrong thing is overwhelming. In the first place, the woman was extremely poor. She was suffering from malnutrition, and without the twelve dollars she would have nothing to eat. And her children would have nothing to eat. Moreover, there are all the other necessities of life that this wretched family lacked. The doctor, on the other hand, was well-off, and twelve dollars meant relatively little to him (although it did mean something). And to make matters even worse, the doctor did nothing to *earn* the woman's money: *he simply took advantage of her helplessness.* All this provides eminently good reason for affirming the truth of (2). Judgments backed by such evidence are anything but arbitrary or dogmatic. On the contrary, it is the denial of (2) that is unreasonable since no comparable case can be made on that side.

"Now we have gotten to the root of the problem. None of the reasons that have just been given in support of (2) would be allowed by the ethical egoist. On his theory, all those considerations would be irrelevant. At last, this shows why our argument begs the question: premise (2) records a judgment that can be supported only by nonegoistic evidence. Thus, we affirm (2) only because we are presupposing a nonegoistic theory of right and wrong, and so we beg the question."

This objection is based on what I think is a mistaken view about the relation between individual moral judgments and moral theories. I take it that theories such as egoism and utilitarianism offer universal generalizations about the characteristics in virtue of which actions are morally right. Utilitarianism, for example, says that all morally right actions produce the greatest possible balance of good over evil results, when everyone's interests are weighted equally, and that is what makes those actions right. And ethical egoism says that all morally right actions are those that best serve the interests of the agent himself. If this is right, then we may test such theories simply by looking to see whether, in fact, right actions do have the characteristics that these theories say they have. Thus, when it turns out that some right actions, such as refusing to hang an innocent man to appease a bloodthirsty mob, do not have the characteristics that (some forms of) utilitarianism say they should have, we conclude that there must be something wrong with (those forms of) utilitarianism. Similarly, if it turns out that some right actions, such as letting the woman leave with her twelve dollars, do not have the characteristics that ethical egoism says they should have, we must conclude that there is something wrong with ethical egoism.

The main point here is that we do not determine what is right *merely* by consulting theories of rightness. Such a theory may be helpful in difficult cases, when we are not sure what to think; but in the *clear* cases, in which it is *plain* what is right and what is wrong, then the theory is tested by how well it corresponds to the moral "facts," and not the other way around. The same can be said of the *evidence* or *reasons* that support individual moral judgments. We do not discover what sorts of considerations are relevant to supporting moral judgments exclusively by consulting theories. Our ability to recognize the relevant considerations, at least in the clear cases, is prior to any speculations we might make about moral theory; and, again, our theories may be tested by the degree to which they do identify the sorts of considerations that we know to be important.

So I do not say that (2) is true, nor do I cite this evidence in support of it simply because I am presupposing some nonegoistic theory of right and wrong. The wrongness of the doctor's action is recognizable independently of any such theory. It is more certain than any mere theory could be: it is one of the fixed, constant points against which proposed theories may be tested, and the whole point of this argument is that ethical egoism does not pass this test.[3]

Notes

1. See, for example, Brian Medlin, "Ultimate Principles and Ethical Egoism," *Australasian Journal of Philosophy* 35 (1957): 111–18; William H. Baumer, "Indefensible Impersonal Egoism," *Philosophical Studies* 17 (1967): 72–75; and Richmond Campbell, "A Short Refutation of Ethical Egoism," *Canadian Journal of Philosophy* 2 (1972): 249–54.

2. In the *Moral Point of View* (Ithaca, N.Y.: Cornell University Press, 1958), Kurt Baier presents an argument against egoism that relies on a premise somewhat like this one. Baier gives an extended defense of this premise in "Ethical Egoism and Interpersonal Compatibility," *Philosophical Studies* 24 (1973): 357–68.

3. I am grateful to Jack Glickman and Asa Kasher for helpful comments on earlier versions of this paper.

BIOETHICS

ELEVEN

The Principle of Agency

I

Suppose a state of affairs could occur "naturally," without your help, or you could do something to make it happen. Further suppose that if it occurs naturally, people will think it is a good thing; but if you do something to make it happen, you will be said to have acted wrongly. On the face of it, this makes no sense. How can it be wrong to make something good happen? Yet there are cases about which many people believe exactly this. Here are four examples.

Euthanasia

It is common for people to think that death, in certain sorts of circumstances, is a good thing. When a ninety-year-old man dies after a prolonged illness, even those who love him may say that "his time had come." Privately they may describe his death as a relief and be glad the ordeal is over. Yet if the death had been brought about by direct action—if it had been voluntary active euthanasia—the person who killed him would be said to have acted impermissibly because, as the traditional doctrine has it, the direct killing of an innocent person is always wrong.

It looks like something very odd is going on here. Normally, we assume that if an act would have a good consequence, then that is a reason in favor of doing it. At the very least, the good outcome cannot be a reason against doing it. In this case, however, the same outcome that is said to be good when it occurs naturally—the "death of an innocent person"—is said to be something that we cannot aim to bring about. It looks like a straightforward case of being forbidden to do good, even when other things are equal.

In Vitro Fertilization

In in vitro fertilization (IVF), we accomplish in a petri dish what normally happens in a fallopian tube—namely, the fertilization of an ovum by a sperm. (We "help nature along a bit," in the words of John Brown, father of the first child born by this method.)[1] The zygote is then placed in the mother's uterus, and this enables otherwise infertile couples to have children. Since couples' having babies is a good thing, we might expect this procedure to be lauded as one of the indisputably good things in modern medicine. But, in fact, ever since the procedure was first used in 1978, critics have argued that there is something monstrous about it.[2] A key problem is that we cannot take one ovum and one sperm and produce one perfect baby. Instead, we must make multiple attempts with multiple eggs, and the result is that we create some imperfect zygotes and some "extras" that are discarded when the procedure is concluded. This, the critics say, is unacceptable.

But this is exactly what happens in nature. In the normal course of human reproduction, about 40 percent of pre-embryos fail to implant in the uterine wall. (This is a conservative estimate.) Many fail because of chromosomal abnormalities. Thus, when the process finally "takes," and the woman learns she is pregnant, it is the end result of a sequence that involves the same mishaps and false starts as IVF. IVF, therefore, is condemned not for some strange distortion of the reproductive process, but for having the same side effects that natural reproduction has always had.

It would be possible, of course, to take the view that natural reproduction is impermissible because it involves the creation of imperfect zygotes and zygotes that do not survive. One might say that since natural reproduction has this side effect, it is on the whole wrong to have children, and, morally speaking, no one should do it. I do not know of anyone who believes this. But if someone did take this view, they would be in a good position to condemn IVF.

Cystic fibrosis (CF) is genetically transmitted; if both parents are carriers, there is a one-in-four chance that their child will have the disease. For such parents, this naturally makes having a baby a fearful thing. Some remain childless rather than run the risk. (How often will both parents have the CF gene? More often than we might think; one in twenty-two Caucasians carry this gene.) Suppose, however, we were to use IVF techniques to create multiple embryos, and at the eight-cell stage we removed one cell from each embryo and tested it for CF. (This would not harm the embryo because at this early stage the cells are still undifferentiated.) Continuing the IVF process, we could implant only embryos without the cystic fibrosis gene. This way we could ensure that the child would not have CF.

We think it is a good thing when natural reproduction results in healthy children—when, for example, parents with the CF gene have children without CF. Yet many people who rejoice at the birth of a healthy child object strenuously to intervening to make sure it happens. It is important to bear in mind that for CF-carrying parents, the natural reproductive process may also involve the creation of embryos with CF that never implant. Thus, what happens naturally is the same as what we can make happen in the IVF procedure.

Cloning

When Ian Wilmut and his colleagues in Scotland announced in 1997 that they had successfully cloned an adult sheep, everyone started thinking about human cloning, and in the United States there was an immediate clamor for a federal law forbidding it. This reaction was supported by some remarkable arguments. Will the clone have the same soul as the original? What is to stop rich people from cloning themselves? Do we want "rooms full of human clones, silently growing spare parts for the person from whom they had been copied?"[3] It would be the worst thing in human history, said one critic; the people originated by cloning would be our slaves.[4] Another added that such people might not be moral agents.[5] These arguments were offered not by fringe figures, but by people regarded by the public as serious bioethicists.

Meanwhile, the National Bioethics Advisory Commission, a government panel charged with making recommendations for federal law, held hearings and invited prominent bioethicists to testify. One expert told them that it is wrong to break the connection between procreation and the combining of the parents' genetic material. By doing this, he said, cloning "aims directly at the heart of the mystery that is a child." Why, exactly? He elaborated, "Part of the mystery here is that we will always be hard-pressed to explain why the connection of sexual differentiation and procreation should not be broken."[6] Hearing such reasoning, the commission was persuaded that human cloning should be banned. Understandably enough, at least some of the commissioners were uncertain what had persuaded them. When asked why the commission had reached this decision, one of its members explained, "There's a very human tendency to know what you want to do but not be clear necessarily about why."[7]

But, of course, cloning only reproduces a common occurrence in nature. A person who was conceived by cloning is the genetic duplicate of someone else, but so are monozygotic twins. No one thinks something terrible has happened when twins are born. The obvious question is, "If there is nothing bad about having twins 'naturally,' why should it be wrong to use cloning techniques to bring about the delayed birth of a twin?" Consider this pair of cases:

1. Ann and Abner Adams had twin sons, conceived and born in the old-fashioned way. Unfortunately, one son died. It was sad, but the three remaining Adamses are a happy family.

2. Burt and Betty Brown had one child and planned to have another. But then their son died, and Burt, for some reason, became sterile. But it turned out that it was still possible for them to have the second child they wanted. Before their son died, tissue samples had been taken. Betty could ovulate, and with cloning technology DNA from that tissue could be inserted into her denucleated egg. (Afterward the zygote would be implanted into her uterus and gestation would proceed as usual. In this way, cloning is very much like IVF.) This was done, and all went well. The new baby was the twin of the child who died. His parents, both biologically and socially, were Burt and Betty. Now the death of the first child is a sad memory, but the three remaining Browns are a happy family.

These stories are fictitious, but they are realistic in a way that the fantasy about "rooms full of clones silently growing spare parts" is not.[8] When human cloning becomes a reality, this is the sort of use to which the technique is likely to be put. Now the difference between the two cases is that in the first there is a twin who comes to exist "naturally," while in the second, people deliberately set out to conceive a twin. Again, the question is, "If it is a good thing for the Adamses to have their son, how can it be wrong to take the steps needed for the Browns to have a similar son?"

II

The preceding remarks appeal to a principle that we may call the *Principle of Agency*:

> If it would be good for a particular state of affairs to occur "naturally," without being brought about by human action, then it is permissible to act so as to bring it about.

Obviously, the principle requires some qualifications. Suppose the state of affairs in question is a complex consisting of both good and bad elements, and we would prefer, if possible, to have the good without the bad. In that case, we might say that it is permissible for an agent to bring about the whole state of affairs only if it is not possible to bring about only its good parts. (For example, if we think it would be better for nature not to produce extra zygotes, then we may say it would be better for IVF technicians not to produce those zygotes.) This sort of qualification does not violate the spirit of the principle. The spirit of the principle is that we should make the same judgment about what people do as about what nature does.

If the Principle of Agency is correct, it would make a difference in the discussion of such matters as euthanasia, IVF, and cloning. It would not settle those controversies because there are other issues involved in them. But it would support the view that these practices and others like them are acceptable.

Is the principle correct? It is hard to find arguments in its favor—not because it is implausible, but because it is too plausible. Philosophical arguments usually appeal to more certain ideas in order to support less certain ideas. But the notion that it is not wrong to do good seems so obviously right that it is difficult to think of anything more plausible that could be adduced in its support. Indeed, if it were not for the fact that so many people, including many bioethicists, apparently reject the principle, defending it might seem like an unnecessary exercise in belaboring the obvious. So we might proceed instead by looking at the arguments on the other side. Why should anyone doubt that the Principle of Agency is true?

Philosophers might be suspicious because the Principle of Agency is a consequentialist principle, and consequentialism is a much-disputed theory. But we must distinguish between consequentialist principles and consequentialism as a moral theory. All moral theories hold that consequences are important; nonconsequentialist theories just hold that other matters are also relevant. So in order to cast doubt on the Principle of Agency, more must be said than merely that it permits us to bring about good consequences.

Nonconsequentialist theorists might prefer to express the basic idea of the principle like this:

> If the "natural" occurrence of a state of affairs would be a good thing, then the fact that performing a certain action would lead to that state of affairs is a morally good reason in favor of doing that action.

This version of the principle obviously leaves room for other reasons that might bear on any particular issue. This version appears to be platitudinous. Even so, it has implications that will trouble some bioethicists. For instance, it implies that although there might be various good reasons for opposing euthanasia in the sort of case I described above, the fact that it involves bringing about someone's death cannot be among them. On the contrary, this fact is a reason in its favor.

But there is another problem having to do with consequences. It is easy to detect in the discussion of such matters as euthanasia, IVF, and cloning a kind of nervousness about the consequences of human power. The feeling seems to be that so long as nature determines the course of events, nothing very bad will happen, but if people take control, things are bound to go wrong. This feeling often gives rise to predictions that are hard to take seriously: if euthanasia is permitted, we will end up killing the inhabitants of retirement homes; or if cloning is permitted, there will be rooms of artificially created people silently growing spare parts. It would be charitable to assume that no one really believes such things and that such remarks serve only to express a general worry about the consequences of people assuming control over too many things.

This worry might lead one to oppose the Principle of Agency with the following line of thought: perhaps, in some instances, people should not be permitted to bring about the specified state of affairs because of what would happen if human beings were generally allowed to do things like that. It is not that we expect bad consequences from any one particular action. Rather, bad results may come about as the cumulative effect of many actions of the same type. Therefore, in order to block the undesirable consequences, it may be necessary to prohibit a whole class of actions, even though this may mean sometimes forbidding someone from doing something good.

This, of course, recalls the slippery slope, a familiar form of reasoning that has often been discussed by bioethicists. The slippery slope is not so much an argument as a recipe for formulating arguments about particular matters. These arguments will differ depending on what practices are in dispute—euthanasia, IVF, cloning, or something else—and on exactly what consequences are feared will result from them. Whether the arguments are persuasive will depend on the plausibility of the predictions being made.

In retrospect, it often turns out that such worries were unfounded. This has happened in the case of IVF. When Louise Brown, the first "test-tube baby," was born in 1978, there were alarmed cries about what might be in store for her, her family, and society as a whole.[9] But nothing bad happened, and IVF became a routine procedure that has been used to help thousands of couples to have children.

In prospect, however, it can be difficult to determine whether such an argument is sound. The predictions are often such that reasonable people can disagree about their likelihood. This makes possible a frustrating sort of impasse: disagreements about the merits of the argument often seem to depend simply on the prior dispositions of the disputants—those inclined to defend the behavior in question think the dire predictions are crazy, while those predisposed to condemn the behavior insist the predictions are realistic.

Where the Principle of Agency is involved, this tendency is brought into sharp focus, for here the slippery slope is invoked to explain why we may not bring about states of affairs *that are admitted to be good*. This being so, we should expect the argument to be used reluctantly and with a sense of regret; and if the fears proved to be unfounded, we should expect general rejoicing. But, at least in the cases we have been considering, this is not what we find. When it turned out that IVF had no catastrophic consequences, the critics did not rejoice and withdraw their objections. Similarly, it is hard to believe that the objections to euthanasia and cloning would go away if it turned out that retirement-home inhabitants were safe and the rooms of spare-part zombies did not materialize. This should warn us that, in these cases at least, the worry about "what will happen" is not really the fundamental issue. While there must always be a prudent concern about the consequences of public policy, it is a mistake to focus too much on the slippery slope. We should instead ask what more fundamental reasons motivate the conviction that bringing about good outcomes is impermissible.

III

Our examples of euthanasia, IVF, and cloning do not involve bad intentions or the violation of anyone's rights.[10] Nevertheless, those topics raise general problems for the Principle of Agency.

Intentions

The Principle of Agency says that if it would be good for something to happen naturally, then we may take action to make it happen. But it may be urged that there is a crucial difference between states of affairs that occur naturally and those brought about by human action. When actions are involved, human intentions are added to the mix, and intentions are morally significant.

It is undoubtedly true that intentions are morally important, but how does this cause trouble for the Principle of Agency? Intentions are obviously important for assessments of character. It is more problematic whether they play a role in the assessment of actions. This is a complicated issue, and fortunately we need not settle it here. We need only to note that in order for there to be trouble for the Principle of Agency, something like the following would have to be true: the intention with which we bring about a state of affairs can make it wrong to do so, even though the existence of that state of affairs is a good thing.

Can this be true? There are two possibilities to consider: we may act with a good or a bad intention. If we have a laudable intention, then it is hard to see how we could be acting wrongly—we would be doing a good thing with a good intention. So we should concentrate on the other possibility. Suppose we act with a bad intention—let's say, we bring about the good state of affairs as part of a larger plan to accomplish some dastardly purpose. John Stuart Mill considered a case like this. In the first edition of *Utilitarianism,* published in 1861, Mill had written that "the motive has nothing to do with the morality of the action, though much with the worth of the agent. He who saves a fellow creature from drowning does what is morally right, whether his motive be duty or the hope of being paid for his trouble."[11] Then, when the book was reprinted in 1864, he added a footnote discussing the objection of a critic (the Rev. J. Llewellyn Davies) who had written, "Surely the rightness or wrongness of saving a man from drowning does depend very much upon the motive with which it is done. Suppose that a tyrant, when his enemy jumped into the sea to escape from him, saved him from drowning simply in order that he might inflict upon him more exquisite tortures, would it tend to clearness to speak of that rescue as 'a morally right action'?"[12]

Mill's response was to distinguish between intention and motive. The intention is what the agent wills to do, and it is relevant to the morality of the action, Mill says, because it determines the nature of the action that is performed. The man who simply rescues another from drowning and the tyrant who saves in order to torture perform different acts. If this is correct, we must know what the intention is before we can establish what act is being done, and therefore we must know what the intention is before we can determine whether the act is right. As for the motive, it is merely "the feeling that makes him will it," and "if it makes no difference in the act, [it] makes none in the morality."[13]

Mill's analysis helps us to distinguish two ways in which intentions can be relevant to the morality of actions:

1. *The Direct Effect View.* Intentions are relevant to the assessment of actions as right or wrong in this way: the same act may be done with different intentions, and an act that is right when done with one intention may be wrong when done with a different intention.

2. *The Indirect Effect View.* (This was Mill's view.) Intentions are relevant to the assessment of actions as right or wrong in this way: actions done with different intentions are different actions. Therefore, because the morality of an act depends on what the act is, and what the act is depends on the intention, the morality depends on the intention.

Both of these views have been held by thinkers who believe that intentions are important.[14] Let us consider what each of them implies for the Principle of Agency.

If we take the Indirect View, there is no trouble for the Principle of Agency. If the agent's intention is simply to bring about the "naturally" good state of affairs, then his intention is good, the outcome is good, and there is no problem. On the other hand, if we imagine the agent acting from some other intention, then she is performing a different action from the one referred to in the principle. Since the principle implies nothing about the morality of this different action, the principle will be unaffected by any moral assessment we make of it.

The situation with respect to the Direct View is more complicated. We should note that there are some fairly strong arguments against the Direct View. First, according to it, you and I might do the very same thing, and yet what you do may be right (because you do it with a good intention), while what I do is wrong (because I do it with a bad intention). But this seems self-contradictory: we are doing the same thing, and how can the same thing be both right and wrong? There is obviously a better way to describe the situation. *Pace* Rev. Davies, it would make for greater clarity to say that while you are doing the right thing with a good intention, I am doing the same thing— the right thing—but with a bad intention. As Mill observed, this might make me a bad man, but it does not mean that what I am doing is wrong.

A second argument against the Direct View appeals to the nature of moral reasoning. Whether actions are right or wrong depends on the reasons that can be given for or against them; but the intention with which the act would be done does not appear among those reasons. Suppose, for example, we were trying to figure out whether you should send money to the United Nations Children's Fund. You would want to know about the reliability of that agency, about how many additional children would receive inoculations against life-threatening diseases as a result of your contribution, and so on. You would also need to think about other uses to which your money might be put. But it would be pointless to start mulling over your intentions—unless, that is, you were trying to guard against motives that might corrupt your reasoning or something like that. Your intentions themselves would not be among the reasons you would need to consider in determining the right thing to do.

There are substantial grounds, then, for suspecting that the Direct View is false. Nevertheless, suppose we accept it. Then, when someone brings about the good situation as part of a dastardly plan, we will concede that she acts impermissibly. Should we, for this reason, reject the Principle of Agency? Yes and no. The principle in its original formulation might have to go. However, there would be a closely analogous principle that would need to be incorporated into any moral theory that includes the Direct View. That principle would be exactly like the Principle of Agency except that the phrase "it is permissible to act so as to bring it about" would be replaced by "it is permissible to act with the intention of bringing it about." Every reason that supports the Principle of Agency would support this modified principle, and there would be no reason against it having to do with intentions.

197

Rights

Finally, another potential problem is that in bringing about the good state of affairs, we could be violating someone's rights. Natural occurrences don't violate rights, but actions do. It will not often happen that we violate someone's rights by doing good. (Usually rights are violated by causing bad outcomes.) But it can happen. Suppose Jones, a competent adult, is sick but unwisely refuses treatment. If we force treatment on him, we make something good happen, but we violate his rights.

Moral philosophers have held a wide range of views about rights, ranging from *(a)* it's nonsense even to talk about them to *(z)* rights are the fundamental and irreducible basis of morality. But even those who look most favorably on rights will not, for that reason, reject the Principle of Agency. Those who believe in rights do not deny that we should seek good outcomes. Instead, they emphasize that there are limits on what we may do in pursuit of such outcomes. Thus, they might insist that a qualification should be added to the principle to the effect that it is permissible to bring about the good outcome only so long as no one's rights are violated. (Those who do not believe in rights, of course, will not believe that such a qualification is needed.) This will not be regarded as an *ad hoc* provision because it reflects the basic structure of theories about rights; as Robert Nozick famously put it, rights are side constraints on the pursuit of goals.[15] Therefore, if the Principle of Agency is to be rejected altogether, it must be for some other reason than that it conflicts with ideas about rights.

IV

The Principle of Agency, or at least some form of it, appears to be inescapable. We should make the same judgments about what people do as about what nature does. But why do so many people think otherwise? A belief as general and prevalent as this should have an interesting explanation. Such explanations are inevitably speculative and should be entertained only with some skepticism. But here is one possibility.

First, we may consider the cases we have been discussing as part of a larger pattern. People seem to be generally willing to accept things in nature that they will not accept from human agency. Environmental issues provide additional easy examples. Species go extinct all the time in the natural course of things, and no one thinks this is a tragedy (unless, of course, it is a conspicuously beautiful species). But if a species is threatened by human action—say, as the side effect of building a dam or an oil pipeline—this is condemned as the irresponsible destruction of nature. Or, to take a different example, it is now generally believed that forest fires are a part of nature's routine for periodically rejuvenating the forest; so if lightning starts a fire in a national park, the fire may be allowed to run its course. Yet fires caused by the carelessness of campers are regarded as disastrous.

What could explain this pattern of judgments and attitudes? It could be that, behind the scenes, there is an unacknowledged religious view of nature at work. It is as though people were thinking of nature as a great mysterious force with its own special kind of moral authority. Hence, we have one standard for "what nature does"—in the main, we must accept it and live with it—and a different way of thinking about what we do. It is not hard to identify the source of this conception. It is left over from medieval Christianity. It attributes to nature the characteristics of God—it is mysterious, powerful, and "other" than humankind. Our ethical thinking contains much that appears to be secular, but really is vestigial religion. The deference paid to nature may be a case in point.

Notes

1. Quoted in Gregory E. Pence, *Classic Cases in Medical Ethics*, 2d ed. (New York: McGraw-Hill, 1995), 100.

2. For a description of the controversy surrounding the development of this procedure, see ibid., chap. 4.

3. *Newsweek*, March 10, 1997, 53.

4. Deborah Sharp and Lori Sharn, "Big Questions for Humanity," *USA Today*, April 1, 1997.

5. Leon Kass, "The Wisdom of Repugnance," *The New Republic,* June 2, 1997, 22.

6. Quoted in Gilbert Meilander, "Begetting and Cloning," *First Things* 74 (June–July 1977), 42.

7. Quoted in Gina Kolata, "Analysis: Commission on Cloning—Ready-Made Controversy," *New York Times,* June 9, 1997.

8. The second case is adapted from an example suggested by Gregory E. Pence in "At Least Talk Before Ban on Human Cloning," *Birmingham News,* March 2, 1997, C1.

9. For details, see Pence, *Classic Cases,* chap. 4.

10. Those who believe that eight-cell preembryos have rights will not agree.

11. John Stuart Mill, *Utilitarianism* (Indianapolis: Hackett, 1979; originally published in 1861), chap. 2, para. 19, p. 18.

12. Ibid., 18.

13. Ibid.

14. Until recently, these views have been the main options. Now, however, a third way of thinking about these issues has been made available by Jonathan Bennett. In *The Act Itself* (Oxford: Oxford University Press, 1995), Bennett argues that in moral philosophy we should avoid the notion of "an action" altogether and make do instead with the notion of human behavior. Thus, problems about identifying and individuating actions, distinguishing between "the act itself" and its consequences, and so on—problems that Bennett thinks come up only because we are thinking about our subject in a confused way—would not arise. If Bennett is right, the problem for the Principle of Agency that we are now considering would not arise either.

15. Robert Nozick, *Anarchy, State, and Utopia* (New York: Basic Books, 1974), 26–42.

TWELVE

BABY M

It is, the commentators agree, a case that was waiting to happen. In 1985, after concluding that his wife, Elizabeth, could not bear children, William Stern of Tenafly, New Jersey, contracted with Mary Beth Whitehead to act as surrogate mother. Mrs. Whitehead, a married woman who already had two children of her own, agreed to be artificially inseminated with Mr. Stern's sperm, bear a child, and then turn it over to the Sterns—for a fee of ten thousand dollars. Elizabeth Stern would then become the child's adoptive mother, and the surrogate mother would never see the child again.

The deal was arranged through a New York infertility clinic. Mrs. Whitehead's involvement began when she responded to an advertisement placed by the clinic. At first, her husband didn't like the idea, but eventually he relented. She was considered by at least one other couple prior to the Sterns, but wasn't thought to be a good "match." The Sterns, however, thought she was perfect—she even *looked like* Elizabeth Stern. So the bargain was struck, and there was celebration all around when the artificial insemination was successful and Mrs. Whitehead became pregnant.

Everything went according to plan, and the child was born on March 27, 1986. But then Mrs. Whitehead suddenly decided that she wanted to keep the baby. "I thought I could go through with it," she said, "but I couldn't." A dispute then followed about possession of the infant. Mr. Stern obtained a court order giving him temporary custody, and the police were sent to the Whitehead home to fetch the child. But when the police arrived, Mrs. Whitehead passed the baby out a rear window to her husband, and they fled to Florida. The Sterns hired a private detective to track them down, and after eighty-seven days the baby and the Whiteheads were brought back to New Jersey. The baby was given temporarily to the Sterns, a judge ordered psychological evaluations of all concerned, and a trial to sort things out was scheduled for the following January. The Sterns called the infant Melissa; the Whiteheads called her Sara; and the court, in a show of neutrality, called her Baby M.

Unlike England and Victoria (Australia), where commercial surrogacy was banned in 1985 and 1984, respectively, the practice is legal here—legal in the minimum sense that there are no laws prohibiting it. But neither are there any laws regulating it. The legislatures of the various states have, thus far, ignored the subject. Questions of law aside, however, polls show that most Americans see nothing wrong with surrogacy. This is not surprising, considering that we have had a generally good experience. Almost six hundred babies have been born to surrogate mothers in the United States during the past decade, and problems have arisen in fewer than 2 percent of the cases. Two or three of the babies have been kept by the surrogate mothers, but without a court fight. (Exact figures are hard to come by because there are no central records.) This relative lack of controversy helps to explain why, until now, state legislatures have felt no need to act.

From the beginning, the story of Baby M captured the public imagination, and the newspapers were full of it. Despite the general public approval of surrogacy, my subjective impression was that, at least in the beginning, most public sentiment sided with Mary Beth Whitehead. Certainly the newspapers seemed to take her side, more often than not. The popular thought seemed to be that Mrs. Whitehead was the mother, and a mother's baby should not be taken away against her will, deal or no deal. (Never mind that William Stern is the biological father.) In support of Mrs. Whitehead, Ellen Goodman, a popular liberal newspaper columnist, urged that "a baby is not a piece of goods, and human emotions do not make for neat contracts."

When the newspapers here want an "expert opinion" on a controversy in bioethics, they turn most often to the Hastings Center, the highly respected think-tank that is no doubt familiar to readers of this journal. The opinions they got about commercial surrogacy ranged from worried to openly hostile. Daniel Callahan, head of the Hastings Center, contributed a piece to the *New York Times* that was printed under the headline "Surrogate

Motherhood: A Bad Idea." Callahan argued that as a matter of social policy, we should reject surrogacy because of what it would do to the institution of motherhood: surrogacy, he said, would mean the creation of a cadre of women "with the capacity thoroughly to dissociate and distance themselves from their own child. This is not a psychological trait we should want to foster, even in the name of altruism." George J. Annas, who writes a regular column on bioethics law in the *Hastings Center Report* opined that "commercial surrogacy promotes the exploitation of women and infertile couples, and the dehumanization of babies." In the Stern-Whitehead case, the issue of "exploitation" arises in the classic manner: the Sterns are well-educated, prosperous people—Mr. Stern is a biologist and Mrs. Stern is a pediatrician—while Mary Beth Whitehead, who never graduated from high school, is the wife of a sanitation worker. This is a theme that would be emphasized in the coming trial.

Not all the arguments were so high-minded. Many editorialists wondered, if the Sterns wanted a baby so badly, why didn't they just adopt one? Why get involved with so complicated and expensive a business as surrogacy? As if to correct the purveyors of this argument, the Associated Press (AP) ran a special report on the shortage of babies available for adoption. In 1984, the AP said, there were two million couples after fifty-eight thousand children. The unsatisfied demand has even attracted the attention of organized crime: "Federal officials," the report continued, "say the rising demand has led to a proliferation of organized rings that smuggle babies, some of them kidnapped, across the Mexican border and then sell them to the highest bidder in this country." William Stern provided his own answer to the argument. He was motivated, he said, by the ancient urge to continue his family line. Both his parents are dead, and all his other relatives were killed in Nazi concentration camps. He is the last surviving member of his family. For what he wanted, adoption wouldn't do.

A digression: last fall, after Baby M had been taken from her but before the trial began, Mary Beth Whitehead appeared with her lawyer on national television and listened passively while he portrayed her as a poor, uneducated woman who had been "taken advantage of." Those appearances were very effective. They generated a lot of sympathy for her, as they were intended to do.

The use of television to influence public opinion in such cases has become increasingly noticeable and increasingly troublesome as "informing the public" shades into crass manipulation. There seems to be an endless number of talk shows and interview programs eager to feature the latest controversy. The format of such programs is (when possible) to have the parties to a controversy appear together and to prod them into public combat. Emotions run high, often with spectacular results. Mary Beth Whitehead's television appearances were small potatoes; others—including professionals such as Susan Carpenter McMillan—have used the medium to much more dramatic effect.

Ms. McMillan was employed by Right to Life of California to represent the parents of "Baby Jesse," an infant born in May 1986 with hypoplastic left heart syndrome. Without a heart transplant, Baby Jesse would die. Of course, there are many more transplant candidates than there are donor hearts available. The first step, then, is to get one's baby on the waiting list. But Baby Jesse's parents had been unable to achieve this first step: Loma Linda Hospital, a Seventh-Day Adventist facility in California—the same hospital where, two years earlier, a baboon's heart was transplanted into "Baby Fae"—had declined to include Baby Jesse on its list of eligible infants on the grounds that his young, unwed parents were less likely than other candidates' families to be able to provide good postsurgical care. But then Ms. McMillan arrived on the scene, and thanks to her efforts the refusal was widely publicized, and public sentiment was aroused against the hospital. The impression was created that the baby was being allowed to die simply because its parents were not married; and the hospital's insistence that the matter was more complicated than that went unheeded. So after the couple had relinquished guardianship to the father's grandparents, the hospital relented, and Baby Jesse was declared eligible.

That was only the beginning. Getting on a waiting list is one thing; actually getting a transplant is another. The next step was to bring Baby Jesse's name to the top of the list, ahead of other infants who had no public-relations agents. This was soon accomplished. Cashing in on the earlier publicity—"Baby Jesse" was becoming a cause célèbre—Ms. McMillan succeeded in getting herself and the parents an appearance on the Phil Donahue Show.

Donahue, a popular champion of liberal causes, specializes in dramatizing controversial issues by interviewing the contending parties before mostly female studio audiences who are invited to join in the questioning. He has often featured bioethical controversies. A year earlier he had presented a hired surrogate mother and a "buyer couple" (much like Mary Beth Whitehead and the Sterns) who were disputing possession of a baby. This time, however, nobody wanted the baby because it had been born defective.

The dispute was resolved when, live and on the air, Donahue revealed to all concerned that blood tests had proven that the surrogate mother's husband was actually the biological father of the child. The "buyers" were elated, and the "surrogate" was nonplussed. In television terms, it was a socko show.

But the Baby Jesse show was even more sensational. After telling their story, Ms. McMillan and the parents had to face some skeptical questioning. No infant receiving a heart transplant had lived longer than seven months, and realists conceded that this particular infant's prospects were bleak. He would likely have lifelong problems, including a significant chance of mental retardation. Ms. McMillan vehemently disputed all such prognoses and assured the audience, with fire in her eyes, that "this baby will be perfect!" But the debate was cut short by a telephone call. A family in Michigan, with a brain-dead infant born on the same day as Baby Jesse, had been watching the program and had called to say, live and on the air, that Jesse could have their baby's heart. The audience cheered as Ms. McMillan and the parents rushed out. There wasn't a dry eye in the studio. Sure enough, the Michigan infant's heart was soon transplanted into Baby Jesse's breast. Another socko show, and nothing to be troubled about, unless one thinks that there might be a better way than this to determine who lives and who dies.

But back to Baby M. The trial for her custody, which began on January 5 and lasted until March 13, was presided over by Bergen County Superior Court judge Harvey R. Sorkow. The trial was divided into two phases: the first phase dealt with the question of the legality of the surrogacy contract, and the second phase dealt with the question of Baby M's best interests. Judge Sorkow maintained throughout that the paramount issue was the infant's best interests; with this in mind, he sought to have the trial closed to the public, but was overruled by the New Jersey Supreme Court.

The proceedings were a disaster for the Whiteheads in almost every respect. Before the trial began, there was considerable public sympathy for Mrs. Whitehead—my impression, as I have already said, was that a majority of people felt that she should be allowed to keep her baby. But as the trial went on, this feeling evaporated.

The Whiteheads had had troubled lives, and their troubles were paraded in court. They were married when Mary Beth was sixteen, and both their children were born before her nineteenth birthday. Her husband, it turned out, is an alcoholic whose driver's license has been revoked twice. Once, when he was unemployed, she worked as a go-go dancer. At various times, the Whiteheads had been on welfare, and they once filed for bankruptcy—

and, they admitted to Judge Sorkow, they perjured themselves in some of the bankruptcy papers. To top it all off, at the time of the trial they were facing loss of their home in a mortgage dispute with a relative.

Unsavory as all this seemed, it was not these facts that hurt the Whiteheads' case the most. Worse damage was done by a tape of a telephone conversation between Mary Beth Whitehead and William Stern, in which she had threatened to kill the baby. While the Whiteheads were hiding in Florida, she had called him to discuss the situation and had said: "You want me to kill myself and the baby?" "I gave her life. I can take her life away." "I'd rather see me and her dead before you get her.... I'm going to do it, Bill. I'm going to do it; you've pushed me into it." And to make things even worse, she had called Stern back the next day and threatened to charge him with sexually molesting her ten-year-old daughter.

These revelations destroyed the Whiteheads' credibility so thoroughly that further demolition seemed superfluous. But there was more. In a bizarre episode, one of Mrs. Whiteheads' character witnesses, Susan Herherhan, a former neighbor, admitted to having forged a letter to Judge Sorkow and to having lied on the stand. (She had written a letter to the judge but had signed Mary Beth Whitehead's name; this was discovered when Sorkow asked Whitehead about the letter, and she knew nothing about it.) The judge threatened to have the character witness charged with perjury.

Both sides, of course, had "expert witnesses" to testify on their behalf. But the court had its own "neutral" experts, and these all sided with the Sterns. The infant's court-appointed guardian, Lorraine A. Abraham, recommended that the baby be given to the Sterns and that all Whitehead's parental rights be terminated. The guardian had hired three mental health experts, each of whom testified that Mrs. Whitehead's emotional problems could prevent her from being a good mother. All three joined Ms. Abraham in recommending that the baby go to the Sterns. (To the surprise of all, Abraham modified her recommendation at the conclusion of the trial, suggesting that Mrs. Whitehead's rights not be terminated permanently, but that they be reconsidered after five years. "People are capable of change," she said.)

The Sterns, by contrast, had an easy time of it. They appeared throughout to be reasonable, responsible people of upper-middle-class virtue. Their only uneasy moment came when it was revealed that Mrs. Stern was not actually infertile: she had decided against pregnancy because she has a mild case of multiple sclerosis, and she feared that pregnancy might aggravate her condition. Mrs. Whitehead expressed surprise and said that she had been deceived. The judge, however, didn't think this revelation was especially important.

Judge Sorkow's decision was handed down on March 31, and it was a complete victory for the Sterns. He upheld the validity of the surrogacy contract; he awarded the child to the Sterns; and he stripped Mary Beth Whitehead of all parental rights—she would have no right ever to see the child again or have anything further to do with it. Baby M was now to be called Melissa Stern.

For the Whiteheads and the Sterns, the most important question was, of course, who would get the baby. But for public policy, the most important question was whether surrogacy contracts are to be considered valid. Judge Sorkow's inclination was plainly to hold that such contracts are valid unless good reason can be shown for thinking otherwise. In the course of his 122-page opinion (much of which was taken up by findings of fact), he considered six arguments against such contracts and rejected all of them:

First argument: Surrogacy contracts should be deemed invalid because they are contrary to adoption statutes and other child benefit laws.

Judge Sorkow's reply: No, they are not. This is a new area of law, different from the law concerning adoption. "Indeed, it is held that the only concept of law that can presently attach to surrogacy arrangements are contract law principles and *parens patriae* concepts for the benefit of the child. These are the only polestars available for this court to chart its course on the issues of surrogacy."

Second argument: Under such contracts, the child's interests will not be protected.

Sorkow's reply: The court's primary duty is to protect the best interests of the child. That is true regardless of the type of legal proceeding. If the terms of a surrogacy contract are enforced, adoption will take place, and the court's duty to protect the child in adoption proceedings comes into play. If there is noncompliance, the court still has the duty to intervene in order to protect the child.

Third argument: Such contracts create the potential for exploiting surrogate mothers.

Sorkow's reply: "To the contrary. It is the private adoption that has the great potential, if not the fact, for the exploitation of the mother. In the private adoption, the woman is already pregnant. The biological father may be unknown or at best uninterested in his obligations. The woman may want to keep the child but cannot do so for financial reasons. There is the risk of illegal consideration being paid to the mother. In surrogacy, none of these 'downside' elements appear. The arrangement is made when the desire and intention to have a family exist on the couple's part. The surrogate has an opportunity to consult, take advice, and consider her act and is not forced into the relationship."

Fourth argument: Surrogacy allows an elite economic group to use a poorer group of people to achieve their purposes, to "make their babies."

Sorkow's reply: "This argument is insensitive and offensive to the intense drive to procreate naturally and when that is impossible, to use what lawful means are possible to gain a child. This intense desire to propagate the species is fundamental. It is within the soul of all men and women regardless of economic status."

Fifth argument: It degrades human dignity to recognize any arrangement in which a child is produced for money.

Sorkow's reply: "[T]o produce or deal with a child for money denigrates human dignity. To that premise, this court urgently agrees.... The fact is, however, that the money to be paid to the surrogate is not being paid for the surrender of the child to the father.... The biological father pays the surrogate for her willingness to be impregnated and carry his child to term. At birth, the father does not purchase the child. It is his own biological genetically related child. He cannot purchase what is already his."

Sixth argument: Surrogacy undermines traditional notions of family.

Sorkow's reply: "How can that be when the childless husband and wife so very much want a child? They seek to make a family. They intend to make a family."

Having rejected these arguments, Judge Sorkow found no reason not to hold the surrogacy contract valid. With what appeared to be something like pride of authorship, he declared the legitimacy of such contracts to be "a new rule of law." He did, however, find fault with one provision of the contract actually used by Stern and Whitehead: it forbade the surrogate mother from having an abortion. Sorkow held this provision to be unacceptable: "Having defined a new rule of law," he wrote, "this court hastens to add an exception. After conception, only the surrogate shall have the right, to the exclusion of the sperm donor, to decide whether to abort the foetus."

As for the question of the infant's best interests, Sorkow did not treat this as an entirely separate matter. He related it to the question of the legitimacy of the contract in the following way. (These seven quotations, drawn from several pages of Sorkow's opinion, summarize the main outline of his reasoning.)

1. "This court concludes and upholds that the surrogate parenting agreement is a valid and enforceable contract pursuant to the Laws of New Jersey."
2. "Mrs. Whitehead had breached her contract."
3. "What are the remedies available to the plaintiff?"
4. "Specific performance is a discretionary remedy."
5. "The court holds that whether there will be specific performance of this surrogacy contract depends on whether doing so is in the child's best interest."
6. "Melissa's best interest will be served by being placed in her father's sole custody."
7. "This court therefore will specifically enforce the surrogate parenting agreement to compel delivery of the child to the father and to terminate the mother's parental rights."

But students of medical ethics shouldn't be too quick to commit this reasoning to memory. Harvey Sorkow is a lower-court judge, and lower-court judges rarely make judicial history. This decision is already being appealed, and higher courts will have their say. That process may take years. Meanwhile, state legislatures all over the country, prompted by this case, will be considering bills to regulate, and in some instances to forbid, commercial surrogacy.

They will do so in an environment that has to some extent been poisoned by this case—or at least that is how it seems to me. The trauma of Baby M has made people wary of the whole business. Shortly after Judge Sorkow's decision was rendered, the *New York Times* published a selection of comments from eighteen "legal experts, ethicists, religious leaders, public figures, and others." Of those eighteen, ten were clearly dismayed at the judge's decision to uphold the contract, four were noncommittal, and only four approved of it. Betty Friedan's comments were among the most scathing: she said that the whole concept of surrogacy contracts is based on a "male model" and referred to the infertility clinics as "surrogacy pimps." The distrust created by the Baby M case seems to me most unfortunate. In almost six hundred cases of surrogate motherhood, things have worked out well enough; in only a few cases have there been serious problems. It would be a shame if our legislators reacted only to the problems.

THIRTEEN

ETHICAL THEORY AND BIOETHICS

What is the relation between bioethics and ethical theory? Since bioethics deals with the moral issues that come up in particular cases and ethical theory deals with the standards and principles of moral reasoning, it is natural to think the relation between them might be something like this:

The straightforward-application model. The ethical theory is the starting point, and we apply the theory to the case at hand in order to reach a conclusion about what should be done.

Utilitarianism is the leading example of an ethical theory that might be thought to solve bioethical problems by the straightforward application of its ideas. Utilitarianism says that in any situation we should do what will have the best overall consequences for everyone concerned. If this is our theory, and we want to decide what should be done in a particular case, we simply calculate the likely effects of various actions and choose the one that produces the greatest benefit for the greatest number of people.

But many bioethicists reject this model. In the first place, anyone who approaches an ethical problem by announcing "I hold such-and-such a theory; therefore my conclusion is so-and-so" will be unlikely to get much of a hearing. We want to know what really is best, not just what this or that theory says. Moreover, many investigators doubt that there can be a satisfactory ethical theory of the kind that philosophers have traditionally sought because, they say, morality cannot be codified in a set of rules. Instead, living morally is a matter of cultivating virtuous habits of action, including, perhaps, the kind of "caring" behavior that some feminist writers have argued is central. And in any case, it is said, bioethical controversies are too complicated to be resolved by the simple application of a theory. Theories are general and abstract, while real life is messy and detailed.

If we reject the straightforward-application model, where do we turn for an alternative? One of the most popular options is an approach that focuses on "case studies"—detailed investigations of specific cases that make use of whatever analytical ideas and principles seem most promising in the circumstances at hand. The case-study approach suggests a different conception of the relation between ethical theory and bioethics:

The physics/car-mechanic model. The relation between ethical theory and bioethics is like the relation between physics and automobile repair. Cars operate according to the laws of physics, to be sure; but one doesn't have to know physics to be a good mechanic, and one certainly doesn't "apply" the laws of physics to fix cars. The mechanic's reasoning does not begin with "For every action, there is an equal and opposite reaction." Instead, it begins with something like: "The problem is either electrical or fuel-related. If it's electrical … "

So, like the car mechanic, the bioethicist will rely on midlevel principles, ignoring the lofty but unhelpful pronouncements of high-level theory.

Case Studies and Midlevel Principles

At first blush, the case-study approach seems to permit bioethicists to make progress without resorting to ethical theory. But this turns out to be an illusion. In ethics, theoretical issues crop up everywhere. Deciding about abortion requires that we think about the nature of persons; the allocation of health-care resources raises questions of distributive justice; and arguments about euthanasia make critical assumptions about the meaning and value of human life. Without the resources of ethical theory, we can make little progress in dealing with such matters. It is also an illusion to think that midlevel principles can, by themselves, yield definitive answers to ethical questions.

Consider the case of Theresa Ann Campo Pearson, an anencephalic infant known as "Baby Theresa," who was born in Florida in 1992. There are about one thousand such infants—babies without brains—born each year in the United States, so Baby Theresa's story would not have been newsworthy except for an unusual request by her parents. Knowing that their baby could not live long and that, even if she could, she would never have a conscious life, Baby Theresa's parents volunteered her organs for transplant. They thought her kidneys, liver, heart, lungs, and eyes should go to other children who could benefit from them. The physicians believed this was a good idea, but Florida law would not allow it. So after nine days Baby Theresa died, and by then her organs had deteriorated too much to be transplanted. Other children died as well—the ones who would have received the transplants—but because we do not know which children they were, we tend not to think of their deaths as real costs of the decision.

The newspaper stories about Baby Theresa prompted a great deal of public discussion. Would it have been right to remove the infant's organs, thereby causing her immediate death, to save the other children? A number of professional bioethicists joined the debate, but surprisingly few of them agreed with the parents and physicians. Instead, they appealed to various principles to support letting all the children die. "It just seems too horrifying to use people as means to other people's ends," said one expert. Another explained, "It is unethical to kill in order to save. It's unethical to kill person A to save person B." And a third added: "What the parents are really asking for is: Kill this dying baby so that its organs may be used for someone else. Well, that's really a horrendous proposition."

Here we see midlevel principles at work. ("It is unethical to kill in order to save" is a typical midlevel principle.) Compared to the abstract pronouncements of ethical theory, midlevel principles are much more like everyday moral rules. They express our commonsense understanding of right and wrong. Therefore, it may be argued, we can have greater confidence in decisions that are supported by widely shared midlevel principles than in decisions based on general theories, which are more remote from everyday life and inevitably more controversial.

Of course, these principles are called "midlevel" because they are derived from or justified by higher-level principles. So aren't we just ignoring an important part of the picture if we are content with only the midlevel rules? To this there are two replies. First, it may be maintained that midlevel principles are not derived from higher considerations. They may be viewed as a collection of independent moral principles, each of which is valid in it-self. (Someone taking this view might like the sort of general ethical theory championed by W. D. Ross in the 1930s.) The problem, however, is that within this approach one has no way of adjudicating conflicts between the independent rules. Suppose a different bioethicist, looking at the case of Baby Theresa, felt that the midlevel rule "save as many children as possible" has priority? Or suppose she favored the rule "saving the life of a child with the potential for a satisfying human life is more important than respecting the life of a child without a brain"? Then, of course, the conclusion would be that Theresa's organs should be taken. So the midlevel rules alone cannot provide a definitive answer to the question of what we should do.

Second, and more interesting, it could be pointed out that the same midlevel rules may be endorsed by *more than one* higher-level principle. Kantians, for example, take it as an ultimate principle that people should always be treated as ends-in-themselves; so they would naturally insist that "it is wrong to kill person A to save person B." But utilitarians might also endorse this midlevel principle. They might see it as a useful rule of thumb because following it will have generally good consequences, just as follow-ing other familiar rules—don't lie, don't steal, and so on—have generally good consequences. Thus, these theorists may arrive at the same midlevel rules despite their different starting points. If so, we do not need to worry about which starting point is correct. On the contrary, our confidence in the midlevel principle is increased by the fact that many outlooks endorse it.

Once again, however, a problem arises about how to adjudicate conflicts. Both Kantians and utilitarians would also endorse, as a midlevel rule, that we should save as many children as possible. But when there is a conflict, they might have different recommendations about which midlevel rule should be given priority. By establishing priorities, each theory gives an an-swer to the question of what should be done. But if the theories ultimately lead to different answers, we cannot avoid the larger issue of which theory is correct.

Of course, the failure to reach a definite conclusion need not be regarded as a defect. There is a way to avoid choosing between theories: when dif-ferent lines of reasoning lead to different outcomes, we can conclude that we are faced with an unresolvable dilemma. This may appeal to those who dislike appearing dogmatic. "Not all dilemmas have easy solutions," it may be said, and the doctors and scientists may be left to fend for themselves, with the bioethicist wishing them good luck. According to taste, this may be considered a realistic acknowledgment of the complexity of an issue or a failure of nerve.

The following episode illustrates an additional way in which ethical theory can aid in the analysis of particular cases. In 1995, an international medical team fought an outbreak of Ebola—a devastating virus that destroys cells and causes disintegration of the internal organs as it spreads throughout the body—in Kikwit, Zaire, in which 244 people died. As the epidemic was winding down, a nurse who had worked throughout the crisis was stricken, and the Zairian doctors formulated a desperate plan to save her. This particular strain of Ebola did not kill everyone who became infected; one in five victims survived. So the Zairian physicians proposed to save the nurse by transfusing whole blood from one of the survivors in the hope that whatever antibodies had saved him would be transferred to her.

The foreign doctors adamantly opposed this plan. The donor blood might contain HIV or hepatitis or some other harmful agent, they said. And suppose the diagnosis is mistaken—what if she only has malaria or typhoid? By transfusing the blood, we might actually be giving her Ebola, not curing her of it. Besides, in a similar procedure using animals, the treatment had failed.

The Zairian physicians met privately to discuss these objections. They dismissed the worries about giving the nurse HIV or typhoid; after all, she already had Ebola. As for the possibility that the diagnosis was mistaken, this was also dismissed. "We shouldn't doubt our diagnosis," said one doctor, "we've seen so many cases." They concluded that although their chances of helping the nurse in this way were slight, it was better than nothing.

With the nurse's consent, the transfusion was given, and she recovered. Eight more patients were then given similar transfusions, and seven of them also recovered. These were the last cases in the epidemic. The foreign doctors did not, however, concede that the treatment had worked. "We'll never know," said a physician from the Centers for Disease Control and Prevention in Atlanta. Other possible explanations for the recoveries were offered—late in the epidemic the virus may have become less deadly, or people may have been getting smaller viral loads when infected.

At first glance, it seems that there was little difference in principle between the views of the Zairian physicians and the foreigners. Both groups were concerned, in a straightforward way, with the welfare of the patients: they merely differed about what strategy would stand the best chance of accomplishing their common goal. Yet, on reflection, we can detect a subtle difference between them. The difference concerned their respective attitudes about action versus inaction. In explaining their unanimous decision to proceed with the transfusion, the head of the Zairian team said, "We felt compelled to try *something*." And before the procedure was undertaken, he challenged the European and American physicians: "Tell us if there is something else we can do, and we'll do it." The one thing not acceptable to them was to do nothing: they couldn't just let the nurse die.

The foreigners, by contrast, were more conservative. When in doubt, they preferred not to act, but to wait and see what would happen. The traditional "first principle" of medical ethics is "Do no harm," and the foreign doctors seem to have been strongly motivated by this thought. It is as though they were thinking: *it is worse to cause harm than merely to allow it to happen.* Or perhaps: *One bears greater responsibility for the consequences of one's actions than for the consequences of one's inactions.* The question of who was right, the Zairians or the foreigners, is partly a question about the soundness of these midlevel principles.

A benefit of doing case studies is that they help us to identify the intuitive principles that influence people. Once exposed, such principles may be subjected to critical examination. Are they, in fact, sound? In practice, however, the critical examination is often skipped, and it is assumed that any principle that seems intuitively plausible is a "relevant factor" to be taken into account in analyzing issues. The chief danger of the case-studies approach is that it can degenerate into nothing more than a systematic description of what people happen to believe.

The midlevel principles we have mentioned—that we may not kill one person in order to save another, that we should save as many as possible, and that it is worse to cause harm than to allow it to happen—are among the items often found in the bioethicist's kit bag. Here is a small sample of additional principles that might be invoked as case studies are pursued:

- that people are moral equals—that no one's welfare is more important than anyone else's;
- that personal autonomy, the freedom of each individual to control his or her own life, is especially important;
- that people should always be treated as ends-in-themselves and never as mere means;
- that personal relationships, especially kinship, confer upon people special rights and responsibilities with regard to other people;

- that a person's intention in performing a given action is relevant to determining whether the action is right;
- that we may not do evil that good may come; and
- that what is "natural" is good and what is "unnatural" is bad.

Obviously, different bioethicists will be attracted to different combinations of these ideas; each investigator will accept some of them and reject others. But on what grounds will they be accepted or rejected? Once again, it is an argument for the relevance of ethical theory that a well-supported theory would provide principled evidence or argument concerning which of these ideas are worthy of acceptance and which are not. Each item on this list can be rationally assessed; it need not be judged simply on its intuitive appeal. But such assessments quickly take one into the more abstract matters of ethical theory.

Justifying the Choice of an Ethical Theory

There are other reasons why bioethicists have doubted the value of ethical theory. Some doubts are prompted by the number of theories available. It is not as though there were only one theory on which everyone agrees. Instead, there are numerous theories that conflict with one another. Confronted with such an array, what is the bioethicist to do? Is there any principled way to choose between the competing theories? Or is the choice merely arbitrary?

This issue was raised in the eighteenth century by David Hume, who argued that morals are ultimately based on "sentiment, not reason." Hume knew that moral judgments require reasons in their support, but he pointed out that every chain of reasoning leads back to some first principle that is unjustified. If we ask for a justification of that principle, perhaps one can be given, but only by appealing to still another unjustified assumption, and so on forever. We can never justify all our assumptions; reasoning must begin somewhere. A utilitarian might begin by assuming that what is important is maximizing welfare. Someone else, with a different cast of mind, might make a different assumption. But reason alone cannot justify the choice of one starting point over another.

Hume is not the only philosopher who has objected to exaggerated claims about what unaided reason can accomplish. A more recent critic,

Alasdair MacIntyre, advances a different sort of objection. MacIntyre argues that "rationality" has meaning only within a historical tradition. The idea of impartial reason justifying norms of conduct binding on all people is, he says, an illusion fostered by the Enlightenment. In reality, historical traditions set standards of inquiry for those working within them. But the standards of rational thinking differ from tradition to tradition, and so we cannot speak of "what reason requires" in any universal sense. In his 1988 book *Whose Justice? Which Rationality?* MacIntyre writes: "What the enlightenment made us for the most part blind to and what we now need to recover is ... a conception of rational inquiry as embodied in a tradition; a conception according to which the standards of rational justification themselves emerge from and are part of a history in which they are vindicated by the way in which they transcend the limitations of and provide remedies for the defects of their predecessors within the history of that same tradition." Thus, in MacIntyre's view, the reasons that would be adduced by a modern liberal in arguing, say, that slavery is unjust would not necessarily be acceptable to an Aristotelian, whose standards of rationality are different; and the search for standards that transcend the two traditions is a fool's quest. No such tradition-neutral standards exist, except, perhaps, for purely formal principles such as noncontradiction, which are too weak to yield substantive results.

What are we to make of all this? If these arguments are correct, then no ethical theory can be anything more than an expression of the theorist's sentiments or the historical tradition he or she represents. But before we accept such discouraging conclusions, there are some additional points that should be kept in mind.

First, even if "reason alone" cannot determine what ultimate principles we should accept, this does not mean the choice must be arbitrary. There are numerous constraints on what principles we may choose, and these constraints provide grounds for hoping that reasonable people will be able to reach agreement. All people have the same basic needs—food, warmth, friendship, protection from danger, meaningful work, to name only a few. We all suffer pain, and we are all susceptible to disease. All of us are products of the same evolutionary forces, which have made us at least partially altruistic beings. And we are social animals who live in communities, so we must accept the rules that are necessary for social living. Together, these facts and others like them impose striking limits on what sort of principles it is rational for us to accept.

Second, it may be true, as MacIntyre says, that the standards of rational thinking differ from one historical tradition to another. But this does not mean that traditions are immune from criticism. Some moral traditions depend on theological assumptions that are inconsistent or arbitrary. Others make assumptions about the nature of the world that are at odds with what we have learned from modern science. Still others are based on untenable views about human nature. Thus, there is no need to assume that all traditions are equal. At the very least, those that do not depend on what Hume called "superstition and false religion" are preferable to those that do.

Bearing these points in mind, we might be a little more optimistic about what reason can accomplish. We might hope to discover ethical arguments that appeal to rational people generally and not just to some subset of people who have agreeable sentiments or form part of an agreeable tradition. But abstract considerations will take us only so far; the real proof that such arguments are possible is to display one. A test case might be slavery, which, as we have noted, is condemned by modern liberal culture but accepted within other traditions. Is there an argument against slavery that must be acknowledged by every reasonable person, regardless of the tradition of which he or she is a part?

The primary argument against slavery is this: All forms of slavery involve treating some people differently from the rest, depriving them of liberty and subjecting them to a host of evils. But it is unjust to set some people apart for different treatment unless there is something about them that justifies setting them apart—unless, that is, there is a *relevant difference* between them and the others. But there are no such differences between humans that could justify setting some of them apart as slaves; therefore, slavery is unjust.

Should this argument be compelling not only to modern liberals, but to those who live in different sorts of societies, with different sorts of traditions? Consider a slave society such as Aristotle's Athens. According to one estimate, there were as many slaves in Athens, in proportion to the population, as there were in the slave states of America before the Civil War. Aristotle himself defended slavery, arguing that some people are "slaves by nature" because of their inferior rationality. Yet the resources available within Aristotle's own tradition seem to have been sufficient for an appreciation of slavery's injustice. Aristotle reported that "Some regard the control of a slave by a master as contrary to nature. In their view the distinction of master and slave is due to law or convention: there is no natural difference between them: the relation of master and slave is based on force, and being so based has no warrant in justice."

Aristotle did not share this enlightened view. Plainly, though, he accepted the principle that differences in treatment are unjustified unless there are relevant differences between people. In fact, this is just a modern version of an idea that he advances in the *Nicomachean Ethics*—namely, that like cases should be treated alike and different cases differently. That is why he felt it necessary to defend slavery by contending that slaves possess an inferior degree of rationality. But this is a claim that can be shown to be false by evidence that should be counted as evidence as much by him as by us. Therefore, even on Aristotle's own terms, slavery should be recognizable as unjust. And in saying this we are not simply transporting our standards of rationality back into a culture that was "different."

Perhaps, then, we may hope for an ethical theory that will specify norms acceptable to all reasonable people. Justifying such a theory, however, will not be easy. (But then, why should it be? Why should justifying a general theory in ethics be easier than justifying a general theory in, say, physics or psychology?) The process will include assessing our intuitions about particular cases; looking at a host of arguments about individual behavior and social policy; identifying and evaluating midlevel principles; bringing to bear what we know about human nature and human social systems; considering the claims of religion; and then trying to fit it all together in one unified scheme of understanding. If there is indeed one best overall ethical theory, it is likely to appear as many lines of inquiry converge. The fact that there is still so much disagreement among ethical theorists may be due not to the impossibility of the project, but to its complexity and to the fact that secular ethical theory is still a young subject.

What does this mean for the question with which we started, about the relation between ethical theory and bioethics? We have seen that the physics/car-repair model won't do because case studies cannot be conducted independently of theoretical concerns. We are now in a position to appreciate more fully why the simple-application model won't do either. It is not that ethical theory is useless or that real life is too messy and complicated to be approached using its tools. Rather, it is that the simple-application model represents the relation between ethical theory and bioethics as a one-way affair. In reality, however, bioethics contributes to ethical theory as well as benefiting from it. In studying cases and identifying and analyzing midlevel principles, bioethicists are pursuing one of the many lines of inquiry that contribute to the development of ethical theory. In this sense, bioethics is part of ethical theory. One flows into the other.

Considering all this, we might try a different analogy that provides a more satisfactory way of understanding the relation between ethical theory and bioethics.

The biology/medicine model. The relation between ethical theory and bioethics is like the relation between biology and medicine. A physician who knows nothing of biology, but who approaches her patients in the spirit of a car mechanic with a kit bag of practical techniques might do a generally serviceable job. But she would not be as good as the physician who does know the relevant sciences. The difference would come out when new or tricky problems arise, requiring more than the rote application of already-familiar techniques. To deal with the difficult problems, she might find herself turning to the scientific researchers for help or even turning temporarily to more fundamental research herself. And what she learns from the cases she encounters in her practice might, in turn, have significance for the further development of the sciences.

At its best, bioethics does not operate independently of ethical theory; but neither does it proceed by simply "applying" a theory to particular cases. Instead, there is an interplay between theory and case study that benefits both.

References

Aristotle. *The Politics.* Translated by Ernest Barker. London: Oxford University Press, 1946.

Briggs, David. "Baby Theresa Case Raises Ethics Questions." *Champaign-Urbana News Gazette,* March 31, 1992, A6.

Halpern, Elliott, and Simcha Jacobovici. "Plague Fighters." On *Nova* (Public Broadcasting System), February 6, 1996.

Hume, David. *An Inquiry Concerning the Principles of Morals.* Originally published in 1751. Appendix I.

MacIntyre, Alasdair. *Whose Justice? Which Rationality?* Notre Dame, Ind.: University of Notre Dame Press, 1988.

Ross, W. D. *The Right and the Good.* Oxford: Oxford University Press, 1930.

ART

FOURTEEN

MOVIES

Knowledge makes a difference to what we enjoy because it makes a difference in what we perceive. To a person who knows nothing about music, for example, Beethoven's third symphony may sound like a confused mass of noise. Listening to it may be quite boring. But then, if he (or she) learns the difference between various woodwinds and strings, he will begin to *hear* the woodwinds and strings. If he learns about symphonic form, about themes and variations, about major and minor keys, he will begin to hear all that, too. Soon, instead of a mass of undifferentiated sound, he will be hearing a complex and wonderful musical composition.

To learn means to put one's feelings at risk: because the acquisition of knowledge makes such a difference, it can change the way we feel about things. Someone who likes country music may, after learning a lot about music, come not to like it so much. It is no accident that those who know the most tend to think better of J. S. Bach than Conway Twitty. On the other hand, it sometimes happens that our earlier feelings are confirmed. Learning something about music will increase, not decrease, one's respect for the compositions of Lennon and McCartney.

Movies are the one new art form that has developed in our century. The rapid development of the new art has been possible because movies have been so popular. Indeed, "popular" is an understatement: the movie business is the ultimate in glamour; to be associated with it is to be a celebrity.

And, of course, one does not have to be *educated* to enjoy movies: the hundreds of millions of dollars in admissions every year are not paid only by a small elite in pursuit of "art."

Nevertheless, what one knows about movies will make a big difference in what one perceives and enjoys, just as it makes a difference in connection with any art. The purpose of this essay is to suggest some ways in which one might think about the movies to increase one's knowledge and heighten one's powers of judgment. I will assume that the reader has seen lots of films (haven't we all?), but I will *not* assume that you have thought much about the experience. Thus, I will emphasize the simplest, most basic elements of movie "education." I will concentrate on the movie equivalents of the woodwinds and strings and major and minor keys.

Movies and the Other Arts

One way to begin thinking about movies is to ask about the similarities and differences between them and other arts. Plays and literature come immediately to mind; in all three we find stories, characters, and dialogue.

In fact, movies are often *based on* novels and plays, and viewers familiar with the "original" may be tempted to assess the movie by comparing them. This is usually a mistake. Even when movies are based on materials from another medium, they should be judged "on their own." A movie should stand or fall according to what it is, not according to how it compares with something else.

However, some moviemakers fall into the trap of *not* making films that are independent of their sources. They only half-tell the story of the original, so that what you see in the movie makes little sense considered on its own. The movie *True Confessions*, about two brothers, one a cop and one a priest (played by Robert Duvall and Robert DeNiro), was based on the fine book of the same title by John Gregory Dunne. It is *almost* a fine movie, but it is marred by episodes that make no sense apart from the background provided only in the novel (the suicide of one character, for example, is explained in the book but is wholly unmotivated in the movie). This is an especially annoying type of failure.

Because a writer can expound the thoughts and feelings of his characters in a straightforward manner, a novel can explore the inner life much more effectively than a movie. On the other hand, by *showing* a face or a landscape, a movie can provide a much more vivid sense of externals than a novelist ever could. An interesting exercise is this: as you read a novel, ask yourself whether parts of it could be translated into cinematic terms and how. You will find that the answer is sometimes yes, sometimes no, and sometimes "with great difficulty!" If you read a novel that has been made into a movie, and you haven't seen the film, ask yourself how *you* would translate it. Then see the movie, and compare your ideas with the work of the filmmakers. The results will be interesting, and you can't help but learn something. .

Superficially, plays and movies seem very much alike. But in reality they are quite different, and the differences stand out when plays are filmed. Plays are, usually, much more "talky" than films, with a lot less action. They are also confined to one or two settings. Thus, the movie version of a play will seem much slower and more confined than other movies.

There are also things that can be done in plays that are very difficult to do in films. For example, in a play a character can make a speech to the audience. This seems, in context, natural enough—it is one of the theater's established conventions. But in a movie it seems terribly artificial. This was a problem that the filmers of *Equus* did not solve—they had Richard Burton deliver his big speeches staring into the camera. It did not work.

Equus also illustrates another important difference between movies and plays. In the play, horses were represented by actors wearing stylized heads and hooves; in the movie, of course, real horses were used. As a result, what was powerful and symbolic on stage became banal on film. Like many other theatrical devices, these turned out to be sui generis—not transferable to another medium.

Before leaving this subject, we should notice what actors say about the difference between movies and the stage for them. Actors typically regard the theater as the "real" medium for performers, with movies a weak substitute. Why? The reason is that, on stage, actors are able to give whole, integrated performances, with instant audience response. In movies, on the other hand, they give their performances in little bits and pieces. A few seconds may be filmed, then a long pause, then another few seconds. The filming may take months, and the "performance" that is ultimately seen on the screen may owe as much to the film editor's art as to the actor's. Thus, it is said that the stage is an actor's medium, while film belongs to others.

The Moviemakers

When we think of movies, we tend to think of movie stars—Clint Eastwood, Al Pacino, Meryl Streep. Certainly, the actors are the most conspicuous of the moviemakers. But movies are the joint products of many hands, and to increase one's understanding of them one must learn something about the contributions of the other artists.

The director is perhaps the single most important person in the making of a movie, so much so that some critics think of the director as the "author" of the film. He is the one in charge as the film is made; the others take their directions from him. Thus, the film is what he decides it will be; it reflects his style and sensibilities.

The idea of the director-as-author is a helpful analogy. The first thing we want to know about a book is "Who wrote it?" Similarly, the first question one might ask about a movie is "Who directed it?" If you read a book you like, you might want to try another by the same author—and if you read several books by the same author, then when you pick up another one you know more or less what to expect. The same goes for films. Suppose you are trying to decide whether to plunk down four dollars to see *Streets of Fire*—it will help to know that the movie was directed by Walter Hill, who also made *The Warriors* and *48 Hrs.*

A knowledgeable moviegoer will learn what to expect from different directors. Alfred Hitchcock made psychological thrillers, done with humor and great style; Sam Peckinpah makes tough, violent movies with a distinctly "macho" flavor; and George Lucas and Steven Spielberg make escapist fantasies with spectacular effects. Of course, a director, like any artist, may surprise us by going against expectations. Yet each one has his own recognizable style.

Other critics object to the analogy of director-as-author because, they say, there is no one contributor who is *the* author of a movie. The medium is too collaborative for that. Consider the tremendous importance of the writer, who devises the plot and puts the words into the characters' mouths, or the editor, who takes the bits of film and puts them together to make a whole.

The editor's contribution is one of the least appreciated. What we think of as a single scene is actually an assembly of many separate shots, spliced together. *How* they are put together can make the difference between an exciting scene and a dull scene. The next time you see the shower scene from *Psycho,* notice the editing. Directors who want to exercise artistic control over their films often demand the right to supervise the editing or even to do it themselves. The producers, whose money is at stake, may respond by reserving final approval to themselves.

There are, of course, large numbers of other artists whose talents contribute to the finished product: the set and costume designers, the cinematographers, the art directors, the composers and arrangers of music, and the special-effects people. Sometimes a movie will obviously show off some of these talents more than others. *Blade Runner* has a wonderfully seedy atmosphere; in a way, the art director, and not Harrison Ford, was the "star" of this film. In movies like *Thief* and *Body Heat*, the musical background is especially noteworthy. In *Star Wars* and *An American Werewolf in London*, the quality of the special effects is obviously important. With the recent popularity of escapist fantasy, special-effects people like Douglas Trumbull have become "stars" in their own right.

The moral is: when you watch a movie, pay attention to the contributions being made by these different elements. Don't just say, "Well, in general I sort of like it." Instead, think about the *parts* of the film. How is the music? the editing? the writing? the costumes? Then, when the last scene is over, don't get up and leave while the credits are being shown. Stay and read the credits. After a while, you will begin to see familiar names and make connections. You'll learn a lot about movies that way, and you'll find that this kind of active, critical viewing makes going to the movies more fun.

The Characters and the Plot

Like novels, movies tell stories. (For lack of space, I will not discuss documentaries and other nonfiction films here.) Thus, we may expect the same qualities from them that we expect from good novels: at a minimum, the characters should be interesting and the story should make sense. It is surprising how many movies—even famous and well-regarded movies—fail to pass this basic test. Both Kubrick's *2001: A Space Odyssey* and Spielberg's *Close Encounters of the Third Kind* had plots with gaping holes.

Sometimes a little knowledge of how pictures are made enables one to understand how plots get garbled: in the editing process, a film may be shortened to fit the theater schedules (showings typically start every two hours—that's good for business), and a scene that would have explained everything ends up on the cutting-room floor. This sort of thing happens much more often than filmmakers like to think about. An extreme example is Sergio Leone's *Once Upon a Time in America,* the gangster film starring Robert DeNiro. The original version of the movie, seen in Europe, was three hours and forty-five minutes long; but for its American release more than an hour was cut out!—and the "plot " of the shorter version, not surprisingly, made little sense. Leone denounced the shortened version, disavowing any responsibility for it.

It is not necessary for a plot to be believable or realistic, but it is necessary for a story to be told *consistently.* Joe Dante's *Gremlins* (which was marketed as Steven Spielberg's *Gremlins* obviously because Spielberg, the producer, has a better-known name) violated a cardinal rule of storytelling when, without any explanation or other preparation, the little monsters began to sing Christmas carols, wear cute little costumes, and drink beers in bars. Where did the costumes come from? How are the monsters supposed to have learned to behave in these ways? Admirers of this movie (I am not one of them) may reply that these are churlish questions—after all, they may say, this was a *fantasy.* But I like fantasies as much as anyone; the complaint is that it was an *inconsistent* fantasy, which did not play fair with the audience. A fantasy may have any wild premise it wants—in fact, the wilder the better—*but,* once the premise is established, the picture should proceed logically from it. It is no fair simply throwing absurdities in, with no explanation, even in a fantasy.

Occasionally a movie will not have much of a plot but will nevertheless succeed because it has wonderful characters. *Tender Mercies* introduces us to people we care about; repeated viewings are like visits with old friends. Such movies often exhibit another quality of fine art: a realism, a truthfulness, that makes us see ourselves and our lives more clearly. *Tender Mercies* reveals more about what it means to love someone than all the maudlin "romantic" pictures put together.

Reflecting on the characters in a movie is a good way to size it up. Compare, for example, *Porky's* and *Fast Times at Ridgemont High,* two pictures that might be lumped together because they both feature teenagers obsessed with sex. But *Porky's* is a despicable movie, while *Fast Times* is really pretty good. Why? Part of the explanation is that in *Porky's* every single character is a creep. It isn't just that they are mean and boring and unlikable people; there is, in addition, a kind of *hatefulness* in their relations with one another. Who'd want to spend five minutes with any of them? In *Fast Times,* on the other hand, we have an interesting variety of people trying to cope with some funny and even poignant situations. We end up liking them and wishing them well.

What happens when a moviemaker neglects to provide either an interesting plot or interesting characters? One answer might be: *Indiana Jones and the Temple of Doom*. There's a lesson to be learned from this disappointing film—namely, that there is a big difference between a satisfying story and a succession of cheap thrills. A good plot is a mixture of various elements. It has *pacing*. Consider *Raiders of the Lost Ark*, a much better movie. We are introduced to the hero and get to know something about him; he is given a job to do that, while surely fantastical, has some interest and point; he then visits a variety of exotic locations for his adventures. The adventures themselves are well paced: after a thrilling escape from danger, the film moves for a time at a more leisurely pace and then builds to the next action sequence. *Indiana Jones*, by contrast, rushes from one hair-raising brush with death to the next—they *seem* to come every sixty seconds—and has no story worth following because it leaves no time for anything so mundane as background, plot development, or getting acquainted with the characters.

The Special Qualities of Good Movies

Unfortunately, there is no simple formula that describes the qualities of a good film because the best movies, like other works of art, have qualities that are not shared by other films. The better the film, the more likely this is to be true. The best movies will surprise you with virtues you didn't anticipate. They won't be easy to categorize or explain. To appreciate a really fine movie, we have to discern what is *special* about it.

Let me give two examples.

The first thing one might notice about *The Godfather*, Francis Ford Coppola's 1972 film about the Mafia, is its superb cast, which includes Marlon Brando, Al Pacino, and Robert Duvall. Each gives a performance that can be watched again and again. There is a special pleasure in seeing the greatest screen actor of the older generation, Brando, playing with our best younger actor, Pacino. At the end of the movie, when Don Vito Corleone (Brando) dies and his son Michael (Pacino) takes over leadership of the family, it is as though the mantle of authority among actors is also being passed on. (Unfortunately, this may be too literally true. Brando has not played a significant role since then and shows no signs of wanting to.)

The Godfather is in some ways representative of a familiar genre, the gangster movie. Certainly it has all the qualities we like in such movies: the clash between good and evil, excitement, controlled violence, memorable characters. We can enjoy it, easily enough, just on this level. But that is not what makes it a masterpiece.

It is a masterpiece for three reasons. First, underlying the story of power struggles in organized crime there is a deeper story of individual corruption. Michael Corleone is, at the outset, not a part of the "family business." He is the son destined for a legitimate life, who may one day be "Governor Corleone, Senator Corleone." But he is inexorably pulled into the life of the family, until at the end he is its leader. (For most of the movie, we think the title refers to the old man, Don Vito. At the end, we realize it refers to Michael.) We see Michael transformed from a sensible, "straight," even idealistic young man into the leader of all organized crime in New York. And it is not greed or viciousness that accounts for the transformation—it is, paradoxically, his *good* qualities that bring him down: his loyalty and love for his family, and the brains and strength of character that enable him, but not his brothers, to save it. He doesn't want his life to go this way, but we see him drawn in deeper and deeper, until he cannot turn back. Although it is a story told on a grand scale, in human terms it is absolutely convincing.

Second, the movie draws us into an alternate moral universe. It is an unsettling, but illuminating experience. The characters do not live by ordinary rules—they break the law, they bribe policemen and judges, they commit murder over and over again—yet they *do* have rules. They live by a strict code of honor, existing within the larger culture but not as part of it. The disturbing thing is that we are so drawn into this "society" that, while watching the movie, we begin to feel the force of its obligations and to respect its code. The "bad guys" begin to seem not so much bad as living by a different set of values. The film accomplishes this by showing not just gangsters, but people who have evolved a way of life—beginning in Sicily—that has its own dignity and its own virtues. Owing to the way this ethnic group is portrayed, we learn to feel what it would be like to *be* different from what we are. Italian-American groups protested that *The Godfather* gave a false picture of Italian-American life: "We are not like that," they said. Perhaps not, but it doesn't matter. Even if the world created in this film were entirely fictional, it would remain high art to have created it so effectively.

But none of this would work if the filmmakers were not expert in their craft, and that is the third thing that makes this a splendid film. The elements mentioned above—the art design, the music, the writing, the editing—work together beautifully. The sense of time, place, and social detail is remarkable. The wedding scene that opens the movie is in itself a little masterpiece, perfectly realized in every detail—we know immediately that we have stepped into another world. The conclusion, playing off the baptism of Michael Corleone's child against the murders of his rivals, is a powerful summation of the elements of this way of life: family, religion, ruthlessness. In every way, it is a terrific movie.

Martin Brest's *Going in Style* is very different from *The Godfather.* In fact, it is unlike *any* other movie with which I am familiar. It is about three old men, played by George Burns, Art Carney, and Lee Strasburg. Their lives have become unbearably empty—they are "senior citizens" irrelevant to the rest of society—and so they decide, for something to do, to rob a bank. They bring it off, have a fling in Las Vegas, two of them die, and the third ends up in prison.

But, as with so many good films, no simple plot summary can convey its special qualities. It is, as one might expect with Burns and Carney in the cast, a funny movie—one laughs a lot. Their preparations for the robbery, as they choose disguises and try to figure out which bullets fit their borrowed guns, are especially hilarious. But even though it is full of laughs, the picture is by no means a comedy. More than anything else, it is about growing old. We see the three men sitting silently on a park bench and making their morning coffee, and these scenes stick in our memories more vividly than the funny scenes. The relation between Art Carney and his nephew—the nephew is in the midst of a life, while Carney's life is, in effect, over—strikes one as absolutely right and true. When death comes, we think: yes, that is what it must be like, both for the one who dies and for the ones who remain.

I must confess, however, that if I heard a movie described in this way, I would not be eager to see it. We want movies to entertain us, and being taught what it's like to grow old hardly sounds like fun. Yet what makes this movie special is that it *is* entertaining—enormously so—while at the same time it deepens our appreciation of the serious matters with which it deals. As in *Tender Mercies,* we come to like these characters a lot, and we enjoy the time we spend with them. And how many pictures could include both a zany bank robbery and a sad monologue about the estrangement of parents from children, without either seeming out of place?

Distinguishing What We Like from What We Think Is Good

The element of personal taste can never be eliminated from our assessment of art, and why should it? The arts appeal to us, first and foremost, because we *enjoy* them. This is certainly plain enough in the case of movies. People pay millions of dollars each year to see them not because they are instructive or edifying, but because they are fun. It is tempting, therefore, to react to them purely in terms of our likes and dislikes.

What we like, however, is not the same as what we think is good. To give one example: I like *The Competition*, a sappy romance starring Richard Dreyfus and Amy Irving, a lot. It's the story of two young pianists at an international competition; they are competitors, and naturally they fall in love. Will they get together, or won't they? I liked the movie because I liked the characters, and I was pulling for them. The corny ending made me happy. But I would *not* cite this as a particularly *good* movie.

What's the difference? The difference is that when we judge a movie (or anything else, for that matter) to be *good*, we must have *reasons* for thinking it so. If someone says that *Conan the Barbarian* was a good movie, you may ask *why* he thinks so. The answer must be some account of the qualities of the movie that support that critical judgment. Those reasons can be discussed, examined, weighed, and in this case almost certainly found wanting. On the other hand, if he merely says, "I *liked Conan*," no reasons are necessary: he is merely stating a fact about his own reaction, a fact that can hardly be disputed. I do not say that *The Competition* was a particularly good movie because I do not think that a critical examination of its qualities will support that judgment. But I liked it anyway.

As you think about movies, it is important to bear this distinction in mind. Each of us has his personal favorites that may or may not withstand critical scrutiny. And in one sense it doesn't matter: we can enjoy our favorites even if they *don't* hold up under inspection. Yet it is also important to be clear about what we think is good. Here is a worthwhile exercise: make a list of the movies you especially like, paying no attention at first to the question of whether you think they are good. Then look at the list. Ask yourself what those films have in common, if anything. (The answer may teach you something about your own tastes.) Then ask whether you think these are *good* films. If you say "yes," then ask *why* you think so—What about them appeals to you? This is a simple, but enlightening exercise. A more sophisticated exercise is to compile a list of films you think are good, but that you did not personally enjoy that much. When you can do this and provide some reasons for your critical judgments, you will have advanced far in your appreciation of movies.

A Final Example

One evening you notice that a movie called *The Conversation* is on the TV late show. *Who is the director?* Checking your handy reference guide, you see that it is a 1974 effort by Francis Ford Coppola, who directed *The Godfather.* Coppola's later films included a number of disappointments—films such as *Apocalypse Now* (a noble failure with flashes of brilliance, but a failure nonetheless), *The Outsiders,* and *One from the Heart.* You think it may be interesting to see what Coppola did immediately following his great triumph with *The Godfather,* so you tune in to find out.

What about the plot? The picture stars Gene Hackman as Harry Caul, a professional "surveillance technician," a man who specializes in eavesdropping and wiretapping. He has been hired to record the conversation of a couple walking in a crowded park at noontime. It seems impossible, but Caul brings it off. But he is disturbed at what he hears—it sounds as if the couple are in danger. He (and we) begin to suspect that Caul's employers are planning to murder them. Our suspicions increase, until at the end we discover that the reverse is true: the couple were plotting to kill the man who hired Caul. Now, as we remember the recorded conversation, we realize it was ambiguous and could have been interpreted either way! It is a neat plot that absorbs us fully.

What about the characters? In addition to its mystery story, the movie turns out to be a character study of Harry Caul. A professional invader of other people's privacy, he is obsessed with his own: he has multiple locks on his apartment door; he doesn't want other people to know his telephone number (he even denies he has a telephone in his home, although he does have one); he is furious when, as an innocent prank, another surveillance specialist plants a microphone on him at a party; and at the end, when he suspects his apartment is bugged, he destroys it completely in a pathetic attempt to find and expel the electronic intruder. Caul is also haunted by the idea that he may be responsible for the uses to which his work is put—he tries to deny it, but this is an attitude he ultimately cannot maintain as he comes to believe the couple will be murdered. We don't like him much—it isn't that kind of movie—but we are fascinated by him nonetheless.

What about the parts of the movie? You will observe that the editing is especially noteworthy: bits of the conversation, recorded by Caul at the beginning of the film, are repeated at regular intervals, building suspense and reinforcing our (false) perception that the couple are in danger. When, at the end, we hear it one last time, we realize the ambiguity we had not perceived before. You may also notice how well the settings establish the mood of the film. Harry Caul and his assistant work in a corner of an otherwise deserted warehouse—a cold, stark place, but one that conveys a kind of emotionless professionalism—reflecting the attitude with which Caul would like to approach his job, but which ultimately he cannot maintain.

What is special about this film? Like *The Godfather*, this film shows us another world—this time, the world of a man operating at the fringes of society. There is great interest merely in seeing how Caul does his unusual job (he is very good at it, and we get a glimpse of what professionalism in this area means). Caul attends a convention of surveillance specialists, complete with seminars and manufacturers' booths showing off the latest bugging equipment, and we realize that here is a whole sleazy subculture of which we have been unaware. But in the end it is Caul's character that defines what the picture is about: it is about the importance of privacy, and about the impossibility of escaping responsibility for one's conduct.

You conclude, then, that this is not only an enjoyable picture, but a good one as well.

James Rachels's Curriculum Vitae

DATES

Born May 30, 1941, in Columbus, Georgia
Died September 5, 2003, in Birmingham, Alabama

JAMES RACHELS'S LITERARY EXECUTOR

Professor David Rachels
Department of English
Virginia Military Institute
Lexington, VA 24450
rachelsda@vmi.edu

EDUCATION

B.A., Mercer University, 1962
Ph.D., University of North Carolina at Chapel Hill, 1967

ACADEMIC JOBS

University of Richmond, 1966–68
New York University, 1968–72
University of Miami, 1972–77
Duke University, 1975
University of Alabama at Birmingham, 1977–2003
    Chair, Department of Philosophy, 1977–79
    Dean, School of Humanities, 1978–83
    Academic Vice President (acting), 1983
    University Professor, 1984–2003

BOOKS

The Elements of Moral Philosophy. New York: Random House, 1986; 2d ed.,
    McGraw-Hill, 1992; 3rd ed., 1999; 4th ed., 2003. Also published in Ital-
    ian, Portuguese, Chinese, Indonesian, and Korean. Fifth edition (by Stu-
    art Rachels), 2006.
The End of Life: Euthanasia and Morality. Oxford: Oxford University Press,
    1986. Also published in Dutch, Serbo-Croatian, Italian, and Japanese.
Created from Animals: The Moral Implications of Darwinism. Oxford: Oxford
    University Press, 1990. Also published in Italian and Japanese.
Can Ethics Provide Answers? And Other Essays in Moral Philosophy. Totowa,
    N.J.: Rowman and Littlefield, 1997.
Problems from Philosophy. New York: McGraw-Hill, 2005.
The Legacy of Socrates: Essays in Moral Philosophy. New York: Columbia Uni-
    versity Press, 2006.

BOOKS EDITED

Moral Problems: A Collection of Philosophical Essays. 1st ed. New York: Harper
    and Row, 1971; 2d ed., 1975; 3rd ed., 1978.
Philosophical Issues: A Contemporary Introduction (coeditor, with Frank A.
    Tillman). New York: Harper and Row, 1972.
Understanding Moral Philosophy. Encino, Calif.: Dickenson, 1976.

The Right Thing to Do. New York: Random House, 1989; 2d ed., McGraw-Hill, 1999; 3rd ed., 2003; 4th ed. (with Stuart Rachels), 2006.

Ethical Theory 1: The Question of Objectivity. Oxford: Oxford University Press, 1998.

Ethical Theory 2: Theories about How We Should Live. Oxford: Oxford University Press, 1998.

The Truth about the World: Basic Readings in Philosophy. New York: McGraw-Hill, 2005.

ARTICLES (MOST REPRINTS NOT LISTED)

"Wants, Reasons, and Justifications." *Philosophical Quarterly* 18 (1968): 299–309.

"On Liking." *Analysis* 29 (1969): 143–44.

"Wanting and Willing." *Philosophical Studies* 20 (1969): 9–13.

"On Moral Absolutism." *Australasian Journal of Philosophy* 48 (1970): 338–53. Reprinted with revisions as "Lying and the Ethics of Absolute Rules" in James Rachels, *Can Ethics Provide Answers? And Other Essays in Moral Philosophy.*

"Egoism and Moral Scepticism." In *A New Introduction to Philosophy,* edited by Steven M. Cahn, 423–34. New York: Harper and Row, 1971.

"God and Human Attitudes." *Religious Studies* 7 (1971): 325–37. Reprinted with revisions as "God and Moral Autonomy" in James Rachels, *Can Ethics Provide Answers? And Other Essays in Moral Philosophy.*

"Reasons for Action." *Canadian Journal of Philosophy* 1 (1971): 173–87.

"Evaluating from a Point of View." *Journal of Value Inquiry* 6 (1972): 144–57.

"Political Assassination." In *Assassination,* edited by Harold Zellner, 9–21. Cambridge, Mass.: Schenkman, 1974.

"Two Arguments Against Ethical Egoism." *Philosophia* 4 (1974): 297–314.

"Active and Passive Euthanasia." *New England Journal of Medicine* 292 (January 9, 1975): 78–80. Reprinted in roughly three hundred anthologies. Reprinted with revisions in James Rachels, *Can Ethics Provide Answers? And Other Essays in Moral Philosophy.*

"Why Privacy Is Important." *Philosophy and Public Affairs* 4 (1975): 323–33. Reprinted with revisions in James Rachels, *Can Ethics Provide Answers? And Other Essays in Moral Philosophy.*

"Do Animals Have a Right to Liberty?" In *Animal Rights and Human Obligations*, edited by Peter Singer and Tom Regan, 205–23. Englewood Cliffs, N.J.: Prentice-Hall, 1976. A revised part of this essay was incorporated into "Do Animals Have Rights?" in James Rachels, *Can Ethics Provide Answers? And Other Essays in Moral Philosophy.*

"Fetal Research." *In Vitro* 13 (1977): 732–38.

"John Dewey and the Truth about Ethics." In *New Studies in the Philosophy of John Dewey,* edited by Steven M. Cahn, 149–71. Hanover, N.H.: University Press of New England, 1977. Reprinted with revisions in James Rachels, *Can Ethics Provide Answers? And Other Essays in Moral Philosophy.*

"Medical Ethics and the Rule Against Killing." In *Philosophical Medical Ethics,* edited by Stuart Spicker and H. T. Engelhardt Jr., 63–69. Dordrecht, Netherlands: Reidel, 1977.

"Vegetarianism and 'the Other Weight Problem.'" In *World Hunger and Moral Obligation,* edited by William Aiken and Hugh LaFollette, 180–93. Englewood Cliffs, N.J.: Prentice-Hall, 1977. A revised part of this essay was incorporated into "The Moral Argument for Vegetarianism," in James Rachels, *Can Ethics Provide Answers? And Other Essays in Moral Philosophy.*

"Can the Egoist Have It Both Ways?" *Philosophia* 8 (1978): 425–28.

"What People Deserve." In *Justice and Economic Distribution,* edited by John Arthur and William H. Shaw, 150–63. Englewood Cliffs, N.J.: Prentice-Hall, 1978. Reprinted in James Rachels, *Can Ethics Provide Answers? And Other Essays in Moral Philosophy.* However, it is so extensively revised and expanded in that volume that it is virtually a new essay.

"Active Euthanasia with Parental Consent: Commentary." *Hastings Center Report* (October 1979): 19–20.

"Euthanasia, Killing, and Letting Die." In *Ethical Issues Relating to Life and Death,* edited by John Ladd, 146–63. Oxford: Oxford University Press, 1979.

"Killing and Starving to Death." *Philosophy* 54 (1979): 159–71.

"Can Ethics Provide Answers?" *Hastings Center Report* (June 1980): 32–40. Reprinted with substantial revisions in James Rachels, *Can Ethics Provide Answers? And Other Essays in Moral Philosophy.*

"Euthanasia." In *Matters of Life and Death,* edited by Tom Regan, 28–66. New York: Random House, 1980. Revised versions of this essay are in the second and third editions of the book (1986, 1993).

"When Does a Person Die?" *Alabama Journal of Medical Sciences* 17 (1980): 328–29.

"More Impertinent Distinctions." In *Biomedical Ethics*, edited by Thomas Mappes and Jane Zembaty, 355–59. New York: McGraw-Hill, 1981.

"Reasoning about Killing and Letting Die." *Southern Journal of Philosophy* 19 (1981): 465–73.

"Barney Clark's Key." *Hastings Center Report* (April 1983): 17–19.

"Do Animals Have a Right to Life?" In *Ethics and Animals*, edited by Harlan B. Miller and William H. Williams, 275–84. Clifton, N.J.: Humana Press, 1983. Parts of this essay were incorporated into "Do Animals Have Rights?" and "The Moral Argument for Vegetarianism," in James Rachels, *Can Ethics Provide Answers? And Other Essays in Moral Philosophy*.

"The Sanctity of Life." In *Biomedical Ethics Reviews 1983*, edited by James Humber and Robert Almeder, 29–42. Clifton, N.J.: Humana Press, 1983.

"Euthanasia and the Physician's Professional Commitments." *Southern Journal of Philosophy* 22 (1984): 281–85.

"Chess as Art: Reflections on Richard Reti." *Philosophic Exchange*, nos. 15–16 (1984–85): 105–15.

"Movies." In *Stepping Out*, edited by Ada Long and Robert Yowell, 63–77. Dubuque, Iowa: Kendall-Hunt, 1985.

"The Animal Rights Movement Comes of Age." *Social and Health Review*, no. 3 (1986): 80–83.

"Darwin's Moral Lapse." *National Forum* (summer 1986): 22–24.

"The Permissibility of Ending Life." *Transactions of the American Society for Artificial Internal Organs* 32 (1986): 674–76.

"Responsibilities for Monitoring and Maintaining Quality of Care: Mistakes." *Ethics in Emergency Medicine*, edited by Kenneth V. Iverson, Arthur B. Sanders, D. R. Mathieu, and Allen E. Buchanan, 196–200. Baltimore: Williams and Wilkins, 1986.

"Baby M." *Bioethics* 1 (1987): 357–65.

"Darwin, Species, and Morality." *The Monist* 70, no. 1 (January 1987): 98–113.

"Lives and Liberty" (coauthored with William Ruddick). In *The Inner Citadel*, edited by John Christman, 221–33. New York: Oxford University Press, 1989.

"Morality, Parents, and Children." In *Person to Person*, edited by George Graham and Hugh LaFollette, 46–62. Philadelphia: Temple University Press, 1989. Reprinted with revisions in James Rachels, *Can Ethics Provide Answers? And Other Essays in Moral Philosophy*.

"Why Darwin Is Important for Ethics." In *Mind, Value, and Culture: Essays in Honor of E. M. Adams,* edited by David Weissbord, 301–25. Atascadero, Calif.: Ridgeview, 1989.

——— "Reflections on the Idea of Equality." In *On the Track of Reason: Essays in Honor of Kai Nielsen,* edited by Rodger Beehler, David Copp, and Bela Szabados, 1–18. Boulder, Colo.: Westview Press, 1991. Reprinted with revisions in James Rachels, *Can Ethics Provide Answers? And Other Essays in Moral Philosophy.*

"Subjectivism." In *A Companion to Ethics,* edited by Peter Singer, 432–41. Oxford: Blackwell, 1991.

"When Philosophers Shoot from the Hip." *Bioethics* 5 (1991): 67–71. Reprinted with revisions in James Rachels, *Can Ethics Provide Answers? And Other Essays in Moral Philosophy.*

"Are Quotas Sometimes Justified?" In *Affirmative Action and the University,* edited by Steven M. Cahn, 217–22. Philadelphia: Temple University Press, 1993.

"Killing, Letting Die, and the Value of Life." *Bioethica: Revista Interdisciplinaire* 2 (1993): 271–83. Reprinted with revisions in James Rachels, *Can Ethics Provide Answers? And Other Essays in Moral Philosophy.*

"The Legacy of Socrates." The 1992 Ireland Lecture at the University of Alabama at Birmingham. Tuscaloosa: University of Alabama Press, 1993. 31 pp.

"Moral Philosophy as a Subversive Activity." In *Applied Ethics: A Reader,* edited by Earl Winkler and Jerrold R. Coombs, 110–30. Oxford: Blackwell, 1993. Reprinted with revisions in James Rachels, *Can Ethics Provide Answers? And Other Essays in Moral Philosophy.*

"Why Darwinians Should Support Equal Treatment for Other African Apes." In *The Great Ape Project,* edited by Paola Cavalieri and Peter Singer, 152–57. London: Fourth Estate, 1993.

"Moral Philosophy in the Twentieth Century." In *Twentieth Century Ethical Theory,* edited by Steven M. Cahn and Joram G. Haber, 1–9. Englewood Cliffs, N.J.: Prentice-Hall, 1995.

"Prejudice and Equal Treatment." In *Ethical Issues in Contemporary Society,* edited by John Howie and George Schedler, 54–77. Carbondale: Southern Illinois University Press, 1995. An expanded version of an argument in this essay appears in "Coping with Prejudice," in James Rachels, *Can Ethics Provide Answers? And Other Essays in Moral Philosophy.*

"Punishment and Desert." In *Ethics in Practice,* edited by Hugh LaFollette, 470–79. Oxford: Blackwell, 1997.

"Animals and Ethics." In *Routledge Encyclopedia of Philosophy,* 1:273–76. London: Routledge, 1998.

"Darwin, Charles." In *Encyclopedia of Animal Rights and Animal Welfare,* edited by Marc Bekoff, 124–26. Westport, Conn.: Greenwood Press, 1998.

"Ethical Theory and Bioethics." In *A Companion to Bioethics,* edited by Peter Singer and Helga Kuhse, 15–23. Oxford: Blackwell, 1998.

"Nietzsche and the Objectivity of Morals." In *Philosophy Then and Now,* edited by N. Scott Arnold, Theodore M. Benditt, and George Graham, 385–412. Oxford: Blackwell, 1998.

"The Principle of Agency." *Bioethics* 12 (1998): 150–61.

"Naturalism." In *The Blackwell Guide to Ethical Theory,* edited by Hugh LaFollette, 74–91. Oxford: Blackwell, 2000.

"Killing and Letting Die." In *Encyclopedia of Ethics,* 2d ed., edited by Lawrence Becker and Charlotte Becker, 2:947–50. New York: Routledge, 2001.

"Theory and Practice." In *Encyclopedia of Ethics,* 2d ed., edited by Lawrence Becker and Charlotte Becker, 3:1706–708. New York: Routledge, 2001.

"Doing Without Free Will." *Dialogue* 19 (2002): 35–39.

"Ethics and the Bible." *Think* (spring 2002): 93–101.

"The Value of Human Life." *Philosophical Inquiry* 24 (2002): 3–16.

"The Basic Argument for Vegetarianism." In *Food for Thought: The Debate over Eating Meat,* edited by Steve F. Sapontzis, 70–80. Amherst, N.Y.: Prometheus Books, 2004.

"Drawing Lines." In *Animal Rights: Current Debates and New Directions,* edited by Cass R. Sunstein and Martha C. Nussbaum, 162–74. New York: Oxford University Press, 2004.

"Egoism." Published as an appendix to Stuart Rachels and Torin Alter, "Nothing Matters in Survival," *Journal of Ethics* 9, nos. 3–4 (October 2005): 311–30.

REVIEWS

Review of *The Central Questions of Philosophy* by A. J. Ayer. *New York Times Book Review,* January 31, 1971, 17.

Review of *Ludwig Wittgenstein* by David Pears. *New York Times Book Review,* January 31, 1971, 22.

Review of *Bertrand Russell* by A. J. Ayer. *New York Times Book Review,* October 22, 1972, 7, 14.

Review of *Applications of Moral Philosophy* by R. M. Hare. *Journal of Philosophy* 71 (1974): 84–88.

Review of *Living Trophies* by Peter Batten. *Miami Herald,* September 5, 1976, 7E.

Review of *Anarchy, State, and Utopia* by Robert Nozick. *Philosophia* 8 (1978): 440–45.

"Sociobiology and the 'Escalator' of Reason" (review of *The Expanding Circle* by Peter Singer). *Hastings Center Report* (October 1981): 45–46.

Review of *Bad Blood* by James H. Jones. *National Forum* (summer 1982): 47.

Review of *By No Extraordinary Means,* edited by Joanne Lynn. *Bioethics* 2 (1988): 353–58.

Review of *Prescription: Medicide* by Jack Kevorkian. *Bioethics* 6 (1992): 258–63.

"Animal Houses" (review of *Zoos and Animal Rights* by Stephen St. C. Bostock). *Nature* 365 (September 23, 1993): 305.

Review of *Life's Dominion* by Ronald Dworkin. *Bioethics* 8 (1994): 268–72.

MISCELLANEOUS

"Linguistic Analysis." *Encyclopedia Americana* 17:523–24 (1972).

"Reply to Critics." *New England Journal of Medicine* 292 (1975): 866–67.

"Reply to VanDeVeer." In *Animal Rights and Human Obligations,* edited by Peter Singer and Tom Regan, 230–32. Englewood Cliffs, N.J.: Prentice-Hall, 1976.

"Reply to Dr. Caso." *In Vitro* 14 (1978): 400–401.

"Moral Education in Public Schools" (abstract). *Journal of Philosophy* 79 (1982): 667–68.

"Reply to Hickey and Fischer." *Hastings Center Report* (October 1983): 44.

"Ethical Relativism." In the current on-line edition of *Encyclopedia Britannica.*

INDEX